Tom Morris

Author of the National Bestsellers
If Aristotle Ran General Motors
If Harry Potter Ran General Electric

Plato's Lemonade Stand

Stirring Change into Something Great

WISDOM/WORKS
Published by Wisdom Works
TomVMorris.com

Published 2020

ISBN 978-0-9994813-4-9

Printed in the United States of America

Set in Adobe Garamond Pro
Designed by Abigail Chiaramonte
Cover Concept by Sara Morris

What is philosophy?
Doesn't it mean preparing to meet
whatever will come our way?

Epictetus

CONTENTS

Preface

THIS IS A BOOK OF GOOD NEWS AND GUIDANCE. THE MOST powerful life skills available to us are among our oldest and simplest discoveries. They are also fully within our control to put into practice. And when we cultivate them properly over time, they can dramatically change our lives. There is, in particular, one broad form of art, or really, a set of wise behaviors, that's been tested for centuries and brings with its proper application all the agility, resilience, and grit we may need in any quest for personal or business excellence in our world of challenge and change. And the art in question can accomplish all this because it also takes us into a dimension of delight that stretches out beyond those other vital qualities and helps us to experience what we truly need in life and work.

An apparently endless stream of business management fads and popular self-help fashions have spread across our culture for the past half-century as ambitious individuals and companies in every industry have searched for the secret sauce or one differentiating factor that can set them apart from all others and propel them to extraordinary and lasting success. On the business side, the genuine insights of such diverse movements as Six Sigma, Total Quality Management,

Re-engineering, Innovation Training, and more recently, Purpose Driven Everything have had measurable results whenever they've been done well. But then all those initiatives have also launched in their wake countless carnivals of faux gurus, profound sounding pretenders, and well intentioned parrots promising us the moon and beyond if we'll just buy their watered down elixirs of excellence, take a swig every morning, and tweet about it to our friends.

Most of the serious business fads in our time focus on measures and methods of increasing product quality, process efficiency, or public awareness. Others are more concerned about niche marketing, Big Data, and AI. Only a very few have highlighted the spirit of the people who do the work. And yet I've found that this is where the real magic happens, where the deep insights and true differentiators of greatness that stand the test of time are to be found. It's the realm of practical philosophy, an ancient deep tech needed anew in our high tech world. It's the domain of wisdom and virtue, true insight and inner strength. And there's a skill or art at the center of it all that this book will describe in detail. When someone masters this art or it gets baked into the corporate DNA of a business through the lives of the people who work there, great things happen. And it's nothing new. The best people have been doing it across cultures and throughout thousands of years of civilization. But it needs to be rediscovered in our time now. We can all benefit from practicing it daily. And in these pages, I'll explain how.

The Real Difficulty That Confronts Us

IT CAN SEEM THAT LIFE IS JUST ONE UNEXPECTED CHALLENGE after another. There are always large-scale problems that impinge on us, like political turmoil, economic craziness, dire environmental threats, social upheaval, and many other forms of uncertainty. In addition to all this, any day could bring unexpected bad news about your health, your spouse, your family, your friend, your dog, or your cat. Your business may face a disaster. Your personal hopes and goals can appear dashed by forces outside your control, or even by the unintended consequences of choices you've made. Experts are now warning that many of us will be out of a job within a few decades due to the rise of sophisticated artificial intelligence, unless, of course, a big wayward asteroid gets here first. Unexpected change surrounds us to an unprecedented degree. And, of course, all this can create severe stress.

> Nothing is so painful to the human mind as a
> great and sudden change.
> Mary Shelley

This book will offer a practical philosophy for how to flex and innovate your way forward in the face of life's irritations, shocks, defeats, disappointments, heartaches, and failures. The good news is that we've long had some profound advice on how to deal with the vast range of difficulties we face. It's as succinct as it is vivid and memorable:

> When life hands you lemons, make lemonade.

It seems like almost everybody in modern times has shared this suggestion of practical wisdom, from the popular writers Elbert Hubbard in 1915 and Dale Carnegie in 1951, to the contemporary mega-star Beyoncé, and on down the line. In the face of a real tragedy, you may think it to be ridiculously trite, or even glib. But it's not at all. Beneath the simple surface image of the advice, there are great depths to be explored and powerful insights to be used. It actually captures a profound philosophy of life.

And yet there's a basic problem with this popular adage. Nearly everyone says it, but no one says how. Nobody tells us exactly, or even remotely, how to do what's so vividly recommended. This book will solve that problem, providing guidance from some of the wisest people who have ever lived on the best ways to deal with the most difficult changes and challenges that enter our lives, as well as the little everyday obstacles that cross our path. It's about adversity in all its forms and how we can best respond to it wisely and well. It's a personal guide for all of us, but it's also a surprisingly powerful look what leaders need to learn to do well and help their associates and partners accomplish on a regular basis.

In recent years, a chorus of voices has been reminding us that the best of our achievements tend to happen on the far side of adversity, that anything worth doing is going to be harder than we might imagine, and that we need certain inner resources in order to keep on track amid the challenges we'll inevitably face on any worthy path. Some astute thinkers have stressed the importance of inner resilience, an ability to bounce back whenever we're knocked down. Others, like the insightful psychologist Angela Duckworth, have identified the attribute of grit, or a dogged mental determination, as a common characteristic of successful people in our world of struggle. I agree that both resilience and grit are indeed vital characteristics needed for any challenging success in our time, as they have been in every other era. But the old adage about lemonade is particularly interesting because it hints at something more.

We're not told that when life hands us lemons, we should just bounce back emotionally and regain our poise, or that that we should perhaps instead grit our teeth and persist in soldiering on despite that sour fruit. It makes a rather radical suggestion that we should do something that involves a transformation, and one that results in much more than the simply tolerable. It doesn't just help us put pain into the past. It urges us on to use our difficulty to create an outcome that's even delightful. Resilience and grit mean doing something because of adversity and even despite it. But there is an alchemy beyond these two qualities that involves doing something immensely creative with the challenge. And this may be where most of our innovation in life happens, in the midst of daunting challenge and difficult change. When life hands us lemons, we're to make cool, refreshing lemonade. We have here a simple and vivid metaphor of metamorphosis for what I've come to think of as a secret to life. It touches on something of great wisdom and power.

Wisdom conquers the ups and downs of change.
Juvenal

In the ancient world and through the European middle ages, up to the rise of early modern science and even beyond, there was an endeavor known as alchemy. In dictionaries and history books, it's often characterized as the pre-scientific forerunner to chemistry, and it's said to have been a quest to find a way to turn base metals into gold, as well as to create an "Elixir of Life" that could endow anyone with a vigorous and youthful immortality. And of course, in a sense, neither desire has disappeared. We're still on a quest for the power of gold and the vigor of youth. We all want resources. And who wouldn't prefer to avoid the decay of old age and death? I recently bought a book entitled, *The Virtues of Aging.* The first thing I noticed was that it's very short. And it has big print, which in a sense almost in itself detracts from the intended theme. Age at times can be as problematic as poverty. In fact, physical aging is at a certain point a form of physical impoverishment. It's been said that if you can do at the age of sixty what you could do at the age of twenty, then you obviously weren't doing much in your youth. The process of aging throws at us changes, challenges, and daunting problems to solve. And yet, so does nearly every new day, completely apart from our growing sense of limits.

We can understand the alchemistic quest for unlimited gold and boundless youth. But beneath all the metallurgy and the wish to bottle eternity into the ultimate pharmaceutical of worldly vigor, alchemy at its best always involved a spiritual quest for the deepest roots of change and positive transformation. It was an endless search for the power to move from ordinary materials and lives into something truly extraordinary, precious, and ultimately desirable. And that's a great way to hint at the philosophical elixir we're going to pursue here. We're going to see what it takes to be existential alchemists in all the challenges of life.

Resilience is rebounding from adversity. Grit is carrying on amid it. Alchemy, by contrast, is embracing it transformatively and using it to create something great. The arc of alchemy is always from struggle to sweetness, or from difficulty to delight.

This quest is the challenge of any business and of any life: how to take whatever comes our way and make of it something great and, even better, perhaps astonishing. This movement from the mundane to the marvelous and even the miraculous is our subject matter here. This is a book about that alchemistic hope. We're going to examine our ability to rise to a challenge, or bounce back from a blow that life has dealt us, however large or small, and then look at how we can take action in response to it, first in our internal emotions and attitudes, and then also in a form of external, creative action that can indeed be transformative in remarkable ways. We'll see how the very famous image of lemons to lemonade can inspire and guide us in the process along the way.

You just have to make lemonade. During my childhood and teenage years, I often heard my mother give this homespun advice. I think she learned it and the perspective it conveys between the ages of six and eighteen when she lived at a Methodist Home for Children in North Carolina, isolated from her mother and two brothers who as older siblings could work to help pay at least some of the bills that came in after their father's sudden death in a farming accident. They were at first a wealthy family, and then due to the deceptions of a corrupt attorney, as well as a broader economic distress in the nation, they became desperately poor and she wound up for that crucial formative decade of her young life in the stark environment of an orphanage. She arrived at its door just as the Great Depression had enveloped the nation. Her long sojourn there gave her plenty of time for learning how to turn life's lemons into what was for her the extremely rare treat of lemonade.

The first few times I came across the famous lemons-to-lemonade advice, I was too young to know what it meant. It just made me thirsty. But as I grew older, hearing other people convey the same piece of folk wisdom in various circumstances, I gradually came to understand what it was recommending. But I still had no clear idea how to do it. Nobody ever told me that part. And yet, the saying stuck with me and managed to inspire in me a sense that we can respond to difficulties and change things throughout our lives in a way that's transformative and good. We can all be in the business of taking the lemons that roll our way and making the changes that will result in great lemonade to refresh ourselves and share with others. And that's a vital thing to know, because the future belongs to masters of change. The world of tomorrow will be created by those among us who can live most fully as artists of adaptation and transformation in the face of surprise, adversity, and challenge.

> Difficulties mastered are opportunities won.
> Winston Churchill

An unexpected flood destroyed my friend's small health food store in Texas. There was no insurance. It looked like the business couldn't recover. But customers, neighbors, and employees spontaneously came together with the right spirit, adapted to the challenge and against all odds creatively transformed the situation, rebuilding the store, and giving us the seeds of what would soon become the amazing national grocery chain for intelligent and healthy eating known as Whole Foods.

In 1971, the night before the rock band Deep Purple was going to record an important album in Montreaux, Switzerland, one on which they were pinning their hopes for the future, their chosen venue for the recording burned to the ground. The musicians watched all their plans go up in flames as thick smoke spread over Lake Geneva. Their shock was intense. But they didn't get discouraged, give up, and go home. Instead, they wrote and recorded their classic hit song, "Smoke on the Water."

Scientist Percy Spencer was visiting the Raytheon Company and stood too close to a magnetron, a tube that released energy as a part of radar equipment at the time. A forgotten candy bar in his pants pocket melted and made a big sticky mess. But the problem sparked his curiosity and set him thinking, which led to the creation of our now indispensible modern marvel, the microwave oven. Lemons can become lemonade. We can go from mess to masterpiece.

A Swiss engineer named George de Mestral was on a walk in the woods with his dog. At some point, he realized they were both getting covered with annoying burrs, sticking to the pants of one and the fur of the other. After the uncomfortable exercise of painstakingly plucking them all off himself and his companion, the man of science examined a few of them closely and, with what he learned, went on to invent the ubiquitously practical stuff we call velcro.

One more quick story: A lady was going through a difficult and bitter divorce. She didn't know how to fight legal battles and was constantly frustrated and discouraged by the awful things being thrown at her by her former spouse. Things would go from bad to worse on a daily basis. She honestly reports that, during this time, she would lie awake at night and imagine ways to kill her ex-husband. But as an otherwise moral person and a meticulously law abiding citizen, she knew she couldn't actually act on those wild visions. So she found another way of dealing with the bitter lemons of frustration that kept falling in her lap each day. She began to write a book about a murder, *A is for Alibi*, which went on to great fame as the first of the bestselling "alphabet books" she would go on to publish over many years. The author, Sue Grafton, reflected later that, as she puts it, "In a sense, I've launched a whole career on homicidal rage." That remark always makes me laugh. Sue found a better way to use what she had been given and ended up creating one of the great detective series of all time.

> All that happens to us, including our humiliations, our misfortunes,
> our embarrassments, all is given to us as raw material,
> as clay, so that we may shape our art.
> Jorge Louis Borges

Floods. Fires. Melted candy. Sharp, irritating burrs, an unfair and infuriating divorce. The world is full of problems that come our way, large and small. But there's some powerful guidance available to help with all this, a wealth of deep and practical insight that's just waiting to be applied in our lives. And it involves ideas that have been put to use by many of the wisest people who've gone before us over literally thousands of years. I've come to realize that our newest challenges in the present demand our most powerful wisdom from the past. But then, again, this has long been true.

The Lemonade Philosophy

I WISH I COULD TELL YOU THAT THE GREAT PHILOSOPHER Plato was himself the first to recommend making lemonade from life's lemons. But I can't, because he didn't. Our first historical hint of something like the beverage we know and love is from early medieval Egypt. There is earlier evidence of lemons grown in and around the Mediterranean, especially in Italy, and even farther back through history in India. But as a resident mainly of Athens, Greece in the fifth century BCE, Plato didn't ever use in his extant works this image, or explicitly give the metaphorically powerful advice based on it. And yet he did live its approach to life. Still, if some enthusiast were to tweet out the aphorism and attach this profound thinker's name as its source, that little piece of false attribution would likely make it around the world a dozen times before any historians or philosophers could object to the counterfeit ascription. Many people would easily believe it originated in such a famous source of wisdom, precisely because it is so wise and renowned a recommendation.

Take a minute and imagine this: A close, longtime older friend—your teacher, mentor, and guide, as well as your main inspiration in life, generally—is arrested one day for doing exactly what he had been training you to do. Powerful forces are arraigned against him. He's put through a big, public, high profile legal trial and, ultimately, as a result of lies and spin and uninformed popular opinion, he's unjustly convicted on false charges, sentenced to death, and killed. You realize that, as his protégé, there's a chance you might be next. How would you react? What would you do? That was the plight of Plato as he saw the people of Athens turn against his beloved teacher Socrates, the man who was his hero as well as his most trusted advisor in life.

Plato faced the worst. He could have panicked, become emotionally unhinged, and even fallen into a deep depression. He could have given up any hope of rising to be the proponent of radical wisdom that Socrates had taught him to seek and provide. He could easily have been overcome by a natural urge to run and hide away in exile to save himself. Instead, he productively confronted the terrible difficulties that had entered his life, adapted masterfully, and as a result transformed forever the enterprise in which he was engaged and, along with it, the future of western thought. He showed himself to be an expert at taking life's most sour lemons and making lemonade.

This is a book about change and transformation that's inspired, initially, by the life and influence of philosophers like Plato and many more great thinkers who have subsequently followed in their footsteps. It's all about what it takes to turn challenging and difficult situations into something positive. Here's what I've learned. Strong people deal with adversity well. Wise people deal with it masterfully. There are a few ideas that can make all the difference when you face your next surprise, catastrophe, or extremely well disguised opportunity, and the most crucial are to be found in these pages.

How do you personally handle a disappointment or setback? Can you take on a tough twist of fate with a positive and optimistic attitude? Or do you easily flinch at pain, cave in to pressure, give up your dreams, and feel utterly despondent as a result? Some people seem to be born resilient, optimistic, and determined. Nothing really gets them down, or at least keeps them there. Others struggle with anything negative, however small. Any obstacles seem overwhelming. Troubles paralyze their thought and action. But in this life, stuff happens. Every one of us is tested frequently by what often appears to be a hostile, stubborn world bent on blocking our wants, needs, and dreams. We can wonder why it all has to be so hard. But, as Plato himself taught us, things are not always what they seem—and in this one realization there is a vast power of possibility.

> I believe that if life gives you lemons,
> you should make lemonade. Then find somebody
> whose life has given them vodka, and have a party.
> Ron White

"When life hands you lemons, make lemonade." We have this little aphoristic guidance with good reason. Positive outcomes in tough situations can depend on our active involvement. A development or change that's initially difficult can lead to something great. The biggest lemons of all could possibly end up as ingredients in some incredibly good lemonade. And that's most often up to us. But to gain such outcomes, we have to know how to respond well and then get going.

There are things we can do, actions within our power, to sweeten nearly any situation we face, however sour it initially might be. This book draws on more than two thousand years of the best advice ever given about how to do that well. Some simple skills, guided by a dose of real wisdom, can turn us all into masterful lemonade makers.

Imagine, then, one of the great philosophers of the ages like Plato appearing in the present moment as your personal guide and expert lemonade maker. You can visit his lemonade stand any time you'd like, bring him the current crop of lemons that life has been handing you, and get his help on how to turn that fruit into some amazing juice. Now, I should be clear that I'm using the name of our predecessor Plato here as mostly iconic or emblematic of all the great philosophers whose advice to us can be of help. But he was in particular an expert of resilience and transformation in life, and had some crucial insights for us that can help greatly when we confront our own problems. And yet, still, he's just one of the many sages from the past who can guide us into how to be trans-formative agents in whatever circumstances we face.

The Lemons-to-Lemonade philosophy offers a perspective that's crucial for successful living, and it starts by giving us a clear image for our most common experience of change. Almost any major change that comes our way and isn't a clear improvement in our circumstances, any substantial alteration in our lives that we haven't wished for, planned on, or dreamed about tends to enter into our consciousness in the form of emotional lemons—sharply sour, even bitter, and with a bite that can even make us groan. Our modern proverb assures us that this is a problem we can do some-thing about, and it provides a vivid image to inspire us into action.

Notice something right away about our image. Taking lemons and making lemonade doesn't mean coming to view the lemons as sweet rather than sour. And applying the metaphor to life doesn't involve concluding that difficult things are really pleasant rather than trying, or wonderful rather than challenging. It means taking the lemons, squeezing out what's in them, and adding anything necessary to make something good. Our metaphor doesn't allow us to stop with a situation that's sour, or perhaps even bad in itself, and urge us to ignore or tolerate it, but rather guides us into doing something that will incorporate the lemons of life into a result that's distinctively good.

If you're like most people, when you actually make the refreshing beverage of lemonade from basic ingredients, you'll toss out most of each lemon after extracting from it what you can use. You don't keep it as a trophy to admire. You use it and move on. The making of lemonade isn't just about changing your perspective on something. It's about doing the right things to be transformative with it.

> Many problems that nature throws in our way
> can be transformed by the exercise of intelligence.
> Livy

Let's reflect a moment on the general fact of change. There are basically two kinds of it in our lives—the change that happens to us, and the change that happens only because of us. Our challenge with difficult change is then also two-fold. First, we need to learn how to deal better with the lemons of change that drop into our lives uninvited and unexpected. When difficulty finds us and shakes us, we need to know how best to respond. And second, we have to discover how to initiate and launch the positive changes we should be making throughout our journey, both individually and with other people. Initiating innovation is never itself easy, even in little things. We have to learn how to deal with any difficulties we may encounter in going new ways and doing new things, and ultimately how to enjoy the often-challenging process of working to attain the results we need. This book is about mastering both sides of the recipe.

Plato believed that life is like art. And every individual form of art is a skilled behavior that we can get better at, as we come to understand it better and practice it well. There is an overall art of adaptation that will give us what we need for making the best life lemonade in times of turmoil. And there's an art of innovation for stirring up fresh results. Each is one of the major skills of life, and is an art for living well. Adaptation involves responding properly to the new and difficult things that confront us. Innovation revolves around our own creative initiatives as individuals and together. Both combined and used in tandem give us the basic secret for success in the world that's been neglected for far too long.

Every difficulty enters our lives as a change. So we all need an art for dealing with challenging change that will help with any failure or adversity. The overall art of change as I understand it, then, has two major components. So we'll distinguish between an art of adaptation and an art of innovation. To give you a hint of what they are, I'll list here the elements of the basic recipe they provide for great lemonade making. Each step will sound simple, but each involves a learned behavior in which we can increase our personal skill.

When life hands you lemons, respond with
The Art of Change that involves:

1. Adaptation

The Art of Self Control
Don't rush to judgment.
Value the right things.
Use your imagination well.

The Art of Positive Action
Govern your attitudes.
Look for opportunities.
Take the initiative

The Art of Achievement
Be guided in your actions by:
A clear Conception of what you want
A strong Confidence
A focused Concentration
A stubborn Consistency
An emotional Commitment
A good Character to guide you
A Capacity to Enjoy the process

These skills for adapting and responding well to the change that comes our way will structure Part One of this book. Then, five steps to initiating innovative change in your life, however difficult, as well as with other people, will guide us in Part Two. These five requirements are the keys to initiating and leading well any form of innovative change or transformation:

2. Innovation

Prepare for the Challenge.
Gather Strong Support.
Communicate Positively and Well.
Focus on What's at Stake.
Take Action to Launch New Habits.

The second part of our study will examine how a good new idea, as well as a threatening or dangerous situation, can lead us to make important changes, either alone or in connection with the people around us. When we come to understand what all this means and how to do it, we can revolutionize our relationship with challenging change and become the pioneers of the possible we're meant to be.

I'm guessing that, if you're anything like me, life has handed you plenty of lemons along the way and will likely continue to do so. It may even bring you a truckload now and then. With the assistance of many great thinkers, we're going to set up the ultimate ideal lemonade stand, one of nearly Platonic perfection. We'll get out some pitchers and make up a sign. Together, we're going to learn how to stir up something great. And it will end up being much deeper and more important than you might initially imagine. So, let's get started.

Introduction

LIFE LEMONADE 101

HOW WELL DO YOU DEAL WITH DISRUPTIVE CHANGE, A MAJOR obstacle, an apparent failure, or any other form of adversity? Do you handle it easily or is it tough? Do you tend to experience any major upheaval or unexpected detour in your life as a massively frustrating ordeal, or can you see it as a potentially enriching adventure? Are you at peace during turmoil, or do outward storms easily enter your own heart in tumultuous ways?

And what about the distinctive challenge of initiating new and needed change? Are you good at making a change when it's right, or even charting a radically new path forward in your life? When facing a call for initiative, do you ever tend to procrastinate, rationalize, grumble, maybe give the new thing a half-hearted effort and then, out of either inertia, worry, or fear, quickly fall back into old patterns? Is it easy for you to help the people around you transform their habits when it's time for something new, or do you feel irked and perplexed by the psychology of others when change is in the air?

Mark this: there is change in all things.
Terence

However well or poorly you might deal with change right now in any of its forms, we have some great insight for how to handle it like a master. The biggest lemons of change can be made into the very best lemonade. And I should make something clear upfront. We're going to talk about how to handle absolutely any adversity or difficulty, any disappointment or trauma in our lives, but every such thing tends to come into our lives as the result of a change in the way things were. So we're going to focus most on that moment of change and its aftermath. But everything we discover will apply just as much to an ongoing plight or struggle that can seem to have been with you forever. Something is going to have to change. And so we come back to that central concept.

We have good days and bad. We encounter delights and difficulties. And we can be thrown off balance by either. There is an important ancient image for how the right thoughts and attitudes can help us cope with the ups and downs we face. Imagine life as a large wagon wheel. If we emotionally live on the outer rim, then as the wheel turns, we'll be spun around to extreme highs and lows in rapid and dizzying succession. But if we can learn to move closer in toward the mid point of the hub, we become much more centered. The wheel will still spin, but we won't be so dramatically thrown about by its motion. That's a position of power. And the best wisdom can help put us there.

The Challenge We Face

TECHNOLOGY IS THE GREAT CHANGE ACCELERATOR, AND THE technological innovations of the recent past have sped up the pace of cultural change in ways we never expected. Things are reconfiguring around us more rapidly and unpredictably than ever before. As a result, we can find it hard to get our bearings and move forward with optimism, confidence, and hope. Sometimes, change comes at a relentless pace, spinning us around and pushing us in uncharted directions, with no chance to catch our breath or regain focus. Even little changes that initially make life easier add up over time and result in a complexity of daily experience that can push us far beyond our comfort zones. Whenever jarring change enters our lives, it can create worry and frustration for everyone involved.

> No sudden change of circumstances
> ever occurs without some mental jolt;
> and that's why you, too, have deserted
> for a while your usual calm.
> Boethius

Questions and Answers

The unexpected twists and turns of life can lead us to raise questions that are philosophical in nature, and yet have the most practical intent. Philosophy seeks understanding. And a measure of genuine understanding is the most secure foundation for effective action. But there are things that defy our best efforts to understand. As the philosopher Immanuel Kant explained long ago, we naturally and necessarily ask some questions we can't ever definitively answer. That's just the way our minds work. We'll never have all the answers we'd like. But still, we may have the answers we need.

Why are so many major changes completely unexpected, catching even top experts by surprise? Will the recent surge in the pace of change ever slow down? How can you tell the difference between important and trivial changes when they first grab your attention? Is there a single best way for dealing with any big change? Some of these questions we can answer. But there are also things about the ultimate nature of change, as well as about many particular changes we encounter, that we may not ever fully grasp. And yet, this doesn't detract in the least from the solid and reliable perspectives we can gain on how to handle change, day-to-day. The uncertainty we might feel about some specific change we face can goad us to explore more deeply the most profound and practical wisdom that's available on how to handle any change well. The more puzzled we are, the more determined we can become to find real answers.

Uncertainty is the very condition to
impel man to unfold his powers.
Erich Fromm

The Challenge of Uncertainty
There are many reasons change can come to us as something hard.
We all have routines, habits, and familiar ways of doing things
that give us some small sense of comfort in a world of uncertainty.
Much about life is unpredictable. Some of it's mysterious. We never know what's going to happen next year or next month, or even
next week, or why. And yet we all crave to some degree a sense of
regularity and control.

If you've ever paid close attention to the typical ten-day weather forecast for almost any major city in the world over an extended
period of time, you've probably noticed that the prediction for a
particular date will be revised, sometimes radically, every few days.
With all our advanced climatology, we can still get things strikingly wrong even twenty-four hours ahead of time, or less. How
often have you wished the weather services would just look out
their windows? Minutes ago, they missed on their prediction of
the present moment. But this shouldn't surprise us. Las Vegas was
built on our inability to predict accurately what will happen *in the
next few seconds* on the slot machine, the roulette wheel, and the
card table. Dynamic complexity allows for a degree of novelty that
can blind-side even the best informed. And we now have widespread complexity swirling all around us. Because of this, we live
in a time of deep unease.

Uncertainty is the air we breathe. To counter this, we cling
to whatever we do know well, and we often cringe at the mere
thought of any substantial alteration in our situation. Even a minor
unanticipated change that disturbs our routine can bother us to a
degree that's completely out of proportion with its real impact. We
long for some measure of certainty in our lives. But the unforeseen
keeps shaking things up.

We are not certain. We are never certain.
Albert Camus

And of course, it's not just the change coming at us that creates this problem. The world is set up in such a way that we have to initiate change in order to grow, develop, and flourish. And yet any big changes we make can initially lead to more uncertainty, which is one of the reasons we often miss or resist opportunities to try something new.

Here's an important insight: We can't eliminate uncertainty by trying to avoid change. True masters of change understand this. Their secret is to find a way to embrace the uncertainty of life and not seek to flee it. They live in accordance with the novelist Graham Greene's understanding that, "When we are unsure, we are alive." They know that uncertainty forces us to learn and grow. It provides us with the basic conditions for creativity. And, in the end, it may be one of the greatest gifts we have.

Dealing well with any sort of change can be a challenge. But it's always potentially beneficial for us, however tough it seems. So change is not just something we should tolerate and manage. It's something we need to embrace and use well.

Mastering Change

THE MOST SUCCESSFUL PEOPLE IN HISTORY HAVE BEEN MASTERS of change. They've typically faced great hardships and deep troubles at various points in their lives, but they were creative enough to learn how to adapt and transform repeatedly, expertly, and in nearly every situation, no matter how difficult. They became skilled enough to take the many lemons of life and make lemonade. To the extent that we follow their lead, we also can become masters of change in our own time, and in our own ways. We can take any bitter fruit we're given and turn it into something fine. We can be among the alchemists of adaptation and transformation in our own day.

What Mastery Is

But can we ever truly master change? It's certainly possible to wonder whether the idea of mastery is at all appropriate in this context. You might think that something as big and varied as change is just as impossible to master as golf, the weather, the stock market, or the unpredictable iron will of a two-year-old child, and it's often every bit as frustrating. On first thought, it can seem that mastering change is an utterly hopeless idea. We can never control completely what life is going to throw in our path. And so we can easily be led to wonder how we could ever master the manifold contours of such a thoroughgoing and pervasive phenomenon as change. The answer to this reasonable concern is actually quite simple. And it can give us hope.

To be a master of anything is to have developed a very high level of skill in the endeavors connected with it. Mastery doesn't demand omniscience or omnipotence, complete foresight, or unbeatable strength. It simply requires a persistent cultivation of all the right skills. Masters aren't perfect in any respect. They're just extremely good at what they do. They develop the inner resources to help with any difficulty. They build their knowledge and wisdom. They know how to approach the next new challenge in such a way as to maximize their chance for success, despite the unknowns that are always involved. They take what they're given and they innovate well.

In any field, the true masters repeatedly seek to expand their level and scope of expertise by experimenting and trying new things. This just means that they embrace and use change often. They have a habit of change. In fact, it's a rarely understood truth that in order to be a master of anything, you must become along the way a master of change.

> All life is experiment. The more
> experiments you make, the better.
> Ralph Waldo Emerson

Change is clearly a challenge we can confront badly or well, along a broad spectrum of skill. And it's involved in every other challenge. That makes it even more important to handle it properly and well. The person who masters change has just cultivated the perceptions, instincts, inner attitudes, and outer activities that facilitate the most positive outcomes from any encounter with the new. And almost anyone who works on the required skills can become, within their own abilities, a master of change.

The Great Lemonade Makers
Some of the wisest people in history, including the most practical philosophers throughout the ages, have understood what it takes for dealing well with any disruptive change. They've been the great lemonade makers of life. And they've often left notes on how they were able to do it. They've given us their recipe. So, fortunately, you and I don't have to face the challenge of change without help and just guess at what we need.

Imagine Socrates, Plato, Aristotle, Lao Tsu, Seneca, Marcus Aurelius, and Emerson—all top mixologists of life—gathered around your kitchen table with a few more of their insightful colleagues, slicing up lemons, measuring out sugar, bringing in special ingredients, working a little magic, and stirring up some incredible lemonade. In the chapters of this book, we'll examine their most important insights about how you can do likewise in your life and work. Their wisdom will help you to become a true master of change. And then, by your positive example, you can guide the other people around you to work better with change. When you employ the wisdom of the ages, your influence will be felt and will make its mark in many ways. The result will be a happy one.

Wisdom is the supreme part of happiness.
Sophocles

Our Philosophical Heritage: The Four Insights

There are initially four insights behind the process of practical alchemy involved in dealing well with life's lemons and mastering change. They come to us from some of the most famous philosophers in history. These insights are important preliminaries to the other tools and techniques we'll investigate, and all involve basic necessities for mastering change and dealing with any new challenge.

In researching all the most useful tools we have for dealing well with difficult change, I discovered something that's interesting in its own right. The best practical philosophers have indeed had a lot to say that can help us with change. But you won't find shelves of books and collections of essays written by them on this subject in the philosophy section of your local library or bookstore. You can't google 'change' and have their wisdom easily available a click or two away. The great thinkers of the past didn't often isolate the topic of change as a major general subject of human concern like we do today. They most frequently tackled it in the course of thinking about something more specific, like the rise and fall of fortune in a person's life, the variable contours of success in the world, or the issue of how to deal with hardship, pain, and disappointment whenever we experience them. But their insights go far beyond those original contexts of reflection. Gathering the best of their ideas about the challenge of change is like a treasure hunt through discourses, essays, and letters from many centuries and cultures.

It will be useful here, at the outset of our journey, to note quickly a few preliminary thoughts from some especially influential thinkers that will give us important perspectives for understanding and applying what's to come. And we can't do any better than to begin with The Big Three, the Troika or Triumvirate of great, Greek, toga clad thinkers who fundamentally launched the enterprise of philosophy as we know it in the west. So we'll consult with Socrates, Plato, and Aristotle. What's important to know, though, is that some of their deepest insights reflect fundamental perspectives from the east as well. Their advice will introduce us to some important clues about what it takes to encounter change productively and embrace it well.

The Wisdom of Socrates and Insight One: Self-Knowledge

Socrates challenged everyone around him and all the rest of us with his famous proclamation: "The unexamined life is not worth living." He insisted that the people of his day examine their lives—their beliefs and values, attitudes and emotions, actions and predilections—and he vigorously urged that they do this on a regular basis, strenuously, and with absolute candor. Of course, as a result, they insisted that he drink poison and die, not exactly an overwhelming affirmation of his recommendation, which was less than wildly popular at the time. But he was still right and continues to be, despite ongoing, equally contrary attitudes in our own day.

However difficult it might be to engage in the comprehensive process of critical self-examination that Socrates recommended, the alternative ends up being worse, as you can see on nearly any Reality TV show, or in the chaotic scrum of the really real. The unexamined life is an existence in many ways adrift, and it unfolds at the mercy of forces it doesn't understand. It never rises to the level of what it could have been. All too often, it's a life of largely wasted potential. And that's a pervasive problem in our time.

For many decades of my own life, I carried around without realizing it a deep, unrecognized emotional wound from my childhood that greatly affected my thoughts, feelings, and actions. I was entirely oblivious to a center of need and a set of forces emanating from that need that in many ways affected almost everything I did. But fortunately, I can say now, there came a time when it all blew up and created some big problems. Life handed me some huge sour lemons. And as a result, I came to realize that I might need to engage in a new and much more difficult level of self-examination than I had ever attempted. So I launched an extended process of inner discovery and reflection that was quite painful at first, but then tremendously healing and liberating in the end. In this deeper form of self-investigation, I enlisted the help of others, and that made all the difference. Socratic self-examination is not just an inner activity played out in pristine solitude. Those who knew the great philosopher frequently had his personal help with the challenge. To work well, such a process often requires the aid of trusted partners. It can be hard and even extremely hurtful at times. But, however difficult it might be, it can yield great consequences, the metaphorical lemonade of sweet results that we need.

> Make it your business to know yourself,
> which is the most difficult lesson in the world.
> Cervantes

When we live unexamined lives, speeding forward on cruise control or even treating the outward form of our existence as if it were a semi-autonomous lift, we're terribly vulnerable to unconscious assumptions, false beliefs, distorted values, unhealthy attitudes, and inappropriate emotions. As a result, we can find ourselves with problems that were in some way our own creation, without at all seeing how this happened and what it might take for a solution. Several well-publicized celebrity disasters and business implosions of the recent past can easily come to mind. But such problems go far beyond the plight of the rich and famous, as many of our political developments show.

According to Plato, Socrates was convinced that most of us live under the spell of serious illusions and chase superficially attractive mirages that won't satisfy us, while also fearing mere shadows that can't harm us. He felt that the goal of philosophy is to help us to escape from these illusions and guide our lives by the clear light of truth that emanates from reality. We can't deal with our false beliefs and distorted attitudes well without knowing what they are, and that requires knowing ourselves.

> No man was ever great by imitation.
> Samuel Johnson

Self-knowledge is the foundation for appropriate and effective action. It's also a support for excellence. You can't confront any difficult change powerfully without understanding your experience, your knowledge, your talents, and your skills—your overall resources—as well as your weaknesses and limitations. My friend David Rendall in his book *The Freak Factor* suggests that actually embracing some of the apparent "weaknesses" and oddities that make us different may give us a surprising key to our future success. He likes to say that when he was a kid, everyone was always telling him to sit down and shut up. And now, as a busy international speaker, he makes his living by standing up and talking. The same traits that in some circumstances got him in trouble, when transplanted into a different context, gave him an edge. In a sense, Dave's entire book is about personal lemonade making based on self-knowledge. A healthy dose of self-understanding, knowing exactly who you are, can help you make the best of any situation, opportunity, or challenge.

The deepest practical thinkers have realized that one of the most enduring sources of power in this world is self-knowledge. And this applies in interesting ways to organizations as well as to individuals. We can't be and do our best unless we're on a track that's right for us. And, of course, you can be true to yourself and your distinctive talents in times of great change only if you truly know who you are. The path to your own best future always starts within.

My father had a remarkable life. He grew up on a large farm in the sand hills of North Carolina surrounded by dense woods.

As a child and throughout his teens, he roamed the land every day. And then the broader world called out to him. He moved to a big city, learned how to build and design airplanes, joined the army, and fought in the Second World War throughout the South Pacific. Then he came back to his home state and set up some of the first radio stations in towns throughout the southeast. But that was just the next of many adventures and careers that would call out to him.

When I was young, he broadcast the baseball games of the Durham Bulls in Durham, North Carolina during the period of time that inspired the film, "Bull Durham," a hit movie developed and produced by the son of his attorney. After that, my dad sold cars, invented toys, ran a bowling alley, and worked for an encyclopedia company. He lived his life as a series of adventures. And with his ongoing, open attitude toward new things, which was quite unusual in his day, he provided a great example for me.

In moving from one adventure to the next with curiosity, excitement, and a pioneer spirit, Hugh Thomas Morris was in many ways far ahead of his time. He used to say to me, "You can do anything as long as you love it and think you have something distinctive to contribute to it. But if either of these things changes, you should make a change." When my friends in college were trying to decide on their major, I often heard them asking, "What do I want to do for the rest of my life?" Because of my father's example, I never felt that pressure. He taught me that the only question about our work and life adventure we ever need to ask is, "What do I want to do next?" The rest of life is yet to be considered and discovered. Whatever thoughts we might have about it now are subject to change. And that's because the human condition is always one of change.

Every man carries the entire form of the human condition.
Montaigne

In my dad's mid-to-late forties, a deep and dawning new level of self-knowledge created a lasting change in his life. It drew him back to the land and to the sort of woods he had roamed and loved as a boy. He became a licensed real estate broker, opened his own small company, and went on to experience the most fulfilling decades of his life in a return to his roots, walking the rolling hills of piedmont North Carolina and planning great residential communities where people could live outside the city and enjoy the nature surrounding them. Almost every major change in his life ended up being good, but this one change that was the most motivated and guided by a deeper self-knowledge was clearly the greatest of them all and resulted in a business that was for him a form of art and a source of joy. My father worked in property development and nature preservation until the end of his life, and was as happy in that work as a person can be. He had his problems, like all of us do, but he was in many ways an artist of change who gave me a special, singular example of the guiding power that self-knowledge can have in anyone's greatest work of art, their life.

In all that I've learned from the wise people who've gone before us, including members of my own family, I've come to believe that there is something like an art to living well, and that it's composed of several distinct arts. And at the very center of the secrets to a good and productive life is a form of alchemy or an art of change that involves the two sets of behaviors that I've called "the art of adaptation" and "the art of innovation." It's these arts that give us keys to making our futures, and the futures of those whose lives are touched by ours, great. They will benefit us throughout our days.

The secret of life is in art.
Oscar Wilde

We can take life's lemons and make lemonade successfully only if we live the advice of Socrates throughout our lives. Ongoing, honest self-examination with the deep and helpful self-knowledge this can produce are key. If we truly know ourselves, we can best evaluate our prospects in any new situation, handle better whatever change enters our lives, and choose the right innovations to make as new opportunities develop around us. This is a connection that will be important for all our reflections on change.

One additional point should be made here. Just as self-knowledge facilitates dealing well with change, things can also work the other way. Grappling with change can greatly enhance our self-knowledge. We can't just introspectively gaze within and fully know ourselves. There are many aspects of our unconscious minds that aren't available to immediate self-awareness. We have to learn certain things about who-we-are by paying attention to how-we-act and how-we-feel in the rough and tumble of the world. We often discover our nature by ferreting out the emotions that lie beneath the surface of conscious thought, and by noting what we naturally do as we deal with change.

Change is one of the greatest sources in the world for increased and deepened self-understanding. It's always a test, and the way we respond to the test can teach us a lot about ourselves that we can realize in no other way. This knowledge will then prepare us a bit more for the next test we'll face, as the process continues. But this depends on our ability to pay attention and truly observe ourselves in what we do.

> To know oneself, one should assert oneself.
> Albert Camus

Everyday alchemy starts in our inner life and moves from there out into the world. A necessary part of that inner work is ongoing, honest Socratic self-examination. Life can hand us lemons, roll lemons in front of us, throw them right at us, or dump truckloads all over us, and we won't be able to make any tasty lemonade without the self-understanding that Socrates urged on us. The best lemonade making of life begins within a self-aware mind. The outer phase of the process can then come to enhance our inner awareness further, as we monitor our progress and derive from this an even greater self-knowledge, which itself will allow even more effective results, in an upward spiral of growth and development as we continue to engage with the world.

Plato's Principles and Insight Two: Ideals

The master lemonade maker Socrates had the tremendous advantage of working with an unusually insightful student, the young man Plato, who would go on to bring many elements of his mentor's life and teachings to the world through engaging, written dialogues. Plato believed that, precisely because we live in a constantly changing world, we should grasp firmly and embrace tightly some things that will never change, such as the ideals of Truth, Beauty, and Goodness.

A champion wrestler as well as a great thinker, Plato took his stand on unchanging values as the ultimate leverage we have for grappling with this unpredictable world. He was convinced that we can attain true success in life only if we first understand the things that never change and use them well as our reference points for moving forward productively through life's uncertainties.

Centuries later, Jesus of Nazareth talked about building the structure of your life on a solid foundation of unyielding rock rather than on shifting sands that can provide no sure support. Many more centuries farther on in time, the great Danish philosopher, Søren Kierkegaard, often known as the father of existentialism, said something parallel about change in his influential collection of essays known as the *Edifying Discourses*:

> When the sailor is out on the sea and everything is changing around him, as the waves are continually being born and dying, he does not stare into the depths of these, since they

vary. He looks up at the stars. And why? Because they are faithful—as they stand now, they stood for the patriarchs, and will stand for coming generations. By what means then does he conquer changing conditions? Through the eternal: By means of the eternal, one can conquer the future, because the eternal is the foundation of the future.

Our highest ideals and deepest values that connect with the eternal can shed light on the often murky and confusing situations we face at work and in our personal lives. A former U.S. President, Jimmy Carter, once showed himself to be, at least in this regard, a true Platonist and Kierkegaardian. In his inaugural address to the nation, he quoted one of his old high school teachers who had taught him that, "In changing times, we must take our stand on unchanging principles." This powerful and ancient perspective on change endures from Plato to the present. The philosopher had wisdom that still carries down to us like a gentle breeze through the centuries.

> All thought is naught but a footnote to Plato.
> George Santayana

I've chosen Plato as our emblematic ideal guide into lemonade making largely because of his own personal resilience and this insight. But there's more to come from him as well. In exploring how to apply this particular perspective in detail, in learning how to use the right ideals to grapple with our challenges, we'll discover the full recipe we need. The overall stand that Plato took in his day will end up helping us to set up the Ultimate Lemonade Stand for our own time. Of course, he didn't get everything right, and neither will we. But if we move in the right fundamental direction with the best basic principles, we can follow him in also becoming masterful alchemists for life.

Aristotle's Virtues and Insight Three: Courage

Plato's star pupil and worthy successor Aristotle was in turn convinced that some of the unchanging things we need to bring to any changing situation are those personal qualities or character traits called "virtues." To the ancients, a virtue was an individual form of strength, a characteristic or quality that could empower us to deal with life well, whatever fate might send to our doorsteps. Many philosophers since then have followed him in concluding that, in particular, the trait of courage is foundational among the full array of virtues. Aristotle saw that only a courageous person could experience what all of us most deeply seek, some form of genuine success, authentic fulfillment, and lasting happiness. A courageous, fully virtuous person is uniquely positioned to be resiliently successful in life and, as a result, in the most complete sense possible, happy.

One of the more underappreciated personal qualities in the business world today—and, even more obviously, within the world of politics—is precisely this quality of courage. Whether you're in an established leadership position or rather work on the front lines in any context, some degree of courage is a necessity for doing the right thing when it needs to be done. Fear and timidity rule too many people's lives. Courage is the great liberator, praised by all philosophers who have come to understand the human condition most deeply, from Aristotle to modern existentialists and into our day.

> To the timid and hesitating, everything
> is impossible because it seems so.
> Sir Walter Scott

Any major change presents us with a measure of the unknown. And fear of the unknown is a nearly universal experience. It takes courage to overcome this fear, to confront big changes well, and to initiate a transformation when it's needed in your life or work.

Timidity holds us back. Courage propels us forward. Therefore, philosophers influenced by the great Aristotle say with one voice: Choose courage. It can even be suggested that the single most important quality for taking life's lemons and making lemonade is precisely this one primary Aristotelian trait.

Dealing with change well also requires several other virtues that Aristotle identified, like a strong affinity for truth, the power of self-control, and a personal capacity to act on a large scale, whenever appropriate. The surprising Aristotelian virtue of wittiness doesn't hurt, either. Any person who can laugh well in times of change and bring others to do so with him has a decided advantage in steering events and people successfully through that change. All in all, this philosopher's conception of the virtues is a powerful aid for dealing with any difficulty or challenge, and will in many ways guide me in what I have to say in this book.

Ockham and Insight Four: A Nose for the Simple Essence
Now, let's fast-forward from Aristotle for at least a millennium and a half, and then some. The profound medieval thinker William of Ockham left us a legacy that prominently features one great idea. Mathematicians, scientists, and other philosophers, as well as theorists in many fields of study have found inspiration and guidance in his insight that a preference for hard-earned simplicity is a useful tool for understanding almost anything in life. In any situation, however complicated, there is a simple essence. If we can identify and master that simple core, we can handle the entire situation better, with all its potential complexity. Our world seems to be formed in such a way that a profound simplicity is often a sign of truth, and it's just as frequently a sign of power.

In the chapters ahead, we're going to look at the simple essence of how to deal with the challenge brought by adversity and any form of difficult change. We'll examine those unchanging things we need to master in order to deal appropriately with the ups, downs, and alterations of our lives. And we'll find that the advice of our wisest predecessors is, in this regard, both simple and powerful. Our exploration of this wisdom and its implementation in our lives will enable us to undergo any change successfully, and position us to initiate change in all the right ways.

> The ability to simplify means to eliminate
> the unnecessary so that the necessary may speak.
> Hans Hofman

In our approach to dealing with difficult change, we'll strip away everything inessential and drill down to the basic skills that can carry us to success in any new struggle. Consider the literal side of our guiding metaphor. In order to make great lemonade, we don't have to master all the intricacies of lemon history, genetics, and chemistry. But there are things we do have to master—the ingredients we need for the results we want, and how to mix them together well. In gaining a command of these things, we'll be able to get the job done.

Our search for simplicity here should spark your own similar quest in any circumstance of challenge and change. The first requirement for responding well to difficulty is identifying with clarity and precision the most basic elements of what you confront. What's the core of the situation you face? What's the simple truth beyond and beneath all surface appearances? What's central, and what's peripheral? Once you know that, you can proceed effectively. A properly developed skill for simplifying is a powerful tool in life. When we can get to the heart of a situation, we can often make immediate progress and not waste our time.

Let's briefly review this beginning philosophical advice, which can be a bit like the array of kitchen tools we need for turning life's lemons into lemonade. To help us prosper in a turbulent world, Socrates recommended a strong habit of self-examination and the resulting self-knowledge that only this can supply. Plato pointed out the importance of unchanging principles and eternal values as our ultimate guides when we deal with change and challenge. Aristotle advised us to cultivate virtues like courage that will help us move forward to the future we desire. And Ockham suggested that we simplify insightfully in order to handle complexity well. Armed with these four things—a keen habit of self-examination, some stable guiding ideals, a cluster of personal virtues centered on courage, and a determined preference for simplicity—we can position ourselves to be true masters of challenging change, alchemists of adversity, and expert makers of life's finest lemonade.

Part One

The Art of Adaptation

Working with Life's Lemons

I

Don't Fear the Fruit

The Truth About the Lemons of Change

There are three basic facts about change in general that we need to consider before we begin to look at the individual skills that make up the art of adaptation for dealing with difficulty. These truths about the world will provide us with our most basic points of reference for approaching the challenge of life's unexpected lemons.

Putting Change into Perspective

THE GENERAL FEATURES OF CHANGE THAT WE SHOULD note here will provide the elements of a big picture we need for approaching this feature of the world productively. The fact that there is some paradoxical tension among these features will lead us to dig deeper into why we tend to react to change as we do. What we'll discover as a result will motivate us to master the many varied components of the more powerful response available to us.

Change is Pervasive

First, there's an undeniable truth that the pre-Socratic philosopher Heraclitus emphasized long ago about our world. Change is pervasive. Change is persistent. Or, as he succinctly put it: "Everything is always changing." Around 500 BC, he was just echoing the same observation traditionally ascribed to the legendary Chinese sage Fu Hsi, who is said to have lived more than two thousand years earlier, and whose teachings on how to deal with change are believed by many to be the original source of the ancient text that's still consulted today, *The I Ching*, or *The Book of Changes*.

What would Heraclitus or Fu Hsi say if dropped into our world today? Most likely, "I told you so." Change is all around us and always has been, despite any temporary appearances to the contrary. It's the normal state of things.

> Everything on earth is subject to change.
> *The I Ching*

What may indeed be new in our time is the sheer number of ways we now encounter change and the vastly accelerated pace of it all. In the mind of astute thinkers like Heraclitus or Fu Hsi, it certainly seemed that at some deep level things were in constant flux even in their day. But these philosophers didn't have to adjust to new technology all the time, hit target work numbers that could shift frequently, adapt to hardware and software upgrades unexpectedly, respond incessantly to an always-on-the-job smartphone, recalibrate a daily commute around the shifting vagaries of weather, traffic, construction, accidents, and last-minute errands, and then arrive at a busy office full of stressed out people to deal with constantly morphing information and new demands on a day-to-day basis. They also didn't have kids electronically connected to everything and everybody all the time, with all the concern that this implies. Even a fraction of our current whirlwind of change would have been more than enough all those centuries ago to get anyone's toga in a twist.

Life is so dynamically complex now that small-scale change swirls around us continually, while bigger upheavals can burst into our lives as suddenly and disruptively as tornadoes in the Midwest or wildfires in California, but much more frequently. This new speed and ubiquity of change is not confined to any geography, lifestyle, industry, or type of business. Change is persistent, pervasive, and nearly universal in its ramped up speed. At this point, we should always expect the unexpected, and never be surprised by surprise. Novelty is reality. The next new unparalleled twist simply awaits us.

Change is Necessary

Our second basic fact is that change is necessary. The Stoic philosopher Marcus Aurelius, who served as Emperor of Rome during its Golden Age, once stated a simple, fundamental realization. Nothing ever happens without change. At first glance, this may seem too obvious to mention. But it has some interesting implications.

As the Emperor put it, you can't use a fire to cook your food or warm your room unless the wood fueling it undergoes a change. You won't grow from childhood to adulthood without change. You can't get a raise or a promotion without change. Healing requires change. So does gaining wisdom. It's simply necessary for so many of the things we value. There could be no biological processes without change, and because of that fact, it's a basic requirement for life. In addition, there's a pretty obvious corollary to this general truth that nothing we welcome as good ever happens without change. And this is clearly something important to keep in mind.

What in the whole universe is more natural than change?
Marcus Aurelius

If modern scientists are even remotely correct in current theories about human development on earth, we owe our front row seats in the stadium right now to the millennia of change that have come before us. And this perspective goes even deeper. Ancient philosophers and early scientists long thought of the universe as populated primarily by solid and relatively enduring things that only accidentally or secondarily engage in change. Some form of a deep and static permanence or stability seemed to underlie any form of transition, flux, or alteration. But the physics of the past century and the present day has revolutionized our sense of what's most fundamental in the world.

Stability of any kind seems now to be what's genuinely secondary, if not altogether illusory and dependent on a more basic reality of continual activity, movement, and transformation at the most fundamental level imaginable, and far beyond what we can even begin to imagine. Reality is more like a dance than any static diorama. In our world, change has been revealed, oddly, to be the most enduring necessity of all. And in coming to this realization, we're looping back to another remark made by our old friend Heraclitus, who long ago surmised that, "The only thing permanent is change."

Whatever is necessary for the cosmic expanse within which we live can't simply cease to be necessary, and because of that fundamental truth, we can't call a time-out on the dynamic flow of ongoing reconfigurations in the world. We couldn't change the fact that things are always changing even if we wanted to, and Marcus Aurelius suggests that we ask: "Why should we want to?" The good things we value most can come our way only by means of transition. So we ought never to regret the reality of change in and of itself. It's not a feature of existence just to accept; it's something for us all to find a way to embrace and use well.

True wisdom consists in not departing from nature,
and molding our conduct according to her laws and model.
Seneca

Certain leading international companies have long employed the concept of continuous improvement. This can be a powerful part of an operating philosophy, and it's an orientation that quickly can take a business to the top of its industry. Continuous improvement simply means engaging in ongoing change for the better. For enhancing quality and service in any business, an adventure of change is necessary, and a positive commitment to it is required. What's true then for companies is also best for us as individuals. Especially in our time of dynamic technological and global interrelations, a clear understanding of change as necessary is more important than ever before.

Change is Scary

We sometimes wish we could slow or even stop the incessant flurry of transition and alteration in the world around us because, and this is our third beginning fact, change is often scary. But in light of what we've just seen about change, this can initially seem to be a puzzle. We're usually not frightened by pervasive things, persistent things, or anything that's happening all around us all the time. We're more typically afraid of the surprising, shocking, eerily unusual, disturbingly novel, or unparalleled phenomenon. And we're not often scared by necessary things—we don't exactly shudder at the truths of mathematics, the principles of logic, or the ironclad laws of nature—with the apparent inevitability of death, of course, as one glaring exception to this otherwise reliable rule. However, death on its surface seems to be an exception to most rules, at least regarding the course of normal experience, and it's in a deep way just the ultimate sort of change we all face. It's a fairly startling and apparently permanent form of interruption whose mere contemplation can unhinge normal people and turn them into brooding poets or existentialist philosophers. But the real question is why the mere threat of any sort of change can create anxiety and even fear, when change in some form is a necessity.

Aside from mortality, the vast majority of necessary things are truths about the world that we usually just accept, and at least most of us can come to accept even this final necessity. "Well, that's simply the way it is." Necessary things are fundamental features of reality we know we can't do anything about, and when we recognize that fact, those of us who aren't logicians, mathematicians, or scientists tend to just stop thinking about them. What would be the point? But change is different. We're inclined to think about change a lot. We can worry about it and can even dread it. But, indeed: why?

Always it comes about that the beginning of wisdom is a fear.
Miguel de Unamuno

What's the reason for widespread negativity about change, and about even the possibility of its intruding into our lives? Understanding some of what's behind our common tendency to be unsettled and fearful in connection with even a prospect of change will move us closer to the practical wisdom available for dealing with it.

Chewing on Lemons

LET'S START SMALL. THINK FOR A MINUTE ABOUT THE WORD "change" itself, and the most common associations around the concept it conveys. How do we most often come across this word and idea in our normal experience? When do we use it? Where do we encounter it? A simple but subtle answer to these questions may begin to explain our common emotional tendencies in even considering change.

First, it may be helpful to recall how we most often heard the word when growing up. It was not usually a pleasant situation, or a positive communication:

"You'd better change your attitude, young man."
"Change that outfit or you're not going anywhere."
"I want you to change that tone of voice right now."
"We're going to have some changes around here, starting today."

As a child, if you were ever told, out of the blue and with no request on your part, that there was going to be a major change in your family life, or that you were suddenly going to have to change schools, it likely wasn't a welcome or encouraging thing to hear.

Then you had to learn to change batteries, change light bulbs, change a tire, and perhaps in college go through lots of hassle to change a room situation or your major. Maybe you got married and had a child and discovered the decidedly unpleasant task requested when you heard the words, "Honey, the baby needs a change." And right when you thought your job was going great, there was a dreaded announcement at work that, "Unfortunately, due to the economy, we're going to undergo some major change."

I could give many more examples of this, but I'm too tired. I haven't gotten a good night's sleep in months. My wife wakes me up every hour tossing and turning and throwing off the covers with hot flashes, because she's going through—The Change. It's not a pretty picture. There aren't a lot of positive connotations surrounding the word.

In addition, consider this: Literally thousands of little transitions, alterations, movements, mutations, occurrences, and developments that play a role in our daily lives typically take place far below the sweep of our general conceptual radar. We don't often perceive them as worthy of any special attention or conscious labeling beyond the particular events they are and, even when we do, they don't usually mean enough to justify our reflectively thinking of them as, or calling them, changes. Only those events that are big enough to grab our notice and disrupt our lives and habits in a distinctively positive or negative way will typically evoke a use of the word 'change.' And for most people, more negatives than positives stand out.

In part, this is because of what scientists call "the survival brain," that group of neural structures that have evolved early on to monitor our environment for threats and dangers. We all have a tendency to notice the negative precisely because of the fact that in our ancient past this inclination had tremendous survival val-ue. And, of course, it still does. The problem comes in when the survival brain gets a bit out of control and, in its hypervigilance, augmented by the fear factor which is its natural companion, it comes to obsess on the negative, hardly allowing us to notice any of the positives around us. And yet the negatives it identifies could be no more than possibilities, rather than actual realities. But that's enough alone to get the survival brain's complete attention.

Then again, the survival brain isn't just whistling in the graveyard and jumping at shadows. As Aristotle pointed out long ago with an image from archery, there are vastly many more ways to miss any target than to hit it. Your arrow can be off to the left, or to the right, or high, or low in uncountably many ways. Life itself reflects this fact. There are always more possibilities for things to go wrong than right. Among the changes around us that are big enough to get our attention, there will statistically be many more that initially bother and block us than that benefit and better us. More will miss the mark than hit it. The inconveniences, irritations, and threats in life, as a result, are many. So, because of this, most of the changes we ever notice *as such* will tend to be negative in their nature. Or, at least, they will at first seem so.

This is an unfortunate general truth about human psychology. We tend to think and talk about change in a positive way only when things are very bad and need to be turned around. But even then, we often seem to suspect that any process of making a change for the better will itself be, at least to some extent, difficult and bothersome to undergo. So even when things are tough and the outcome of any substantial change in that circumstance should be perceived as good, the process of transition itself can still be thought of in at least a minimally negative way.

> Change is not made without inconvenience,
> even from worse to better.
> Richard Hooker

Of course, when things are good, change can be especially scary. Most people prefer the known to the unknown and the comfort of the familiar to the challenge of the new. Even on an upward path from good to great, people who are initiating change that's intended to be for the better can still worry about any unanticipated consequences of the changes they're making. There aren't a lot of thoroughly positive associations in most people's minds surrounding the whole general idea of change.

Wait: It Gets Worse

IF YOU'RE A FOOTBALL FAN OR ARE RELATED TO ONE, YOU may remember from years ago the great former Notre Dame football coach and philosopher, Lou Holtz. To the consternation of many diehard Notre Dame fans and sports journalists who favored a faster-paced game, Lou loved to have his teams run the ball. As a result, he was often asked in press conferences, "Why don't you throw the ball more often?" Following several coaches at other famous football schools who had made the comment long before him, he liked to say, "Whenever you throw the ball, only three things can happen, two of them bad. I don't like the odds." And fans immediately got what he was saying. But it will be useful here for us to make his point a bit more explicit.

The American Football Analogy to Change

For any of you who might not be American football aficionados: When you throw the ball in an effort to advance the team downfield toward the goal line, three basic things indeed can happen. The pass can result in an incompletion—the intended receiver drops the ball—and this, of course, is bad. Or, it can be an interception—the wrong guy, a player on the other team, catches the ball and takes possession of it—and that's very bad. Or, finally, it can be a completion, which of course isn't bad at all unless, unfortunately, the play ends up with a net loss of yards, in which case we can really start to understand the coach's hesitation even beyond the literal import of his words.

"I don't like the odds." A lot of people consciously or unconsciously approach the idea of change in exactly the same way. Their operative thought seems to be: "Whenever there's a change, three things can happen, two of them bad. I don't like the odds."

> Just as nature abhors a vacuum, humans resist change.
> Nikki Giovanni

The parallel here is interesting. When there's a change, what three things can happen? Well, first—and this is obviously what we worry about—the dreaded possibility for any change is that it will be a change for the worse, which is clearly bad. Everything was rolling along and something terrible happens. Or: Things were fine and now we've blown it. Or: it never was great around here in the first place, but with this change we've suddenly gone from bad to worse, out of the frying pan and into the fire. In her great novel *Middlemarch*, the very philosophical author Mary Ann Evans, who wrote under the penname George Eliot, refers to this attitude and says of a character that his viewpoint "consisted in holding that whatever is, is bad, and any change is likely to be worse." And this, of course, captures a sadly common mindset with precision. Plus, it's a deep well that's fed richly by the ever-flowing underground stream of interpretation habits known as confirmation bias. But I'll say more about that later. The unfortunate truth is that we typically worry that any change we're contemplating now or already going through may be negative, deleterious, actually wrong for us, and consequently such as to end very badly. There's no mystery at all as to why such a potential outcome is feared.

Perhaps surprisingly, there is also a negative possibility number two, an additionally dreaded result: A particular change can sometimes be one that promises great improvements but that ends up being amazingly difficult and quite disruptive, and then doesn't in the end make things a bit any better; so why did we have to go through all the trouble it caused us? The time used, the energy expended, and all the inevitable accompanying worry end up clearly making this option a net loss and so, ultimately, bad in its own way as well. A change that takes up limited time, resources, and energy and yet gets you nowhere better as a result is definitely worse than no change at all.

And then, finally, there's the third and positive possibility: A change can be a change for the better, which is of course good, although even that happy result may take more time and trouble than we would have liked. A transition to The Promised Land may involve quite a bit of wandering in the wilderness before anyone crosses the threshold of paradise. The process of getting to that happy ending may have put us through more hard work, discomfort, and anxiety than we ever could have imagined. And yet, still in the end, good is good, and better is better, despite any pain and aggravation along the way.

When we anticipate or contemplate the possible outcomes of any change that might be looming on the horizon, lurking at the door, or already altering our lives, we see that of the three possible ways things might work out, it's not an overwhelmingly positive picture we face. So we worry. We feel stressed out. And we brace ourselves inwardly for unpleasant results.

A lot of people, whether consciously or subliminally grasping this overall set of possibilities—when there's a change, three things can happen, two of them bad—in effect say, like the coach, at least, deep in their unconscious minds, "I don't like the odds." That's one of the main reasons so many of us tend to worry about change and seek to avoid it whenever we can. Why take the chance?

Change doth unknit the tranquil strength of men.
Matthew Arnold

But the best practical philosophers, the real alchemists of possibility throughout history, have had a simple and yet profound perspective on this that we all need to hear. The likelihood of a particular change bringing us good or ill isn't always independent of our action. In fact, the outcomes of most changes depend at least in part on us. How will we respond? What will we choose to do? Our reactions to a change can create a new environment for the change itself and spin it, or affect it, in new ways.

Changing the Odds
What indeed are the real odds that any particular change will be, overall, a change for the better or a change for the worse? The truly wise view of change is that this is not a fixed, determinate matter set once and for all, or a feature of reality that's devoid of our input. The best perspective on the general question of what the odds might be that any given change will help or hurt us is simple:

The odds aren't unchangeable. We can change the odds.

Here's something also worth noting. In my years at Notre Dame, if memory serves me at all well here, when Lou Holtz lost a football game, it tended in many cases to be against a team that often threw the ball. I'm reminded of the University of Miami in the late eighties when they were often contending with the Irish for the National Championship. Their recruitment, practice, and strategy changed the theoretical odds that otherwise might haunt a heavy passing offense, and often positioned them to win.

This gives us a good response to the coach's cleverly repeated aphorism about passing and its application to change. The deepest philosophical perspective is to think that we can affect the odds concerning the potential outcomes of change in our lives by what we do in our preparation for change and in our handling of it. That is exactly what those successful football teams that threw the ball a lot managed to accomplish. It's also what, in our own different ways, each of us can do as well.

So don't fret about change. And don't fear it. Take charge of it. It's all around us and it's not going away. Use it properly. Take any lemons that drop at your feet and start gathering the ingredients you need to sweeten the deal. It's going to be up to you to make the lemonade. That way, you can win in the end. But you'll be able to accomplish this reliably only if you can master the overall art of change. And what that amounts to, we'll begin to see in the next chapter. This will be a main part of the way you can make great lemonade.

2

HANDLING THE LEMONS
The Art of Self-Control

Have you ever been in a situation where things suddenly go wrong and everyone goes ballistic? Maybe there's an unexpected development that threatens to derail an important project. Disaster looms. Something's gone haywire or someone's dropped the ball. Tempers flare and angry words fly. The lemons aren't handled well. I've seen people spin out of control at the first hint of a big problem. And this just makes the situation worse. We're unlikely to find the best solutions when we're busy losing our heads.

The art of transformative change is all about dealing with the stress of the new, whether in the form of the demands of difficulty, or the unknowns of opportunity. This vital art is the source of the practical alchemy that's always needed in our lives. When sudden change knocks at your door, how do you adapt and create the best way forward? The first component within the overall art of change that's focused on adaptation is the art of self-control. This art, or form of cultivated, skilled behavior, has three simple requirements or basic rules. Together, these three key behaviors give us the foundations for masterful self-management in the face of challenge or change.

The Art of Self-Control
1. Don't rush to judgment.
2. Value the right things.
3. Use your imagination well.

Each of these requirements is necessary for dealing with difficult change or any form of adversity appropriately and powerfully. Linked together, they can produce important results. Let's look at each of them in turn and dig into the details.

Don't Rush to Judgment
THE FIRST RULE FOR HANDLING CHANGE WELL IS ALWAYS THE same, and it's crucial. When a major change looms on the horizon or suddenly enters your life, don't rush to judgment. Never conclude too quickly that the new development is either terrible or great. Avoid a hasty verdict.

> Things are not always what they seem.
> Phaedrus

We admittedly tend to admire people who can size up a situation quickly in the blink of an eye, but only if they can do it well. In most matters of belief and life, accuracy is more important than speed. Living in a fast-paced world, we admittedly benefit from a capacity to notice things right away and rapidly draw conclusions on which we can act. But being too fast in forming judgments about whether some novel development is either good or bad can get us into trouble by impairing our ability to think clearly and creatively. It can prejudice us at the outset and keep us from seeing more deeply into the situation as it really is.

Snap Judgments: Good or Bad
The problem with most snap judgments in the face of a new development is that they tend to be the result of surface appearances

rather than real understanding, and such appearances notoriously can deceive us. Because of this, many ancient philosophers cautioned us not to form our assessments too quickly, and this advice applies helpfully to most beliefs of the form: "This is very good," or "That's really bad." We should use a measure of caution in sizing up new things, and the more important a situation is, the more careful we should be in drawing any strong conclusions about it. Things are not always, or even often, exactly what they at first seem.

When a big change comes our way, we far too easily rush to judgment based on appearances and adopt a heated opinion of the situation. We get too excited or alarmed. The philosophers advise us to slow down and give ourselves time to process the new things we're confronting. Their recommendation is simple: Don't rush to judgment.

> We don't know a millionth of one percent about anything.
> Thomas A. Edison

A top executive decided to change many of his company's computer systems and methods of interfacing with customers. People panicked. He told me he had never seen such a wave of resistance, almost amounting to rebellion. He kept assuring everyone that, if they would just hang in there and learn the new process, they'd all soon be able to work more efficiently and productively. Common jobs would become quicker and easier, and the range of things they could accomplish would be extended by a lot. It was due to his hard work, constant cheerleading, and elaborate hand holding that people eventually came around, mastered the new setup, and concluded that he had been right all along. They finally realized that their initial snap judgments had been completely off the mark.

Their transition could have been much smoother, a lot less trouble, and not at all traumatic if everyone had simply refrained from rushing to a conclusion about the new changes. Sometimes, we just need to suspend judgment, hit the pause button on our emotions, allow the dust to settle, and do a little detective work on the situation that faces us, realizing that our initial impressions might have been wrong and shouldn't be allowed to spawn emotional reactions that could be, in the end, unhelpful and even self-defeating.

Appearance and Reality

What may be the most memorable image bequeathed to us by the ancient world came from the pen of Plato. It's called "Plato's Cave." The great philosopher imagined all of us as lifelong captives in a deep cave, chained down and gazing at a wall across which fleeting shadows dance, due to the light of a fire far behind us. We habitually mistake these shadows as solid realities and things they aren't. The true philosopher, he said, is the person who breaks his chains and gets out of the cave, escaping to the daylight above where he can finally see what's real under the illumination of the sun. He then returns to the cave in hopes of freeing the other prisoners, helping them to liberate themselves from the false appearances, or illusions, that hold their minds captive.

Plato highlighted what could be the most important distinction ever made in antiquity, and what may be the single most useful contrast for responding well to things that can seem to be lemons of change, the simple and necessary distinction between appearance and reality. Appearances rule us. But to live well, we have to get beyond any that are illusory and grasp instead the realities beyond them. With many of the changes we face in life, the appearance often can suggest we've been handed sour lemons that are good for nothing. The reality instead may be that we now possess the most crucial ingredients for some incredible lemonade. But if we can't see that, we won't begin the process of creative adaptation that's required.

The Stoic philosophers of first and second century Rome, people like Epictetus, Seneca, and Marcus Aurelius, loved to remind us that, typically, nothing in this world is either as good as it seems or as bad as it seems, so we should all just calm down. They understood that we have a natural tendency to react to first appearances and become so worked up and excited about things-as-they-seem that we inhibit our ability to grapple well with things-as-they-are. We far too often react to a big change with discouragement or elation, and without sufficient investigation or consideration. But the new thing that we welcome with abandon or dislike to our bones can often end up being completely different from the way it first struck us.

> Appearances are often deceiving.
> Aesop

I grew up hearing vivid stories of this disparity between appearance and reality. My father was completing his basic training in the army when he came down with the worst case of flu he had ever experienced. He was miserable. He had to be hospitalized and put on IV fluids. He was the only one in his outfit to get sick, and he was consumed with thoughts like, "This is just awful," and "Why is this happening to me?" While he was being treated, everyone else in his unit was shipped out to fight in Europe. He was suddenly separated from all his new friends. That added a new level of frustration and dismay to his ordeal. Things seemed to have gone from bad to worse. And then, one day shortly afterwards, an officer came by and told him he was very lucky to have been so sick, because all the other guys had been killed in transit. They'd never made it to their destination. He was stunned. And he was alive, thanks to many days of a severe illness. The truth can be radically different from any first appearance.

We tend to get too excited about what seems good and too agitated about what appears to be bad. And this is a problem. Irrational exuberance or unnecessary despair can equally unhinge us and distort our capacity for making the right choices in a new situation. Most of us understand the ways in which falsely negative judgments can hinder our benefiting from situations that are really good. But wildly positive excitement can also be the result of a rush to judgment that's equally problematic. Think about all the people who were investing in dotcom companies during the early days of the Internet and making so much money in technology stocks that they rushed to judgment and decided to put everything they had into those exciting high-tech enterprises. Their enthusiasm for how things seemed set them up for terrible losses and in a very short time. The same thing happened in the later massive real estate bubble, when so many people who were caught up in appearances and gripped by easy money mania diverted all their savings into building or buying condos and houses to flip for quick profits. And then the bottom fell out and many experienced disasters that could have been avoided if they had just been more cautious and prudent about what seemed to be the greatest thing ever.

Consider also the oddly similar case of the now-legendary mega-millions state lottery winner who reacts immediately and naturally by proclaiming, "This is the greatest thing in the world!" Then, shockingly often, and in as little as five years or so, the initial delirium of winning has led to enough bad decisions that all the winner's family members and former friends are completely alienated, his reputation has been destroyed, he's had a nasty divorce, he's now in deep legal trouble, and, perhaps most surprising of all, he's flat broke. The unexpected development of fortune wasn't at all what it initially seemed.

> Things often love to conceal their true nature.
> Heraclitus

The most important point here is that we can be wrong in either a positive or negative way when we rush to judgment. First appearances aren't reliable guides to reality. You may have heard someone say, "Getting fired was the best thing that ever happened to me." You actually may have said it yourself. I've come across this surprising report made by many people through the years. And yet, imagine what we might have seen and heard if we could travel back in time to the event itself:

> "Bill, I'm so sorry, but we're having some cutbacks and your position has been eliminated. I hope there are no hard feelings. You've done a great job and are admired around here. It's just the harsh realities of the economy right now."
>
> How do you think we'd see Bill react at that precise moment? "Wow! This is the best thing that's ever happened to me! I can't believe it! Can I take a minute and call my wife to let her hear the news?"
>
> "No, I'm sorry, Bill. We have to escort you out of the building as soon as possible, and in fact, right now."
>
> "Oh, man! That's even better!"
>
> "If you'll just gather up your things, these gentlemen will see you to the door and out to your car."
>
> "Awesome. This is just awesome. I can't wait to tell the kids!"

I doubt this was the reaction at the time. Bill may have felt a knot in his stomach, a suddenly dry mouth, perhaps some light-headedness, and then the room might have seemed to close in on him as he mentally tried to process the words he was hearing, while a dark abyss of anxiety opened up at his feet. He likely rushed to judgment right away with the thought, "This is awful." But then, look at what he later says to you or me just a few years down the road. "It was the best thing that ever happened to me." We then hear about how the unexpected blow set him on a new path that has produced wonderful things for him and his family beyond what they at the time ever could have imagined.

Remember: you must never, under any circumstances, despair.
Boris Pasternak

Even something as serious as the sudden loss of a job can end up being very different from what it initially seems. Many great and successful people have rebounded well from the difficult experience of this sort of unexpected change, and have gone on to prosper because of it, including such luminaries and existential alchemists as Steve Jobs, Robert Redford, Larry King, Donna Karan, George Foreman, J.K. Rowling, and, in a former generation, Walt ("not creative enough") Disney, along with the son of a failed businessman we should also mention, whose teacher told him he'd never amount to anything, either, and who seemed to confirm that view by his early string of temporary, low paying jobs—the eventual, nicely above-average achiever, Albert Einstein.

Literature is full of things not being what they seem. To give a few nearly random examples, in such classic stories as the 1766 novel by Oliver Goldsmith, *The Vicar of Wakefield*, Jane Austin's 1811 *Sense and Sensibility*, and Frances Hodgson Burnett's delightful 1905 novel, *A Little Princess*, matters seem to go relentlessly wrong until a final revelation that all has worked out in the end. In situations of dramatic, unwanted change, and even what can seem to be decimating failure, we need to resist the lure of panic, clear our heads, and consider the real possibility that the challenge we're facing may ultimately lead to good outcomes. Every major change pushes us beyond what we know. And our knee-jerk reaction is often fear. But the realm of the unknown can contain delight as well as danger. The slamming of one door may open a better one. As many astute thinkers have advised us, we can change the odds of positive or negative results in most situations by how we react in our judgments, attitudes, and actions.

In most business and life contexts, a negative rush to judgment in the face of apparently challenging realities or even ambiguous change seems to be more common than a positive rush to judg-ment. Because of this, it will be beneficial to look for a moment at a major tendency that appears widespread in many corporate contexts and that can be poisonous for stirring up great lemonade. It's found outside business as well, in politics, all the professions, and throughout other endeavors within our personal lives.

Pessimism and Optimism
The grumpiest cynics and worst gloom-and-doom types among us most often attempt to justify their customary negative rush to judgment and their resulting bad attitudes by claiming to be hard-nosed realists. But always believing and expecting the worst isn't a proof of realism. It's more often a sign of self-defeating pessimism. Admittedly, we live in a time when it's often easy to believe the worst. But it's rarely helpful to do so.

> No horse named Morbid ever won a race.
> Ernest Hemingway

Positive psychologists like Martin Seligman and Ed Diener, among many others, have noted how our pessimistic or optimistic tendencies can affect outcomes in the external world. The predic-tive ability of both states of mind is at first surprising, but in the end can make perfect sense. These divergent attitudes each tend to be self-fulfilling in interesting ways. Pessimists can limit their ability to use available resources. They think, "What's the point?" And then, as feared, things are more likely to go wrong. Optimists, by contrast, can empower themselves by drawing deeply on their available resources. And then, in a nicely self-fulfilling manner, things are often more likely to go well. Our attitudes often deter-mine our actions, or our lack of proper initiative in the face of any difficult challenge.

And yet, as the ancients counseled us in other connections,

moderation is almost always a good thing. Not rushing to judgment means that we should bring a measure of caution, and even healthy skepticism, to any new situation, but we need not follow the pessimist onto a path of stubborn negativity, however minimal or tentative. Likewise, the positive and hopeful orientation of optimism can be very good, as long as we avoid the ungrounded, incautious mindset that rushes headlong into a new situation without sufficient thought or care. Overall optimism, enacted with the sort of detail-oriented skeptical concern that never allows easy assumption to substitute for hard work is simply an attitude more motivating for the accomplishment of good things than a determined pessimism, lived out with its own dimly jaundiced eye. It seems to me that, all things considered, a moderate and cautious optimism beats any form of pessimism by a mile. We're overall much better off as balanced and responsible optimists who have, as a result of this attitude, a motivation to adapt and transform as circumstances may require.

> 'Twixt optimist and pessimist
> The difference is droll
> The optimist sees the doughnut,
> The pessimist, the hole.
> McLandburgh Wilson

Many pessimists think they're just being worldly wise, hardheaded, no-nonsense, and tough-minded people. But the truth is often sadly different. They live in constant danger of being the self-limiting and unintentionally self-defeating victims of their own rush to judgment, based on nothing more than habitual bias. A realist isn't by nature the same thing as a defeatist, even in harsh and daunting circumstances. A true realist can be a rational optimist by also being a determined activist, by having an appropriate action orientation to life. In this sense, activism is just a sound philosophy of successful living.

When we take initiative to create good outcomes within the range of our ability to act, and in that way seek to make the most of the changes and challenges that come our way, we lay the groundwork for positive long-term outcomes. It's often to a surprising degree up to us, at least in part, how things turn out. But we give up the possibility of exercising our power to the fullest extent when we rush to judgment and set our thoughts and emotions running off in an unhealthy direction that can diminish our potential.

> The pessimist complains about the wind; the optimist
> expects it to change; the realist adjusts the sails.
> William Arthur Ward

The first rule in the art of self-control is simple: Don't rush to judgment. And especially, don't allow negativity to rush in. But also, when things look delightfully good, take care not to let an improper giddiness overwhelm you. Be calm. Chill out. Pause. Give yourself time to process what you've just seen, or heard, or learned. Often, new things will reveal their true nature only with time. Investigate what the real truth might be. Then be open to what you find. This is the first inner step in the alchemy of everyday life, that interior practice that gives us the power to change well and make tasty, refreshing lemonade out of any lemons that may come our way.

Value the right things
By refusing to rush to judgment in situations of unexpected or dramatic change, we provide some measure of inner peace for ourselves and a little breathing room, a mental and emotional space within which to watch, think, and act most effectively. But the art of self-control isn't just about refusing to rush to judgment. It also requires some inner guardrails, and something like a proper guidance system for our reactions and action. And that can be called into play by a personal values-check. Our values are our

most basic and enduring general commitments that determine how we view and respond to the world, as well as how we plan to act in it with specific goals and aspirations. Our deepest values are the ultimate lenses through which we see everything that happens around us. They give rise to our interpretations, beliefs, emotions, and choices. They can blind us to the obvious or liberate us from the misleading.

> People only see what they are prepared to see.
> Ralph Waldo Emerson

The ancient alchemists, the metaphysical lemonade makers of the past, on the surface of their activities pursued the creation of gold and the provision of greater life. But that's also a great metaphor. What's your gold? Where do you see real wealth? What's your idea of a greater life, a full and flourishing human existence? There you'll find your values, the appreciative and aspirational grid through which you see and react to the world. The importance of those values for your perceptions and choices can't be overstated. They open or close the most basic interpretive possibilities for categorizing the things around you and the changes that come your way. They give rise to what you think, feel, and do. They comprise your deepest guidance system.

We react to change and challenge in the calmest, strongest, and best ways when we value the right things to the right degrees and in the right ways. Any skewed, unbalanced, or inappropriate twist in our personal values, however subtle it might be, can prevent our having the best perceptions and reactions in a new situation. And this should lead us to understand a problem that needs our attention.

Few of us at any given moment have a personal value structure in operation that's perfectly healthy and in no need of review, renewal, adjustment, or augmentation. Not all values are equal. And not all are right. And this can create a difficulty. When we value the wrong things and an alteration in our circumstances threatens to take away something we're unhelpfully attached to, we can become needlessly frustrated, tense, angry, and anxious. And then the agitation we experience can cloud our ability to deal well with the overall situation. False values create false problems. And so it will be in our interest to pay more attention to whether we have the exact values we need.

The Power of Our Values

What we think our values are, and what they actually are, can be two very different things. Knowing the difference requires ongoing and completely honest Socratic self-examination. Our actual values are the implicit interpretive grid through which we assess new things, identify our options, and evaluate possible paths of choice and action. As our deepest preferential commitments, pro and con, our real values determine how we see the world, how we feel about what we see, and what we do in response to it. They can help us to perceive more clearly or distort our vision badly, depending on what they are.

Consider a simple short list of possible values that might govern a person's life and affect his or her perceptions and choices, in each of these distinct vertical columns:

Money	Love
Power	Learning
Status	Growth
Fame	Friendship
Security	Health
Winning	Serving
Control	Freedom

The things we value most will always determine how we view and react to the world around us, and especially how we perceive the challenges and opportunities it brings us.

A person whose primary values are dominated by the concerns named in the column on the left will normally see, act, and feel quite differently than someone whose chief values are captured better by the terms on the right. There may be no value in either column that is in itself always bad or false as an overriding concern, or intrinsically wrong as a commitment. But the extent to which we embrace any such concern, prioritize it, and allow it to dominate over other values can be either healthy or detrimental, and in that sense, right or wrong.

By contrast, a reasonable short list of simply false values would certainly include such things as:

Brutality	Cruelty	Manipulation
Racism	Hatred	Destructiveness
Sexism	Greed	Dominance
Anarchy	Deception	Objectification

Just as we can have false beliefs and unhealthy, inappropriate emotions, we can have false values. But we live in a time when this is not widely understood, so perhaps I should say a bit more. We all understand the difference between true and false beliefs, because that can mean the difference between life and death. We can't always determine with full accuracy what's true and what's false, but we all get that there is a difference, and that in most circumstances it matters. But many well-intentioned people recoil from the notion of false values, or even emotions that are inappropriate. We certainly have the emotions we have, and sometimes they can be good guides to reality. They can often track well the true nature of a situation. But at times, they can be an over-reaction, or at the other extreme, they can fail to register the full seriousness of a situation. Healthy emotions guide us well in the world. Unhealthy emotions cause us problems. It's just that simple. And it's the same with values.

It's natural for the mind to believe, and for the will to love;
so that, without true objects, they must attach
themselves to the false.
Blaise Pascal

We can speak of false values without being unjustifiably judgmental, or without presuming to know more than we do about the deepest levels of human nature or the ultimate structure of reality. And when we talk generally of valuing the wrong things, or having false values, we can variously mean to refer to values that are in themselves unhealthy, or to those that can be healthy to a degree, but are prioritized wrongly, or held more tightly, or applied more stringently or comprehensively, than is healthy. Many philosophers follow the spirit of Aristotle here and see good values, or healthy values, as those that are conducive to the living of a full and happy life, allowing for genuine human excellence; and false values, or unhealthy ones, are simply those that tend to create needless problems and detract from individual and communal flourishing. The distinction is fairly easy to draw in a general way. What's harder may be the challenge of knowing in a particular instance how to assign a value, or judgment of importance, to the category of true or false. That's a matter for personal wisdom. And it's also in itself an art.

I conceive that the great part of the miseries
of mankind are brought
upon them by false estimates they have
made of the value of things.
Benjamin Franklin

False values are no recipe for true success. Inappropriate or exaggerated values can cause us to misinterpret and miss out on great opportunities. For example, if you place too high a value on your perceived status in an organization or among your peers, then you'll tend to resist mightily any change that seems to dilute or undermine that status. Over the years, I've heard a similar story in different versions. A person who had performed well in a particular job and had been promoted to a prominent executive position within a large company was suddenly invited to move out of his comfort zone and organize a potentially important start-up venture for the organization. The new assignment at first would involve a dramatically lower budget and a much smaller team, and it would come with nearly zero built-in public prestige, along with a completely new level of risk. The initial reaction many people might have to such an offer is easy to understand. Who would want to leave an important, high status position with all its many perks to go into an obscure new job and start from scratch?

In situations like this, the person asked to launch the new venture will typically respond well to the opportunity only if he or she values the right things like challenge, adventure, personal growth, creativity, the overall good of the organization, and the chance to make a difference in a new way. If that person's dominant values are current prestige, status, power, comfort, and security, the change being offered will seem threatening, and may be rejected or else only grudgingly accepted with an underlying attitude of ambivalence, or even a measure of disappointment, resentment, or frustration. In either case, what could have been a very positive opportunity is not likely to be utilized well to create great good for both the organization and the individual. The wrong values generate attitudes that can block great results. Anyone who holds the wrong values uppermost in their motivations, values that in a dominant position will not be conducive to genuine personal or social wellbeing, will often miss out on what could have been an incredible and rewarding adventure. Our values help us or hold us back. Not all are equal.

This is a much more common problem generally than most of us would imagine. An unexpected change in financial circumstances may enter the life of a family. They need to alter their spending habits and economic commitments quickly in order to deal with the new reality. But they are embarrassed to make those changes, fearing that a certain status or prestige in the community, or among their acquaintances, will be lost. Because of this, the situation is scary to everyone involved in a way that it need not be. An emotional cauldron is stirred up that makes the new circumstances much worse for everyone. It's easy to see how, in both personal and professional contexts, the wrong values—valuing the wrong things, or valuing perfectly legitimate things to the wrong degree, or with the wrong priorities—can block the way to a positive future.

When we value the wrong things, we can easily come to dread change in many of its forms, even a change that could actually improve our situation. With the wrong values, we won't recognize good opportunities for what they are. We'll see instead a pile of sour lemons that we don't want. And by perceiving the situation that way, we will have given ourselves those lemons. It's ironic that the people most likely to offer themselves such bitter fruit by the way they interpret their circumstances through the wrong values are then the least prepared to take productive action, get busy, and make lemonade. When false values block your ability to perceive a great new opportunity for what it is, no positive process tends to result. And an unseen opportunity is like a locked door. It can't be the threshold for entering into something new. By contrast, when we value the right things, we're more likely to realize the fundamental importance of ongoing change in our lives and spot positive opportunities for what they are.

Know your opportunity.
Pittacus

As a philosopher and student of the human condition, I'm firmly convinced that life is best seen as a series of adventures. The right values focused on personal learning, positive growth, opportunity, improvement, and healthy adventure will support us through change like nothing else and lead us into a rewarding future. They are the foundations for masterful alchemy, the values that help us make great life lemonade. To the extent that we embrace them, we flourish. If we ignore them, we end up diminished.

When we value the right things, we're more likely to experience productive responses to any change that comes our way. And we're also more inclined to make the best choices as we see new opportunities developing. We'll even tend to initiate the most appropriate changes in our lives to create new paths forward, involving both adjustments and new directions that result in real improvement. But it's not always easy to get our values right. And the culture around us doesn't typically provide good guidance for this.

Our Values Can Help Us Or Hold Us Back
I believe that at our time in developed nations, we tend to value comfort and security too highly. And this obviously can affect our attitude toward change. Of course, there's nothing wrong with comfort or security. In fact, I'm sure we all wish they weren't as relatively rare as they've become. The great psychologist Abraham Maslow helped us to understand at a deeper level how these values are both important. It's sensible to hold them desirable, precisely because they make other and greater things possible, like proper growth. And these things then reinforce them in the right ways.

> Only in growth, reform, and change,
> paradoxically enough, is true security to be found.
> Anne Morrow Lindbergh

As we can see around the world, when people don't have basic security in their communities or personal lives, very few other good things can result. Even simple comfort is an important condition to value because of how it allows us to rest from our work, refresh ourselves for new challenges, enjoy our families, and embrace our lives with a positive attitude. We should value both comfort and security. But we should value even more the different and sometimes contrasting qualities of growth and learning.

If we fixate on comfort and security as ends in themselves, or as our highest aims, even subconsciously, we can block important forms of personal growth as well as the learning that's always involved in healthy growth. Even valuing these basic conditions disproportionately, or a bit too much, can breed a visceral fear of change, lead us to become stagnant, and result in our missing the full sense of being alive that's necessary for ongoing fulfillment and personal happiness. This is a danger most of us face, in part, because of the dominant cultural values around us.

From every direction, we're offered promises of security—locks, alarms, surveillance cameras, personal protection devices of various kinds, gated communities, password codes, special protective software for our computers and homes, various forms of insurance, and even new investment strategies to keep us and our money safe. Beyond that, we're also constantly encouraged to focus on whatever forms of comfort we can attain. We've come to feel we need our many conveniences and small luxuries, and we'll firmly resist any change that might seem to threaten them in the least. In relatively affluent cultures, the natural importance of comfort and security easily gets magnified into such a social and psychological role that it eclipses the equally important values of growth and learning. Signs of this in our society are everywhere.

> We can tell our values by looking at our checkbook stubs.
> Gloria Steinem

Where we put our money tells a tale. If we all valued growth and learning more, for example, we'd pay our teachers better, all our elementary, middle school, and high school teachers, as well as instructors in community colleges, and the many dedicated pro-fessionals in our four-year colleges and universities. Many of them can barely get by and have to take on second and third jobs in order to pay their most basic bills. What we spend the most mon-ey on can tell a revealing story about what we value the most. The incomes we provide for our top entertainers and athletic stars, as contrasted with the pay of our very best schoolteachers, for exam-ple, clearly show some of the dominant values of our time. If we seek to value growth and learning properly, we can find ourselves swimming against strong currents that in subtle ways pressure us into conformity with deeply flawed priorities. And this is not as it should be. Allowing the ascendant values of our day to define us can keep us from what we most deeply need.

In the world of work, what feels safest or most secure is not often what's really best. When security becomes a focal goal of high priority, it oddly becomes more elusive. It's only when we concentrate on other and better things that some form of security can arise as a nice side effect. When I decided to leave my tenured, lifetime position as a Professor of Philosophy at the University of Notre Dame, a friend reminded of all the security I was giving up. He said, "How do you know that business groups and others in the broader culture will want to hear you speak six months from now?" I told him my view on the issue: The only real security in life is in living our own proper adventures.

A strong preference for comfort can also be problematic. It can keep us from flexing our talents and developing our skills in ways that may be genuinely necessary for our future wellbeing and long-term comfort. Staying within a tight circle of perceived safety and comfort in the present may end up ironically being the least safe strategy we can adopt, and it can lead in the future to unexpectedly uncomfortable results. Great careers, businesses, and lives tend to grow out of great adventures.

It's always the adventurers who accomplish great things.
Montesquieu

If life is best viewed as a series of adventures, then it may well follow that the only true comfort and security right for any of us will arise out of living our best adventures. And that requires the growth and learning involved with change.

The Values of Proper Adventure
Adventure essentially involves the unknown. It means embracing change and challenge and new opportunity. The best forms of comfort and security will then come to us as positive side effects or by-products of living our adventures well. We don't get what we need by focusing on comfort and security as primary goals, but rather from a determined pursuit of growth and learning. Valuing the right things gets the best results.

Not everyone is equally open to new adventures. And that can have serious consequences. A few prominent business thinkers have commented recently on the surprising failures of previously successful companies that can be tracked over the past half century. In many cases, the tremendous achievement that these firms experienced at one time had created a culture of arrogance, presumptuousness, and smug comfort that was closed off to learning and resistant to necessary change as circumstances evolved. Resting on their laurels, the leaders of these enterprises often weren't able to embrace or even acknowledge the changes they needed to make in order to stay competitive and successful. Their values had become distorted. And so they were not able to guide their organizations into the new and adaptive behaviors they needed. As a result, their enterprises stopped flourishing, became stagnant, struggled, and even ceased to exist.

Resting on your laurels is as dangerous as resting when you are
walking in the snow. You doze off and die in your sleep.
Ludwig Wittgenstein

We should never allow success in one adventure to close us off
from new journeys that may be right for us and important to experience. If we truly value such things as discovery, learning, growth,
creativity, and improvement, we can bring a humble openness to
any changing situation that will allow us to embrace the new initiatives it might show to be necessary. The future demands new
things. And those among us who don't understand that important
truth won't get there very happily.

Philosophers have commented for a long time on our common resistance to change, which is one aspect of human nature
that seems, ironically, not to change. In the sixteenth century, the
political thinker Niccolò Machiavelli, the immensely controversial
author of the famous, or infamous, little book *The Prince*, noticed
the pervasiveness of this problem through history, as well as in his
own day. With great verve and typically characteristic overstate-
ment, he wrote about it in the pages of his highly regarded but
seldom read *Discourses*. At the end of the passage I have in mind,
he verbally plays off the classical personification of fortune as gen-
dered and says:

> There are two reasons why we cannot change our ways.
> First, it's impossible to go against what nature inclines us
> to. Secondly, having got on well by adopting a certain line
> of conduct, it's impossible to persuade men that they can
> do well by acting otherwise. In this way, it comes about
> that a man's fortune changes, for she changes his circum-
> stances, but he does not change his ways. (III.9)

Substituting the more modest term 'difficult' for 'impossible' in Machiavelli's claims here, we get some real insight about

how successful individuals and organizations set themselves up to fail. Our first achievements are most often due to following what comes naturally to us, which is the result of our talents, training, and experience. We develop a tight comfort zone that arises from those accomplishments and then have difficulty venturing outside it. And when doing "what nature inclines us to do" brings great results, we can become, as a consequence, reluctant to change our ways even as the world around us begins to shift in such a manner that our habitual actions no longer have their former, customary results.

If we've become famous for our iced tea or strawberry smoothies, we may be hesitant to try our hand at lemonade, even when surrounded by mounds of lemons. We easily become bound to the methods of the past and blind to the need for change. We're comfortable with the familiar and uneasy with what we don't yet know. This inability to embrace something new has led to the downfall of companies, political parties, nations, cultures, and many highly accomplished individuals along the way. Because of this, the fundamental causes of resistance to change are important for us to understand.

The Snare of Excessive Pride

Too many successful people fall prey to the subtle temptations of excessive pride, or of what's called pridefulness. We're properly proud of what we've accomplished and how we've done it. But we let that pride shade into a closed self-certainty and arrogance that blocks learning and further growth. We're sure we're already doing things the right way. Our results have proved it. So why should we even think about changing? We can find the mere suggestion of change to be outrageous, and even insulting. The false certainty that too often results from any form of success can blind us to our need for ongoing innovation. This is one way in which good fortune can set us up for bad fortune, if we don't handle our times of achievement properly and well.

Bear good fortune modestly.
Ausonius

Excessive pride, or the cluster of distorted values that create a bloated self-image, can also express itself in another way. Sometimes we're afraid that if we make any major changes in what we're doing or how we're doing it, this will be seen by others as an admission that we didn't already have everything figured out—as if making changes in changing times signals a reversal of thinking and amounts to an admission of error. But of course, it doesn't mean that at all. In fact, it frequently displays the same flexibility of mind we most likely needed in order to attain our initial success in the first place.

The influential twentieth century philosopher Wittgenstein wrote a note to himself in 1937 expressing a thought that's relevant to all of us whose past victories may have created a wall of pride that can't easily be breached and now holds us back from the possibility of changes we might need to make. The note said, simply: "The edifice of your pride has to be dismantled. And that is terribly hard work." The philosopher was right. But this job of dismantling is worth all the effort it takes.

Pride is said to be the last vice that the good man gets clear of.
Benjamin Franklin

Sometimes the problem we face, the obstacle holding us back from our next proper adventure, is indeed nothing but excessive pride, arrogance, or an overly robust sense of self-satisfaction. But at other times, this is merely a disguise of the real problem. When confronting the possibility of change, or the pressure to adapt to changing circumstances, we often simply recoil in fear from the unknown, or from the possibility of facing failure in a new challenge. We're apprehensive about any loss of standing with our peers that could result. We may even fear a crack in our own self-image that could come from stretching too far beyond where we already are. And we don't want for a second to acknowledge, even to ourselves, that fear is really what's holding us back.

A Fear That Comes From Success
It's been a breakthrough in my own journey to be able to come to realize how often some form of fear can creep into my personal or professional life, most often disguised as something very different, and it either slows me down, or temporarily stops me from making progress at all. I've also found over the years that this problem is common among highly successful people. Too many of us unconsciously fear a new adventure precisely because we've been so successful in the past and feel as a result that people's expectations for us, as well as their continued esteem, depend on the appearance of an ongoing smooth trajectory of assured accomplishment in our path forward. Something really new may trip us up. If we now launch out into a very different adventure, it's possible that a completely unanticipated obstacle, something as yet unknown, may block our efforts, cause us to fail, and diminish us in the eyes of others. And this, of course, is not an altogether irrational worry. Careers can end over a loss of image. But the people around us whose opinions should matter to us the most will know enough of the world not to have such unreasonable expectations for us in the first place. We should give them credit for a little more wisdom. The world can be recalcitrant now and then for the best of us. There are no smooth paths to anything worthwhile.

We often fear failure because we're simply afraid of losing face with others, and perhaps even because we dread a possible drop in our own self-esteem. Of course, the causes of our trepidation can go beyond this as well. We may be afraid of risking our position, power, income, or status on a new experiment that just won't work. And yet, we most often can't see that it's precisely this sort of fear that's holding us back, largely because that realization by itself might tarnish our carefully cultivated self-image.

Formidable is the enemy that lies hidden in a man's own breast.
Publilius Syrus

The CEO of a successful company told me a few years ago that he sometimes worried about whether his top executives who had helped him turn the company around and raise their stock price to new heights may as a result of their own accomplishments ironically fear any new and daunting challenge that lay ahead. But, he told me, the future in his industry and for his particular company demanded even higher and more ambitious goals to be set and pursued quite soon. His imagery was vivid. "We've climbed a very steep hill. It's been tough. And we made it. We should be very proud of what we've achieved. It's the envy of the industry. But now it's my job to convince everyone that what comes next is going to be more like scaling the nearly vertical face of a new and much higher mountain. I don't think people want to hear that at all. It strikes fear into their hearts. And so they'll resist with all their might."

Most of us would naturally assume that the leadership team of such a high achieving organization would be very confident because of their recent victories and eager to take on nearly any new challenge that could provide even more astonishing results. But this wise chief suggested that it's precisely the sense of accomplishment and self-esteem resulting from all the success they've had in reaching their current pinnacle of attainment that had set these leaders up to mistrust and even fear anything that might threaten their newfound position and image in the minds of others. As a leader of leaders, it was now his job to help this intelligent and talented group of people to identify and overcome the subtle and insidious fear that might otherwise now hold them back.

He has not learned the lesson of life who
does not every day surmount a fear.
Emerson

In most situations, when we find ourselves dismissing the possibility of a new adventure because of fear, we have no explicitly conscious experience of the emotion as such—no physical trembling, no jolt to the gut, no racing heart of chill of dread—and so we're able to rationalize our reticence over the new challenge as being due to something other than fear. That's why this obstacle can be so effective in constraining our creativity, blocking our growth, and keeping us back from the heights of which we're capable. It's a general truth in life that when you don't know what's impeding your progress, you can't easily overcome it, because you won't be motivated to deal with it properly. We typically need to identify and understand a problem before we can solve it at all.

A fear of the unknown and untried often hides itself behind something that seems positive and reasonable. It frequently takes on the disguise of pride, or a well-earned feeling of entitlement to stay put and enjoy where we are, along with a hearty sense of self-congratulation on the successes we've had to this point in our lives. I've often heard people say something like, "We don't need a new challenge. What we do need is to stop and take some time to enjoy what we've already accomplished." And there are some core insights behind any such statement. Any form of success certainly should be inwardly acknowledged and relished. The people who have attained it need to be recognized and applauded. Furthermore, such instances of celebration and enjoyment are indeed important in life. But a feeling that they are deserved and should be extended through time can be used to mask an underlying fear of moving forward and accepting a new adventure. Fear can easily find a crowd of friends to help it hold us back.

It logically follows that the more successful we've been, the more vulnerable we are to this obstacle as a result. When we unmask the fear that's at work and identify it as what it is, we can gain the power to overcome it and move on courageously to the next opportunity that awaits us. Adventure calls for courage. And courage allows for change. As Plato's star student Aristotle understood, this primary virtue makes it possible for us to put our inner potential to work. It gets us up and going. And by doing so, it opens us to all the good things that a fear-based complacency can easily prevent. It's been the insight of many great philosophers and all the best lemonade makers through history that courage is a virtue we can cultivate successfully in our lives and, in this way, liberate ourselves for the full range of excellence we're truly capable of attaining. Courage doesn't eliminate fear, or even require judging it to be utterly unfounded. It just allows us to move forward in the face of it.

Courage is the best gift of all.
Plautus

We need to be very clear on this one thing. Rational courage doesn't ignore fear. It's not the same thing as foolhardiness. An experience of fear is sometimes a good warning sign to stop and rethink or turn back. It's nature's hard-wired, motivationally powerful danger-and-damage avoidance system. And yet on many occasions, it becomes simply a by-product of ego, habit, comfort, and complaisance. It can be a result of distorted values, of simply valuing the wrong things, or valuing perfectly acceptable things to the wrong degree. A twinge of fear in the face of change or challenge is often no more than a sign that we're indeed entering into something new. And crossing a new threshold is a necessary precondition for learning and growth. So, if we can cultivate the ability to reign in the initial anxiety we instinctively feel in connection with any consideration of the new and unknown, we can learn to treat this inner reaction as just the indicator of potential adventure that it so often is. Then we can reserve the most powerful emotion of fear for where it will do the most good, in the stark presence of genuine danger.

The lemons of life can be quite sour, but few are poisonous, and so don't typically pose any real danger. The only actual risk we most often face with them is the possibility of a loss that stems from inaction, or failing to make the lemonade they allow, due to a fear that should not have frozen us in place. The bold among us embrace new paths and positive possibilities as creative pioneers. They're existential alchemists who take what life gives and work to squeeze it into something great.

Difficulty, Struggle, and Growth

One way of cultivating courage to overcome any fear that often holds us back is by coming to understand that the hardest things we experience can result in the deepest growth we need. True courage requires a measure of real wisdom. It's no surprise that the philosopher Socrates was reported during the time of his military service to have been tremendously brave in battle. His personal foundation of wisdom allowed him to approach many things well. Plato then, in turn, displayed his own form of wise courage by continuing on in the work he had begun with Socrates after the Athenian public had turned against their enterprise and condemned Socrates to death. Plato's courage to tell the story and articulate what he had learned from his mentor then changed the course of western thought forever. In both their lives, I believe, hard things resulted in real growth.

Even when fear has a proper place in the challenges we confront, our experience of it needs to be tempered with this deeper insight. One of the greatest surprises life has brought me is the realization that our most profound personal learning and growth tends to come out of our most difficult adventures. The worst things we go through can bring us some of the most ultimately instructive and even gratifying results. Struggles and keen suffering can produce life revelations with an enduring value of an irreplaceable nature, along with a strength that can't be attained in any other way.

Great winemakers talk of a simple parallel. Grapes with plenty of nutrients and abundant water make poor wine. Vines that are deprived and pushed to the limit of what they're able to endure can produce the richest results. We shouldn't allow the concept of life adventure to be glamorized or sanitized and stripped of its actual dangers. The greatest and most beneficial adventures can involve both frightening hazards and arduous struggles. But they can also because of that have the most transformative results. This truth derives from an alchemy of the spirit that transmutes difficulty into depth.

> Either the human being must suffer and struggle as the price
> of a more searching vision, or his gaze must be shallow
> and without intellectual revelation.
> Thomas De Quincy

A few years ago, there was a sudden but temporary change in my physical health. An onset of odd and alarming symptoms sent me straight to Google and I quickly discovered thirty-seven possible causes of my symptoms, maybe thirty-five of which were fatal. First appearances were not good. But then, I learned within a day that I was fortunate to have one of the two conditions whose description did not end with the otherwise seemingly ubiquitous statement, "Death ensues." I experienced my first and hopefully only bout with the legendary scourge of kidney stones.

After a series of unexpected and unpleasant experiences, my doctor explained to me that I had two large stones in one kidney that were "too big to find their way out on their own," unaided. In honor of their reported magnitude, I first named the stones Mick and Keith, and then gladly subjected them to the lengthy procedure and many odd discomforts of lithotripsy, where ultra-sound waves were used to break the culprits into smaller bits. The problem was that a day later, all the particles, pebbles and grains that had resulted sought to make their great departure at the same time, creating what's known in the technical jargon of medicine as a "log jam" up inside the body, and resulting in what's often claimed to be the greatest physical pain that a human being can experience, far worse than that of normal kidney stones and their notoriously nefarious movements. A security guard told me later that he was once shot while serving in the military, and that he had also experienced a kidney stone in a similar way. He said, "If I ever had to choose which of them to have again, I'd say just shoot me."

Having undergone extended waves of an unimaginably deep and searing pain for one endless night and most of the next day, largely on hands and knees and vomiting uncontrollably for the first time in my life, I gained insights about myself and our human capacity to endure that were amazing to me. When it was all over, I said to my doctor, "That's the worst thing I've ever been through, with no close second, and I sure hope it never happens again, but I'm really glad I experienced it."

He looked surprised and replied, "Well, this is the first time in a long career that I've heard anyone say the last part of what you've just declared. Could you explain it?"

> Your pain is the breaking of the shell
> that encloses your understanding.
> Khalil Gibran

I told him that the self-knowledge and existential understanding of pain that had resulted from the ordeal was too important to have been missed in this life—at least, by a philosopher like me. It greatly expanded my conception of my own inner strength and capacity to endure, and it helped me to understand other people in new ways. It took me deep. I fully opened myself up to it and embraced the suffering, moment-to-moment. I had no idea beforehand what such an experience could be like, or how it can teach. That openness and embrace of the ordeal were then what allowed for the alchemy to happen, and for the monumental lemons of the moment to be processed and stirred into something genuinely great. I would never have guessed that such an unwanted twist of events could bring me something good and even precious, strange to say.

But let's go a bit deeper. I hadn't been in touch with an old friend in our nation's capital for over a year. I wrote him an email to ask how things were going, and he answered in a way that stunned me. Several months before, he wrote, while a doctor was looking for what he called, "an errant kidney stone," he had been shocked with a diagnosis of pancreatic cancer. In his first email reply to my general inquiry, he said:

> "As to how I am: 2013 has been an interesting year. Just before Christmas I was diagnosed with pancreatic cancer. Yikes! After a little while of wondering whether I had only a few months to live, I started getting every break imaginable and, after surgery by a fantastic team at Hopkins, I appear to be cancer-free. No chemo; no radiation! For a disease whose 5-year survival rate is under 2%, it looks like I may be the rarest of rare birds—with a low probability of recurrence. Looks like I'm more likely to be impaled by a DC Metro-bus."

He then signs off with the word, "Cheers!" Remarkable. It was hard to process it all. When I wrote back to ask more about the situation and his current state of mind, he then surprised me even more with this unexpected description:

> "I had a truly joyous experience with the whole cancer episode, and learned a few things about myself in the process. I had a great time with positive visualization, etc., and

the Hopkins medical team embraced whatever I threw at them. I wouldn't wish pancreatic cancer on anyone, but I wouldn't trade the experience for anything. (That may have something to do with the end result, of course.)"

What could seem worse than a medical diagnosis of pancreatic cancer, with its sudden and dismal short-term prognosis? And yet, this remarkable man characterizes the subsequent adventure as "a truly joyous experience." He wouldn't trade it for anything. That's how utterly stunning the disparity between appearance and reality can be. And it's why the philosophers who have been practical alchemists and expert lemonade makers advise us never to rush to judgment in the face of a sudden change, but always to make sure the right attitudes and values are guiding us.

> When the mind is pure, joy follows
> like a shadow that never leaves.
> Buddha

Now, let's go to what's perhaps even a deeper level still, or at least a different angle on the depths at which we have arrived. I once had a long telephone conversation with a brilliant philosopher, a formerly athletic outdoorsman and esteemed intellectual who had suffered a catastrophic accident at the prime of his career and the height of his powers. He was rendered quadriplegic and, with near total paralysis years after the accident, could speak very slowly with only the greatest of exertion. He hinted to me that day, and described in more detail to one of my colleagues who had visited him, that the adventure of his disaster had involved the attainment of spiritual insights and realizations so great that, if he could go back in time and choose whether to suffer such an accident or avoid it, he had to say that what he had learned as a consequence of the event was too rare and precious to be missed. He would go through it all again.

I could hardly process the thought. Even to recall this many years later and to write these few words about this extraordinary man and his attitude, I feel a nearly biblical sense of being an unworthy fellow treading on holy ground. And yet, this perspective on even the worst of suffering is thoroughly consonant with what many of the wisest people through history have intimated about their own greatest challenges.

Suffering is the sole origin of consciousness.
Dostoevsky

In one of my favorite little books, *The Measure of My Days*, Florida Scott Maxwell, an astute psychoanalyst and playwright, looks back on her life from the high perch of her energetic eighties and writes of the surprising intensity and insights of older age. She also reveals her unexpected realization that the things in her life that were so very hard, extremely difficult, and almost unbearable at the time, events that she went through with pain and regret and consternation, turned out to be what produced in her heart and soul the qualities that she's most come to appreciate and respect, a cluster of characteristics that she sums up with the word 'hardi-hood.' She then wrote: "Life does not accommodate you, it shatters you. It is meant to, and it couldn't do it better. Every seed destroys its container or else there would be no fruition." When we come to value the fruition, the hardihood that can arise in no other way than through challenge and difficulty, we're able to manage that challenge and difficulty much differently, and perhaps embrace it. In a key passage, Maxwell says:

> Suddenly I wonder—Is all hardness justified because we are so slow in realizing that life was meant to be heroic? Great-ness is required of us. That is life's aim and justification, and we poor fools have for centuries been trying to make it convenient, manageable, pliant to our will. (85)

And a bit later:

> What I cling to like a tool or a weapon in the hand of a
> man who knows how to use it, is the belief that difficulties
> are what makes it honorable and interesting to be alive.
> (118)

Struggle can make us capable and strong in ways we could
not have anticipated, and can take us to extraordinary depths we
never suspected might exist. This is the true story and ultimate
source for the spiritual power we have. Life can test us to our limits
and beyond. It's meant to be a path for developing the heroic in
our souls. Sometimes the worst we face can produce the best of
which we're capable, and that can encompass even the most difficult things we ever experience. To dare to think or speak of taking
life's lemons and making lemonade in such a connection can seem
to involve the most unseemly trivialization of enormous suffering
that's imaginable. But the core lesson is always exactly the same.
In the end, it's what we do with what happens to us that matters
the most, whatever it might be. In even the most extremely hard
things, it's possible to experience an almost inconceivable form of
metamorphosis that's, in a deep and universal sense, profoundly
spiritual.

In the fifth century BC, the historian Thucydides made two
successive statements that are relevant. He said: "The secret of happiness is freedom. The secret of freedom is courage." When we
glimpse some of the deeper lessons of our experience, we can come
to see a link between difficulty and growth that's invisible to the
casual glance. Great hardship can open us up to great wisdom. And
wisdom both signals and can further create profound growth. The
more fully we understand this connection, the better we can confront our worst fears with the courage to move forward in a way
that's truly best, knowing ultimately that only courage can provide
us with the genuine freedom to live our proper adventures in this

world. And freedom of this order is necessary for the deepest form of happiness. The courage we need to take all of life's lemons and make from them great lemonade bears profound connections to some of the most hidden secrets in life. Therefore, as the great existential alchemists would say, choose courage. Embrace adventure. Make the most of difficulty and suffering. Open yourself to personal growth.

Deep down we've somehow always known that life is meant to encompass challenging adventures and what they bring. As the political philosopher Montesquieu once pointed out long ago, "It is always the adventurers who accomplish great things." Legendary among the ancient Greeks, Odysseus was a storm-tossed man of disasters and sorrows. His long journey of ordeals has been told and read and studied for over three thousand years by at least a hundred and fifty generations of those who have followed him and who, as we read, wonder at his capacity to endure and prevail, and then at our own. We can begin to realize that we are to be among the adventurers. And then we can be among the heroes. That's our calling. And it can be our joy.

> The great achievements of the past
> were the adventures of adventurers of the past.
> Alfred North Whitehead

One more quotation from Florida Scott Maxwell may be insightful here and help us to catch a glimpse of the capacity we have for adventurous living. She wrote:

> No one lives all the life of which he is capable. (139)

"I can't do this. I can't manage it. I can't stand it." How often have we heard, or perhaps even spoken, words like this? And yet, a deeper view of life holds that we can in fact do and manage and stand whatever is presented to us, and in the process we can grow stronger and deeper, until those words one day unavoidably become literally true, and the adventure of adventures here in this physical world comes to its end. But until then, we should explore and live with confidence in those abilities and capacities we have that most often go far beyond what we might even be able to imagine.

I think we all may realize at some level that we have what it takes to live a great adventure, wherever we are and whatever we're doing. And yet, this is an insight we too easily forget to apply to our careers in the world. We might dream of adventure in our innermost thoughts, but thrown into an actual one, we often react with anxiety, aversion, and fear. In order to shed these emotions and attitudes of avoidance, we need to practice the art of self-control. We should refuse a rush to judgment, value the right things—like learning, growth, and adventure—and then take charge of our imaginations in positive ways to empower us to move bravely into the next challenge, one that might already be calling us onward, or that may recently have caught us off guard and spun us around.

The most important thing we'll need to consider next, then, is the power and use of the imagination. It's a major resource for the art of self-control, and through it, for the art of change. It's severely underutilized in the modern world. And it's always required for the magical transformation from lemons to lemonade.

Use your imagination well

IN THE FACE OF LIFE'S LEMONS, IT'S VITAL TO REMEMBER WE have a power that can help us deal creatively with any challenge, the power of the imagination. And this resource is immense. A piece of advice follows from this fact: Use your imagination well. This is the third rule in the art of self-control: Don't rush to judgment; value the right things; and use your imagination well. When we put our imaginations to work in service of our ideals, we position ourselves for the best response to change.

Imagination, not invention, is the supreme master of art as of life.
Joseph Conrad

Our imaginations can affect powerfully the way we frame and interpret our circumstances, determining in the most basic manner how we understand what's going on around us. And this is something we easily forget, as surface appearances may suggest an obvious but misleading take on any new circumstance, and sometimes forcefully. But situations rarely arise in life that are one thing only, and contain all their implications on their face. Most events can be interpreted in a number of different ways and, as a result, molded in divergent directions. Much about the world is, in this respect, at any given moment, inherently ambiguous and conceptually malleable. Because of that, it's always to some extent up to us how we choose to view the things that happen in our lives. This is a type and measure of freedom that's important for our experience of the world. And it's also up to us, as well, how we imagine what can possibly come next as the result of how we choose to act on the challenges those circumstances might pose.

Interpretive Framing
I like the image of framing, not in the sense in which a contractor puts up the bones of a new house, or in which an innocent man might be set up for a crime he didn't commit, but in the way we frame a painting or a photograph and by our choices either enhance or detract from its beauty. I've had this experience many times. I might buy a painting from a gallery and know that its current frame is not the best presentation for it. I then have it masterfully reframed to complement and augment its subject matter, colors, and style. Then in its new immediate context of the right frame, it instantly takes on different qualities that enhance its beauty and can have an overall visual impact quite different from its original look. The change can be dramatic and even astonishing.

The interesting point of analogy for us as we deal with challenge and change in our lives is that imagination can become like a great framer and learn by practice precisely how to present everything to our inner gaze at its very best.

> Imagination is not a talent of some men,
> but is the health of every man.
> Emerson

What we often fail to realize is that our imaginations are at work in some way much of the time, and when we aren't in control of its projections, we can find ourselves hindered rather than helped by how it might frame new events that come to us. The imagination can interpret almost any situation that arises in our lives in such a way as to cause us some form of worry or distress. The first imaginative framing of a new development can be simply a result of how our emotions and attitudes have been primed by past habits to see things. And the fact is that our imaginations may in the past have been influenced in such a way that, operating now untutored by us, they aren't the most reliable guides to the real nature of any new event. When we don't cultivate any form of control over our imaginations, we allow them to be manipulated and distorted by our worst fears, and even by wayward and inappropriate desires that, on consideration, we wouldn't endorse or countenance. We easily forget that it's up to us how we use the power of the imagination to frame or reframe for ourselves the circumstances we face. Sometimes, this involves simply engaging in positive visualization. At other times, it requires brainstorming possible paths of response. And often, it flourishes best through something like a meditative openness to the creative resources of the unconscious mind.

Used properly, the imagination is one of our most vital resources. With the interpretive freedom that's always available to us in an uncertain world, we should employ our imaginations to empower us and not to undermine our own prospects. We need to view any situation of challenge or change in such a way as to raise the probability that our way of looking at it will enhance our capacity to move forward productively in it.

I'm not talking about fooling ourselves, or engaging in anything like self-hypnosis or inner "spin" as we confront new situations that arise in our lives. To spin a situation is to distort its representation for the purpose of manipulative deception. To frame a situation well is to interpret it productively and highlight its various potentially positive elements for the purpose of personal empowerment, whether of ourselves, or also of any other people we may seek to help deal with the situation. Of course, the imagination can also show us hidden potential obstacles in our path. But it then also can go on to envision paths around those obstacles. Our ability to frame a set of circumstances positively is one of the greatest sources of power in life. It can help us see a way forward in any challenge, however difficult. In fact, reframing difficulties as providing opportunities is a key ingredient for mastering any adventure and making the most of whatever confronts us.

> Opportunities are seldom labeled.
> John A. Shedd

It's important to understand the powerful role of the imagination in our beliefs, emotions, and attitudes. The seventeenth-century scientist and mathematician Blaise Pascal saw clearly that the imagination might actually be the most important natural power we have. We should learn to use it and not be victimized by it. The advice of the philosophers regarding the imagination would then be simple: Take control of this vital power. Block unhelpful negative images and boost positive visions for what's possible.

The Perils of Imagination Running Wild

The practical sages of ancient Rome were masters at working with the most sour lemons of life and stirring them into great lemonade. Their number included individuals from quite different walks of life—in particular, Epictetus, a slave who later gained his freedom and became a great teacher; Seneca, a lawyer and top political advisor; and Marcus Aurelius, an effective Emperor of Rome. These three individuals, living within three distinct social strata in their day, spoke with nearly one voice about what matters most in life. They all said in some form or another, "Take control of your imagination or it will take control of you." Our imaginations can have immense power over us, for good or ill. Whether this inner power enhances or detracts from our lives is ultimately up to us.

I've had many experiences of imagination out of control. You may also have felt this often in your own life as well. Let me give you a small but vivid example from mine. When I was about forty years old, my dentist stood looking over some X-rays on my yearly visit and said: "We've got to take out all your wisdom teeth."

I was shocked. I said, "Wait a minute, I'm a philosopher, and that sounds bad for my business. I need all the wisdom I've got."

He quickly smiled in his best you're-not-really-very-funny way and replied, "Well, we take out everybody's wisdom teeth." I guess he wanted to convince me that I'd at least end up on a level playing field with everyone else. But that wasn't good enough. I explained that I have a personal policy not to give up attached body parts, however small, without a good reason. He rose to the occasion and said, "The problem is, your wisdom teeth are all partially or fully impacted, and we need to take them out now to avoid trouble later. Impacted teeth tend to become infected over time, and that can be a real problem." At that point, he gathered together some papers and explained, "For the procedure, we'll have to use some serious anesthesia, so please sign these forms."

The forms were all about possible disaster and death. That got my attention on a new level. It was no joking matter. I was instantly and seriously worried. Sure, it wasn't brain surgery or a heart transplant we were talking about, but still. My imagination began to spiral out of control, latching onto the tiny probability revealed by the documents in front of me that this could indeed be the unexpected end of an otherwise fulfilling life.

Imagination is everything.
Albert Einstein

I played out in my head all the worst-case scenarios that were even remotely possible, or at least those that involved my demise, mentally hearing: "Cut down in the prime of life! He was so young!" and "What a tragic loss!" My imagination got carried away. I actually saw in my mind's eye the formal obituary in the local paper, the stricken family, and all my terribly shocked Notre Dame students sitting at my surprisingly well-attended memorial service where there was actually a nice-looking buffet afterwards, but it wasn't going to do me any good. I would be gone from this terrestrial orb.

Every day, and especially at night, I dwelled on all the potential dangers of the upcoming procedure, however remote, and was sure that it would be at least a terrible, even if not terminal, experience. I had three miserable weeks like this with my poor imagination running wild. I read about weird anomalies that people can experience with any general anesthesia, and it was not a pretty picture. My level of concern may strike you as a bit odd, so perhaps I should explain.

In my entire life up until then, I had experienced minor surgery only on one occasion with my tonsils and adenoids when I was ten years old. And during it, I had been given a serious overdose of ether, the preferred anesthesia of the day. In the end, though, the patient was fine and only the doctor died. It turned out that right after the procedure, my surgeon committed suicide. Yeah. Really.

Years later, in graduate school, I asked a Yale physician if that over-dose of ether could have done any damage to me. Hearing the details, he said, "You're lucky you're walking and talking." Wow. So as a consequence, I didn't have the most positive associations with medical interventions involving anesthetics and excision. At a deep emotional level, this previous brush with the unexpected had primed my imagination to go into overdrive over any such thing.

Then the dreaded day arrived. You would have thought I was driving to the front lines of a battlefield or the likely location of a predicted terrorist incident. As a result of all the mental images that had arisen out of my panicked imagination, I was the most nervous I had ever been for anything in my life, however well I kept it hidden. But, then, because of the particularly impressive pharmaceuticals they chose to employ on the occasion, I ended up having the very best time ever at a dental procedure or on any medical occasion. It was great. I recommend it highly. I'd do it again tomorrow, and almost any afternoon.

The experience was completely delightful and of course the polar opposite of what I had expected. Indeed, I obviously lived to tell the story. In addition, I'm pleased to report that the oral surgeon is fine, too. Everyone as it turned out went home that day, healthy and happy. The only bad thing to come out of the entire sequence of events was the misery of bad imagination out of control that I had experienced for literally weeks. And it was entirely my own fault.

> How much pain they have caused us,
> the evils which have never happened.
> Thomas Jefferson

I learned something important from that experience. The untethered imagination is not to be trusted. It can create a rush to judgment and a flow of powerful emotion that's totally out of step with the way things are. It can be endlessly productive of anxiety and fear. In the vast majority of situations, our worst fears are more likely to be the product of our overactive imaginations than of reality itself. When dealing with dramatic change, this is absolutely crucial to keep in mind.

Worst Case Scenarios
Any major change or bit of disruptive news is to some extent a transition from the known to the unknown. And the unknown by definition gives free reign to the imagination. It's a blank canvas on which we can paint. We easily project into the future the worst of our worries, creating an inner state of negative expectation and high anxiety that's rarely helpful in dealing with the actual realities we confront. This tendency to project worst case scenarios is often just a well-intentioned attempt to prepare for any challenges that might materialize, in part to motivate ourselves to take whatever precautions might prevent or mitigate such eventualities. And yet very often, the ironically unexpected side effect is to create an unsettled emotional state in which we typically can't make the best decisions or take the most appropriate actions. An emotional fixation on worst-case scenarios is rarely helpful in life, and the fear of change that's generated by an imagination out of control naturally results in exactly that.

> You can't depend on your judgment
> when your imagination is out of focus.
> Mark Twain

My experience in the dentist's office parallels what many people go through in their working lives whenever an unexpected and apparently negative development threatens to upend their world. Of course, it's rare for thoughts of anything like personal death to generate fear in a business context involving even radical change, but product lines, companies, and even industries can in their own way die. Jobs end, careers come apart, and even our working conditions can sometimes be altered in such a way that we imagine and fear the demise of everything we depend on and need. It takes a real inner effort to resist the downward spiral of a negative imagination when we confront radical and unexpected situations that can seem to threaten disaster. But this is exactly what the best philosophers and alchemists of the soul have counseled us to do.

Imagination out of control can literally make us sick and shorten our lives through the stress it creates. The connection this displays between mind and body is often amazing. The good news is that the imagination can affect us just as powerfully in a positive way as in a negative manner. Our imaginations can create positive or negative beliefs, attitudes, and emotions that then go on to have good or bad effects on our physiology, our overall psychology, and our prospects for personal success.

Here's the key. The imagination is malleable through inner as well as outer suggestion. We have the freedom to reinforce its imagery or to redirect it completely. It's up to us more often than we think to determine how it works. That in turn will then be conveyed back to us both mentally and physically in a positive or negative reinforcement loop. As the imagination goes, very often, so we go too.

> As a man thinks in his heart, so is he.
> Proverbs 23:7

It's a crucial insight that our emotions and attitudes are often more tightly tied to our imaginations than to outer reality. And this is partly because everything outer is mediated to us through the filter of inner states like desire, hope, fear, value, belief, and aspiration that give direction and content to our imaginations. We wrongly think of perception as passive and inert, as if the world merely impresses itself on us through our open senses. But psychologists and philosophers have amply demonstrated the impressive creativity with which our minds are always actively editing and molding our experience. Imaginative mental filters can mediate the world to us in either productive or badly destructive ways and, in turn, the imagination then engages our emotions like nothing else can. This is perhaps at least one of the reasons Einstein famously declared that, "Imagination is more important than knowledge," and thus gave the world one of its more enduringly memorable aphorisms for sweatshirt and dorm poster presentation.

We easily imagine the worst whenever major change happens or threatens to enter our lives. And this can lead to bad reactions. But we should never leap from the fact that we have these vulnerabilities of imaginative projection to a conclusion that imagination is bad. When we use our imaginations wisely, we can see things that are invisible to the unimaginative glance. And this can empower us. Imagination is the wellspring of creativity. So it's vital to use this power well. And that will support the self-control we should bring to any situation where lemons may need to be made into lemonade.

Taking Charge of the Imagination
How we use our imaginations to frame the particular circumstances we face can make all the difference in how we're able to proceed. Many executives and managers have told me over the years that they always get very nervous before giving a big presentation in front of a room full of people. I'm able to assure them that this sort of performance anxiety is experienced by many of the most accomplished people I've ever known, and that they're able to turn their nervous energy into something good because of how they use their imaginations. Anxiety can actually be used to power performance.

> Anxiety is the essential condition of
> intellectual and artistic creation.
> Charles Frankel

I once had a two hundred and eighty-five pound National Championship Notre Dame football player come into my office nearly shaking like a leaf in a breeze the day before the first big exam in Philosophy 101. He stepped through the doorway and said right away, "Professor Morris, I'm scared. I'm really worried about the exam tomorrow." I invited him to sit down for a minute and told him I might be able to help.

It was important for me to start by getting him imaginatively back into his normal comfort zone. So I asked him: " Do you ever get nervous before a big game?"

He looked surprised and said, "Sure, all the time." Ok, now I had a point of contact on which to build. I just had to use it well.

I probed a bit more and asked him: "What happens with your initial nerves during the game?"

He said, simply, "After I take the first hit, everything's just fine."

I was tempted to tell him that on the first question of the exam the next day, he was likely to take a really big hit, but I didn't, since, in light of what he had just said, he might take it the wrong way. So, instead, I said, "Listen, nervous energy can be a very good thing. The best people most often have lots of it. They have it because they care. You have it for the same reason. You're nervous because you care about doing well and worry you might not. So a form of energy is there. You can let it shut you down, or you can surf on it. It's up to you. Successful people use it well." I then advised him to let the energy power his preparation for the exam. He should let it push him to do the right things. I suggested that he study all he could for the rest of the day, and then try to get a good, solid night's sleep, so he'd be able to think clearly during the test the next morning. Study and sleep is nearly a magic formula for any upcoming challenge.

I counseled this anxious young man not to worry about his worry, but to use his imagination to turn that energy into some-thing that could benefit him both before and during the test. I even suggested that he should vividly picture in his mind's eye the next day's events, see himself answering the exam questions well, feel a real sense of confidence in his upcoming performance, and envision turning in his exam with a smile. He followed my advice, took control of his imagination, and by doing that, he gained control of his anxiety, tackled every question on the test, and did just fine.

> The world is but a canvas to our imaginations.
> Henry David Thoreau

I could definitely relate. Throughout fifteen great years as a professor, I always got at least a little bit nervous before teaching any class. But some days, it was worse than others. I can recall vividly one particular class session that I had worried about for nearly a week in advance. I had experienced trouble getting to sleep the night before that class day. I was going to be trying out a new philosophical gimmick to illustrate an important theme and, if it worked well, the students would likely remember the experience vividly for years, but if it flopped, I'd look like a real idiot.

I finally got to sleep by giving myself a step-by-step positive imagination of the next morning's class as vividly as possible with a vision of smiling students and a spectacular new teaching trick that worked like a charm, featuring everyone laughing hard, applauding loudly, and then leaving at the end of class with a buzz of enthusiasm to tell their friends, "You won't believe what happened in philosophy class today!" I imagined them all taking the experience with them throughout the week, beyond the end of the semester, and even after graduation, and having it bring back to them now and then the important ideas we'd been discussing on that day-to-remember.

My use of positive visualization, which is just a common and effective application of a healthy imagination, nullified the jittery queasiness I'd been feeling and gave me a real emotional lift. After finally enjoying a good though abbreviated night's sleep, I drove to campus, taught the class, and tried the new trick. It worked like a charm. My positive vision had been right. I was relieved. And more than twenty years after the event, a successful businessman who is a former student came up to me in a large convention center, greeted me like a long-lost friend, and spontaneously described with enthusiasm exactly what happened that day in class. My initial anticipation of the performance had brought me a large load of lemons. But by using my imagination well, I was able to make some great lemonade. Our imaginations can be crucial for the alchemy we need.

In my early years of teaching, whenever I felt my heart rate going up before class, I'd think to myself, "I'm getting nervous." I eventually learned to reframe those sensations very differently. Now when I feel the same thing, I smile and say to myself, "I'm getting ready." I then immediately imagine the positive consequences this good energy will have. The resulting state of mind is an unusual and powerful combination of preparation, eagerness, and inner calm that gives top performers in any field some of their distinctive edge. Positive imagination and positive inner talk can turn your emotional state around and prepare you well for even the most daunting challenges.

> Nothing can withstand the powers of the mind.
> Manilius

Recall our earlier words about wisdom and the ancient image of life as a large wheel. Change turns the wheel. Are you out on the rim, where every revolution whips you around, up and down to great highs and lows of emotion? Or are you near the hub, and more centered? Every rule in the art of self-control helps move you to the center. Don't rush to judgment. Value the right things. Use your imagination well. The wheel still turns, but you're not flung wildly about to unhelpful extremes when you're near hub. You're centered. You're in a position of power.

Everyone who really cares about what they're doing feels a quickened heartbeat or a churning stomach at important junctures in their work, and especially when they face new challenges that are brought their way by unexpected change. Excellence is not immune to anxiety, it just knows the alchemistic procedure of partnering up with the imagination to direct that energy appropriately toward the target of deeply satisfying success. So, the advice of the philosophers on using your imagination well is important. Combined with a refusal to rush to judgment and a grasp of the right values, this is the capstone to the art of self-control, which is the first component in the art of adaptation, the leading edge of the overall art of change and a vital ingredient for making exceptional lemonade out of life's lemons.

3

FINDING THE SUGAR
The Art of Positive Action

MAKING NORMAL LEMONADE IN THE KITCHEN OBVIOUSLY involves taking action in a variety of ways. It requires several different steps. If you had the great philosophers over to your house to help mix up some of this sweet and refreshing libation, they wouldn't just be sitting around contemplating the lemons or pondering the pitcher. They'd be busy and engaged in all the required forms of action: raiding the cabinets, slicing the fruit, finding the sugar, boiling some water, mixing ingredients, getting the ice, and stirring away. The alchemistic lemonade making of life just as clearly involves taking action too. In order to turn any sour fruit of change or challenge into something really great, we need to launch out in positive action of just the right sort. And, here again, there's an art.

An artist is a man of action, whether he creates a personality, invents an expedient, or finds the issue of a complicated situation.
Joseph Conrad

Let's get our bearings first with a quick word of review. I've suggested that dealing well with the lemons that roll into our lives requires an array of behaviors that together constitute an art of change. There's an art of responding well to change, and a distinct art of innovation, or launching new change. The first component within the overall art of adapting or responding to the challenging change that comes our way, as we've seen, is the art of self-control. The second major component is the subject of this chapter, the art of positive action. Many people think of action in connection with change only when they're considering the difficulty of initiating a transformation in their lives or their organizations. But positive action is just as important for dealing with the change that happens to us. We shouldn't react to any new difficulty like a possum paralyzed in the headlights of the unexpected. We need to respond actively and productively in order to accommodate, absorb, and benefit from any source of adversity or new and confounding situation that might drop into our path.

Let me quote from a classic American novel *The Scarlet Letter*, first published in 1850 by Nathaniel Hawthorne, who was in all his stories a philosophical analyst of the human condition. The story is set in the Puritan Massachusetts Bay Colony in the years of 1638 to 1649. Hester Prynne, a woman who has suffered much and learned masterfully, is speaking to the Reverend Arthur Dimmsdale, a man who feels broken by adversity and sees his future as bleak. Our real hero is urging him in this passage to leave his worst experiences and failures behind him, as well as any sense of disgrace that might have arisen from them, and to take the right action to create a new future. She says of his past:

> "Leave this wreck and ruin here where it hath happened! Meddle no more with it! Begin all anew! Hast thou exhausted possibility in the failure of this one trial? Not so! The future is yet full of trial and success. There is happiness to be enjoyed! There is good to be done! (172)

Moments later, she exclaims, "Act! Do anything, save to lie down and die!" She's trying to impress on her friend that, ultimately, it's up to us how we interpret what we face and what we have suffered. And it's up to us to move on and take proper action.

> Action is the foundational key to all success.
> Pablo Picasso

Think about what often happens in business. When a corporate merger is announced, there's a shakeup in a leadership team, a major new initiative is put into effect, the overall competitive situation alters dramatically, or the market undergoes a shift, a common tendency is for people to become frustrated, pessimistic, and inert. Those caught in the whirlwind often just duck and cover, hunker down, and hope the storm will pass with minimal damage to their territory, reputations, and prospects. But that's the wrong reaction to nearly any change. A responsive process of positive action is called for instead, and certain ingredients are necessary for any such thing to take place. We can think of them as three simple requirements, or three rules, for the art of positive action.

The Three Rules of Positive Action
Like the art of self-control, this second main ingredient in the art of adaptation also involves three basic rules, or habits of action. Together, they are:

The Art of Positive Action
Govern your attitudes.
Look for opportunities.
Take the initiative.

If we pause briefly to consider the essential nature of these three requirements, we can see something interesting about their comprehensiveness:

Govern your attitudes: This has to do with what's going on inside you.

Look for opportunities: This focuses on what's happening outside you.

Take the initiative: This actively connects the inner with the outer.

What you have inside you—the cluster of inner states that includes your beliefs, values, attitudes, interests, feelings, dreams, ambitions, talents, proclivities, habits, and intentions—needs to move outward in a healthy way and have a positive effect in the external world through the opportunities available to you, and this always requires a measure of personal initiative. You may have heard an old saying that relates well to this. There are three kinds of people in the world: those who make things happen, those who watch things happen, and those who go around wondering, "What happened?" The advice of the great lemonade makers in life is simple. Be in the first group as often as you can. Make things happen. To do so well involves mastering and practicing each rule in the art of positive action. And we're going to see in this chapter what that means.

Our actions, of course, don't just come out of nowhere. On one very common philosophical viewpoint, they arise ultimately out of our beliefs, values, and attitudes, mediated by feelings. Those three primary realities, working through the energizing mediation of our emotions, determine our desires, and our desires fuel the choices that result in our actions. It's important for us to understand this inner dynamic of action. Reading the arrow as, roughly, "give rise to," we have something like this:

Beliefs+Values+Attitudes→Emotions→Desires→Choices→Actions

Fully parsed out, there is also a looping back from action to belief. For example, if you as a child were guided and habituated to act in a certain way, perhaps out of parental or community beliefs, values, and attitudes, you could in this way have come to form within yourself as a result of those actions over time the same beliefs, values, and attitudes. And in adult life, we can find the identical process. We can begin acting a certain way, and then find ourselves as a result eventually changed in beliefs, values, and attitudes.

Here's a trick that applies this insight. You'll typically act as if a change that comes your way is a positive opportunity for you only if you believe it is. But sometimes, you can come to act in that way because of the different belief that it's in your interest to do so, and the course of action itself will come to produce the more directly natural accompanying conviction that the change is indeed a good chance to learn and grow and improve. Action can at times lead the way. Beliefs, values, and attitudes will follow.

We've already touched on the importance of our beliefs and values in guiding our reactions to change and challenge. Our attitudes are just as important, and we can't get out of the starting gate in any productive way when we face a new situation without some fundamentally positive attitudes to guide and move us properly forward.

> The greatest part of our happiness depends
> on our dispositions, not our circumstances.
> Martha Washington

The most perceptive practical philosophers have said something about attitude that parallels what they've told us about imagination. We should govern our attitudes well, so that they won't rule us badly. Negative attitudes can be corrosive and are by nature opposed to positive, creative solutions. They can narrow our vision, sap our strength, unravel our relationships, and alienate the people around us whose help and support may be most needed during times of change. When we appreciate the full role of attitudes in life, we can understand why the first rule for positive action focuses on this inner reality.

Govern Your Attitudes

IF SOMEONE ASKED YOU TO IDENTIFY YOUR ATTITUDES, YOU might for a moment be completely stumped. We all have attitudes, but we don't ordinarily tend to think about them much. They're a bit like lenses through which we view the world. People who put on prescription glasses or pop contacts into their eyes every morning don't usually spend much time throughout the rest of the day thinking about or looking at their lenses, unless they've come to realize that something is wrong. Then they might inspect them closely. The same thing is true of our inner attitudes. We don't tend to think about them or look at them directly unless we've come to suspect something's wrong. The problem is that something can be wrong long before we become aware of it. And in the meantime, we'll likely suffer in some way from the inappropriate or unproductive inner lens. Because of this, we all need to ask ourselves on a regular basis: What are my dominant attitudes right now, and are they healthy for me to have? Or do I by contrast have any problem with my attitudes that I need to solve? Are those that I have now blocking me or are they boosting me forward in positive ways? This is again just part of the Socratic self-examination that's required throughout our days for the creation of a life that's best worth living.

> Attitude is a little thing that makes a big difference.
> Winston Churchill

One of the difficulties we face in examining our attitudes and identifying whether they're helping us or holding us back is that our typical working vocabulary for them is so general. We most often talk about people having good or bad attitudes, positive or negative ones, and perhaps those that are healthy or harmful. We may speak of a helpful or unproductive attitude. But we're not often as accustomed to much more by way of specificity. And yet, we have plenty of concepts for various positive and negative attitudes. Consider, for example, this short and very incomplete list of terms used to describe people's attitudes, either typically, or in particular situations:

Cheerful	Sulky
Joyous	Glum
Confident	Discouraged
Exuberant	Depressive
Enthusiastic	Reluctant
Committed	Apathetic
Trusting	Suspicious
Hopeful	Cynical
Thankful	Bitter
Respectful	Condescending
Encouraging	Derisive
Forgiving	Resentful
Accepting	Judgmental
Naïve	Worldly
Lighthearted	Serious
Frivolous	Somber
Friendly	Surly
Welcoming	Hostile
Open	Stubborn
Fair-minded	Discriminatory

We certainly have plenty of other negative terms for attitudes, like: Disdainful, indignant, and contemptuous. In fact, we may have available for our daily use more negative than positive attitude identification terms. At least, that often seems to be the case in our common, working vocabularies. Of course, many of these terms can be used to described outer behaviors as well as inner attitudes, but in all such cases they offer an assessment of the behavior with respect to the attitude it seems to show.

Emotions are consciously felt states of mind, body, and spirit. When you have an emotion, you consciously undergo it. You literally experience it. You feel something, either pleasant or unpleasant. You may not be able to identify it accurately in words or specify precisely what it is that you're feeling at the time, but an emotion isn't the sort of thing that's ever completely hidden away, utterly out of view from the person having it.

Attitudes can be quite different. They are more like unconscious tonalities and tendencies that in various ways can be hidden from the person carrying them around. Certainly, on many occasions, we can be completely self-aware regarding our attitudes. But they can sometimes instead be kept from our conscious awareness, tucked away and yet nonetheless active, underlying our emotions, desires, beliefs, and actions. In fact, whenever there is a habit of belief formation of a specific type, or a tendency toward a particular sort of emotional experience, there is likely an attitude lurking in the background, connected with that habit and driving it forward. It can often take a bit of digging to root out the hidden attitudes that may be affecting us in unproductive ways. And this is an endeavor where the opinions of trusted others can be of great help.

> He that would be superior to external influences
> must first become superior to his own passions.
> Samuel Johnson

Our attitudes can lift us up or bring us down. If I have an attitude problem, it might create all sorts of trouble for other people, but it will always cause difficulties for me. I can prevent such problems only by monitoring and governing the sometimes obvious, and yet often subtle and even clandestine attitudes that affect everything I do.

We all have patterns of reacting to what happens around us, emotionally and behaviorally, whether we consciously realize it or not. These are among our inner and outer habits. It's important to become more explicitly aware of these patterns and decide whether they're healthy to have. Some people seem to have been born with a natural tendency to feel thankful or appreciative. Others may have a disposition toward jealousy or envy. Some appear innately celebratory. And others seem judgmental. We retain the freedom to choose whether to indulge what comes naturally, or to cultivate a different response. It's one of the most wonderful realizations in life that our attitudes, along with their accompanying emotional tendencies and habits, can be changed. This is another important freedom that we have, and it's one crucial for the making of life lemonade.

Emotional habits can become deeply entrenched over time. I've known people who when driving a car will let any disruption or delay, even of a second or two, elicit irritation and hostility. It's become a habit. By allowing ourselves to continue to react to situations we didn't expect or don't particularly like with negative thoughts and feelings, we promote a tendency of inner behavior that can harden into a persistent attitude. And this inner behavior, with its naturally accompanying actions, will eventually give rise to problems. It's always surprising to see people react to the lemons that life gives them by becoming active lemon farmers themselves, growing their own supply of the bitter fruit and multiplying their problems far beyond what the world around them already might provide. The best way forward is a very different path.

Anger, Resentment, and Forgiveness
There's a simple reason we often drag so many negative attitudes and emotions through the day. Our reactions of anger, resentment, and irritation have a side to them that actually can feel good. We're

hurling an inner dart at the person or situation that's offending us. We think to ourselves that a particular individual deserves to be the object of our umbrage or inner scorn. If no one felt irritated at his past history or current behavior, he'd be getting away with something. We'll take care of this situation. So we fume. We tense up. We direct a mental tonality of severe disapproval in his precise direction, or something like an emotional glare, as if our inner feelings could directly inflict any form of damage on anyone other than ourselves.

> Anger would inflict punishment on another;
> meanwhile, it tortures itself.
> Publilius Syrus

Complaining, accusing, and resenting, whether aloud or just within the privacy of our own minds, can feel cathartic or cleansing, even while it actually fans the flames of negativity and turmoil in our hearts. We need to face a simple reality: If we're all balled up in negative emotions, we're not going to be able to experience the positive attitudes that are the most conducive to long-term success and satisfaction in our world. Because of this, one of the most liberating actions and resultant attitudes in life is that of forgiveness, which is, at its core, an emotional letting-go. It's also something rarely discussed in the context of modern business, politics, or any forms of organizational life.

A manager once told me that many of the people in his company were having serious problems because of the simple fact that two senior vice-presidents could not forgive each other for something that had happened many years ago. No management tactics, motivational techniques, or strategic planning innovations had been able to overcome the ongoing damage that a lack of forgiveness between two top people was inflicting on the business. And the problems that were being created as a result were completely unnecessary. These accomplished individuals were weakening their overall enterprise and their own personal power to act in the world through that business because of deep, simmering resentments they refused to put behind them. Forgiveness could have confined the past to the past. A lack of it was allowing the worst of the past to infect the present and distort the future in ways that weren't good for anyone involved.

> We have to do with the past only as we can make it
> useful to the present and the future.
> Fredrick Douglas

One of the reasons forgiveness is so rare is that it's so widely misunderstood. Genuine forgiveness is not the misguided gesture of reinterpreting an unacceptable action as having been just fine after all. It's not a delusional act. It's also not an irrational refusal to draw conclusions about likely future actions from the evidence of past behavior. And this is a good thing since, after all, past behavior is one of the most reliable guides we have to future conduct. People certainly can change. And sometimes they do. But far too often at a basic level and in the most desirable ways, they don't. As I understand it, forgiveness is not mainly about interpretations or predictions at all. It's an act more centrally involving our emotions and attitudes than those particular operations of our intellects. It's about letting go and putting behind.

And despite what the philosopher Nietzsche long ago famously seemed to suggest, forgiveness is not a servile reaction of the weak to the strong, merely rationalizing what's actually a fearful reticence to retaliate as being instead a generous dismissal of grievance. The truth is very different. Forgiveness, at its purest and best, is always an act of strength. And it's not properly understood if it's thought in any way to lead to weakness. To forgive is not somehow to become naïve or defenseless. You can forgive a person fully, while also protecting yourself well against further hurt or harm from him. Letting go of certain inner emotions and attitudes never means abandoning your own proper self-interest, self-defense, or greater good. In fact, done right, it can promote all those ends in a distinctive way.

Forgiveness is perhaps the last freedom and is tied to the highest freedom we have: the authentic choice to move forward with love and creativity. As the holocaust survivor Victor Frankl movingly reminds us in his classic book *Man's Search for Meaning*, when everything else has been taken away and every other freedom has been lost, we still retain as our last freedom the ability to choose our attitudes, and in fact, the freedom to forgive.

The Choice to Forgive

The ultimate sign and exercise of moral strength is the ability to rise above a situation of personal injustice or offense, overcome the potentially universal instinct for revenge—the nearly mechanical twitch that would perpetuate a cycle of recriminations and harmful actions, whether in a family, a business, a community, a nation, or an entire part of the world—and forgive the offender. Forgiveness is a decisive existential act that in a transformative way can allow you to move on powerfully to a more positive future.

> To forgive much makes the powerful more powerful.
> Publilius Syrus

A weak person nurses grievances. A strong person rises above them. When you forgive an offender, you no longer allow that person's past action to tie you down and hold you back with resentment, bitterness, or any desire to get even. You choose instead a calm and untroubled spirit. You rise to a state of positive power unsullied by the stain of anger. You free yourself and, ideally, the other person for a brighter future. Jesus told his followers to love each other, their neighbors, and even their enemies. Forgiveness is perhaps the most difficult act of love there is, especially as offered to an enemy, or maybe worse, a former friend who has become an adversary. It involves choosing to treat an individual from the heart as a fellow human being also struggling in this world with hopes and dreams and hurts, rather than as a hated foe, a resented source of pain, a resistant obstacle, or a simple irritant. The act of forgiveness peels off the negative effects from layers of personal history and accumulated emotion and penetrates down to a core identity, person-to-person, soul-to-soul. As such, it's what the great religious thinkers see as a powerful act of creative love directed to another self as a child of God or fellow lively production of our mysterious universe. And, of equal importance, it ends up being an outgoing act of grace that can even more deeply benefit our innermost selves.

Forgiveness involves shedding sometimes deeply entrenched feelings and attitudes that can erode our effectiveness in the world as well as our enjoyment of life. It lays down a burden. It lets go. It turns a page. By contrast, an unforgiving spirit fetters us to the past and to corrosive emotions that rarely help us build a better future. To forgive is not the same thing as to forget. It most often means relegating past feelings and reactions to the past. It means refusing certain emotions and attitudes in reaction to things in the present. It's a matter of the inner spirit that's ultimately guided by the heart and mind, and implemented by the will. It involves choosing to treat something or someone differently than you would otherwise, and it results in a personal liberation from the poison of negativity. When you forgive someone for something he's done or is doing, you may think you're just freeing him, but you're also liberating yourself.

In fact, forgiveness is about inner freedom on two levels. It's first about freeing yourself from the negative attitudes of resentment, bitterness, anger, and vengeance. Then, at its highest, it's also about freeing yourself to experience compassion and show kindness. In some situations, that will lead to reconciliation and a restored relationship to the forgiven person. In other situations, it won't be able to attain that ideal, but will result in other positive spiritual and emotional consequences for others as well as yourself.

We often naturally push back from talk about forgiveness. And we can ask plenty of challenging questions about this idea. What if the offending party has never apologized, or shown remorse, or asked for forgiveness? What if he doesn't deserve to be forgiven? And am I then supposed to forgive even Hitler for what he did to all his victims in his day? But wouldn't that in itself be a further instance of wrong? Am I supposed to forgive the selfish politicians, rapacious business-men, and destructive criminals of my own day for their many lies, injustices, and heinous actions that bring great harm to the world? These are of course deep and honest questions. And I suspect that the only possibility for arriving at wise answers must begin at home.

We're to act to forgive the people closest to us, like our family members and friends and neighbors, whether they have apologized or shown any remorse, and whether we initially think they deserve any such thing. We deserve it. That's what matters most. And then, as we grow in our ability to forgive those close to us, we can per-haps consider more distant individuals properly. In the most exact sense, I'm never in a position to offer primary forgiveness to an individual for wrongs committed against someone other than me, unless the harmed person is someone very close to me who can't offer that forgiveness himself but ideally would if he could. And there can be a spiritual reaction to anyone who has harmed oth-ers that's closely akin to forgiveness, where we drop any feeling of hatred or revenge and seek instead a measure of inner peace and compassion in the face of even great harm. If those wrongs are ongoing in our day, we can work hard and tirelessly to stop them and ameliorate their implications, but we need not maintain an inner feeling or attitude of unforgiveness in order to accomplish those forms of good.

Ironically and paradoxically, I believe that we're ultimately called to be both more empathetic to sufferers and more forgiving to wrongdoers than is typical. Yet, the more empathy we have for a victim, such as someone very close to us, the more difficult forgiveness is to achieve toward anyone who has injured that person. And while we may seem to be forgiving toward distant wrongdoers, separated from us in space or time, that can sometimes be merely an absence of negative emotion flowing more from a lack of empathy than from any alchemy of genuine forgiveness. Forgiveness can't arise from ignorance or indifference. It requires knowledge, understanding, and care, even to the point of grief, and can work its true alchemy only with those ingredients in place.

A properly forgiving spirit cares deeply about right and wrong, and yet is never vindictive or malicious in reaction to harm. It's never tinged with hate, but is free from the ugliness of descending down to anywhere near the moral indifference or depravity displayed by the worst offenders among us. And it's never meant to leave us defenseless, either unable or unwilling to work to stop ongoing injustice and harm, or render us reticent to protect ourselves and any other potential victims from further wrong. It's rather a spiritual transformation of the why and how of our reactions and actions in the world. It's a core shift that for a Christian will mean seeking to emulate Christ as much as possible. Any of us may find similar guidance and benefit in also looking to more recent role models like Gandhi or Martin Luther King, who never acquiesced to evil, but resisted it firmly, and yet without any hint of the inner ugliness that descends to its level. The spirit of forgiveness distinguishes acts from persons, and people as they actually are from the better selves they're capable of being. But it doesn't mean failing to surround yourself or others with protective care. And it doesn't require that you refrain from taking action to stop evil and hold wrongdoers accountable to the laws and mores that rightly govern our lives together. We can embrace some things while letting go of others. We can do what has to be done, but in the right spirit, however hard that might be.

Forgiveness is better than revenge.
Pittacus

When we authentically forgive someone, we accept him as a fellow creature of flaws and imperfections. We decide to value him as a human being and to give more weight to him as a person than to his mistake. As we choose not to hold his misdeed, or series of offenses, against him in the arena of our own inner attitudes and emotions, we cleanse ourselves of harmful inward emotions and, with that act, we also put ourselves into a position to improve our outward circumstances, as others see our behavior and discern anew what's really possible in attitudes and relationships. Grace tends to elicit grace. Forgiveness can lead the way down a better path. In this sense, an act of forgiveness can be an act of moral leadership. We wrongly think that forgiveness must always await repentance. It's sometimes the only force that can elicit a genuine transformation of behavior and a change of heart. It is, in itself, a sort of alchemy of the inner and outer as well, and as such can be astonishingly potent in its effects.

I came across a philosophically interesting post on Twitter. The prominent pastor Tim Keller said something that struck me immediately as both true and important. And it sparked an additional insight. He tweeted: "The essence of forgiveness is absorbing pain instead of giving it." I'd never quite thought of it like that, and on reflection I completely agree. Forgiveness does absorb pain rather than dishing it out. But I think it's also equally important to add the next step: Then the real alchemy begins, transforming the hurt or pain that's been absorbed into something of immense personal and spiritual worth, spinning it on the loom of the soul's weave into something greater than gold.

Forgiveness is all about metamorphosis. It doesn't change a bad act into a good one, a flawed situation into a flawless one, or a sinner into a saint. It's a transformative act of moral alchemy that starts inside us, and then almost inevitably has results on the outside. As we grow in our spiritual maturity and power, we get better at it until finally, ideally, it becomes as natural as breath. And in specific instances where it's still a thing that's hard, we have an opportunity to learn where we are in our own growth toward that place where the alchemy is instant and the repercussions are deep. As parents, my wife and I did what many families do, and put pencil marks on a doorway to measure the ongoing growth of our children in their early years. It was exciting to see their progress. Our ability to forgive can mark our own spiritual growth like almost nothing else. We should try to keep track. We may find that we have a long way to go, but it's good to see when we're making progress, however small.

The Power of Transcendence

Are negative emotions or attitudes of any kind getting you down? Are they hindering anyone around you? Often, they can hold back a family, a community, a business office, or an entire organization. Nations even fall victim to their corrosiveness. But this unproductive weight can be released at any time. We all have the power to rise above any negative situation and unhealthy response. It's up to us whether we exercise that power or not. One of the defining attributes of personal maturity is the capacity to transcend difficult circumstances and release the felt need for negative responses.

Our English verb, 'to transcend' comes from two Latin root words that meant to climb above or go beyond. And the verticality of the metaphor is interesting. We labor under heavy burdens. Hardships wear us down. In difficulties, we feel low. The solution is to rise above the problem. In the midst of a bad situation, I try to remember to tell myself to just let go of whatever's bothering me. And then I go vertical. I like to imagine myself releasing the problem from my grip, detaching from it, and then rising above it, coming to view it sequentially from the emotional distance of

300 feet above, then 3,000, and finally at an altitude of 30,000 feet. Eventually, I may go even higher in my flight of fancy, as I leave the negative behind. The higher I rise, the smaller the situation looks.

Distance has the same effect on the mind as on the eye.
Samuel Johnson

I once had a memorable flight home to North Carolina from a talk I had given to one of the world's most profitable companies, headquartered in Bermuda. The session was great and the hospitality of my hosts was amazing. But seriously bad weather was moving across the Atlantic. The plane I got on for the ride home, a new state-of-the-art Gulfstream 550, took off at an incredibly steep angle, cut through the clouds quickly, and leveled off at a perfectly smooth cruising altitude of 47,000 feet, far above any turbulence the lower-flying commercial airlines might be experiencing that day. Even the biggest storm clouds below us seemed small as an attendant prepared a wonderful meal for the three of us on board. I remember enjoying the view out the large windows and thinking to myself that there's an inner emotional analogue of the G5, and yet unlike the plane, it's free and available any time. Whenever bad weather is moving in emotionally, threatening our equilibrium and overall attitude, we can take off mentally, climb out, and cruise along at our own smooth psychological version of 47,000 feet. From that inner altitude, we can then see any problem as being every bit as small as it really is, in a cosmic and historical sense.

It can help in the midst of challenge to remember the true immensities of the universe in space and time and allow this perspective to remind us of the actual size of any difficulty we're currently undergoing because of the actions of another person, a group, the forces of nature, or even the economy. This is just a matter of reframing the situation in a way that can help us deal with it. In his dialogue, *Phaedo*, Plato used his own memorable, smaller scale image for this way of putting things into perspective when he wrote, "The true earth is enormous, and we live around our sea like ants or frogs around a swamp." We shouldn't let the toads get us down.

Most distressing situations that look so big and daunting to us in close-up are, within the greater cosmic context, ridiculously small and transient, quickly passing away. In real life, there are no ten thousand pound lemons. And even if there were, that would just offer us the possibility of making much more lemonade, with the right approach to the challenge. This again demonstrates the vital importance of attitude for us all.

> Every man takes the limits of his own field of vision
> for the limits of the world.
> Schopenhauer

When we grow more accustomed to putting things into a big picture perspective, we're much better able to avoid allowing the actions of others or our perceptions of those actions to trap us in negative attitudes and emotions. A useful mental technique or image can help us to overcome any bad reactions that may threaten our progress in life. Let me describe another simple one that's meant a lot to me. The first toy telescope I owned as a boy gave me a helpful analogy for the inner action we all need to take. I was at first amazed that when I looked through the small end of the foot-long handheld device, objects around me seemed so much bigger and closer and that, viewed through the other end, they looked so much smaller and farther away. Either view changed my experience of my surroundings. This is a basic image for what we all can do with our problems. When we first notice any new challenge, we tend to turn an emotional telescope on it and look through the small end like almost everyone else. And this gives us a false perspective that makes those problems look much bigger and closer than they really are. For our own sense of balance and perspective, it helps imaginatively to flip that inner telescope around and see how small the difficulties we face can actually appear, viewed differently in the larger sweep of things. Turning our emotional telescope around allows us to shrink and diminish what may previously have seemed big and overwhelming, so that now we can feel some measure of emotional power and control over it. The many times when I've personally tried this have each surprised me with the instant inner effectiveness of such a simple imaginative trick.

The Social Impact of Attitude

As Aristotle was quick to realize long ago, we are essentially social beings. Because of this, the people around us and their moods are important to us. Due to a social and psychological tendency related to basic survival needs in our biological past, moods and attitudes are contagious. One unhelpfully negative person in an organization can cause an incredible amount of trouble and do damage over time just as a single individual. But what's worse is that such negativity rarely dwells for long in only one heart. Negative emotions easily spread through any office or group and can infect many people in different ways over a short period of time, without anyone's necessarily realizing what's going on. Bad feelings can spread like the flu.

> An isolated individual does not exist.
> He who is sad, saddens others.
> Saint-Exupery

It's not just cynics, skeptics, anger management class dropouts, and the worst doom-and-gloom personalities who can have a deleterious effect on their co-workers. Even vocal doubters, nervous second-guessers, chronic complainers, glum energy drainers, and casual gossips can undermine the positive prospects of a group, especially in times of transition and upheaval. And in precisely such times, the presence or absence of a particular attitude or cluster of attitudes can make all the difference between gaining or losing an important edge in our ability to deal with the new realities that have come our way.

I won't for a moment suggest we should all take positivity pills in the morning and hand them out around the office, or make an effort to engage in some form of ungrounded, enthusiastic, happy "group think" at work that's oblivious to difficulties, blind to probabilities, and innocent about ambiguities. People can be realistic in difficult situations, hold properly high standards for corporate decisions, speak up responsibly with divergent viewpoints, and insist on proceeding with due caution and an eye on risk in everything they do while yet maintaining, overall, a good attitude along the way. Attitude isn't magic, but it's always important.

The first rule within the art of positive action would have us govern our attitudes well, both as individuals and as groups. This just means that as we seek to control our own inclinations, we should encourage those around us to do the same. Ultimately of course, with even the best of intentions, we can't directly control the attitudes of other people and assure that a positive climate prevails. But we can remind our associates in various ways about the power of attitude, and how all our inner perspectives, whether positive or negative, can be surprisingly self-fulfilling as they work themselves into our actions and out to the world. Sometimes, this alone can have a degree of persuasive influence on others and enhance the overall atmosphere wherever we happen to be confronting change. But our actions will persuade others more than our words.

What's most important to realize is that the same mechanism of social psychology that helps to spread negativity through groups can also be used to propagate a more positive atmosphere. When you're engaged as an individual in all the activities of lemonade making recommended by the art of change, the reality of group contagion can help to spread your spirit and approach out to others and move them in the direction of emotional transcendence and positivity that will make your work together much better.

> Every man is like the company he keeps.
> Euripides

This tendency in human nature that allows emotions and attitudes to spread through a group is often called "social tuning." I like to think of it as "emotional resonance." It's something like a natural default position for human beings. We generally tend to become like the people we're around, in beliefs, emotions, attitudes, and even physiological states. And we're normally not aware of this movement toward conformity while it's happening. It seems to be hardwired into our unconscious behavioral tendencies.

In the presence of a visibly angry person, your own heartbeat increases, moving in the direction of his. You'll be agitated right away and even without knowing why. If people around you seem suddenly frightened, you can feel something like that knot of fear in your own stomach and go into a heightened state of mental alertness before you have any idea as to what exactly the danger might be. This is just part of nature's way of preparing us to move quickly when we may need to, for our own safety needs. And it's often a tremendously helpful tendency to have. But it sometimes can result in our being caught up in emotions and attitudes that aren't healthy at all.

When people around us are frustrated and worked up in response to a problem that we're all facing, the negative emotional resonance of the group can pull us into a pattern of thoughts and feelings that isn't conducive to actually solving the problem at hand in anything like an optimal way. In order to put ourselves into the best emotional and mental state for dealing with the situation, we'll have to lift ourselves out of the psychological climate of the moment as it is and take on a more positively productive attitude. That may require a cleansing breath or two, or more, the use of some helpful mental imagery, and maybe a quick walk outdoors to clear the mind and heart. Or it may even mean speaking a few positive words to your co-workers with a reassuring tone, perhaps validating them in their feelings, showing some empathetic understanding, and then getting down to work. Nothing dispels negativity quite like the mental focus of getting involved in coming up with positive resolutions for whatever problem we face. We're by nature problem solvers, and when we wholeheartedly throw ourselves fully into that enterprise, any negativity we may have experienced will most often just melt away.

Ultimately, of course, each of us is responsible for our own inner states, despite the ongoing realities of social tuning or emotional resonance. We have an obligation in particular to govern our attitudes well. This is the path of wisdom, the way of health, a source of power, and the first rule of positive action in response to change. It gives us the right foundation for moving forward in a productive way.

> Wisdom is to the soul what health is to the body.
> La Rochefoucauld

Once we do take control of our own attitudes, we can begin to use the mechanism of social tuning to recruit other colleagues of the heart. With empathy, and by adopting a healthy and positive approach to an initially challenging situation, we can indeed help to change the attitudes and emotions of those around us. In fact, this may even be a moral duty we have throughout our days. We all live within the weave of a social fabric. It's part of our individual responsibilities in life to see to it that our actions strengthen this fabric and don't weaken it overall. When others abandon that duty or are oblivious to its demand, it becomes even more important for us to rise to the occasion and initiate positive action. Any time we take the vital step of turning in a productive direction and alchemically adapting to whatever we face, we can begin to recruit others onto that same path of healthy metamorphosis as well. And then the power of partnership becomes available for the next stretch of the path.

Look for Opportunities

Within the art of positive action, the first requirement is to govern our attitudes. That provides a positive base for anything we do. And it allows us to get started on the right footing in any new situation on any given day. The second requirement, then, is to look for opportunities. An unexpected change, challenge, or difficulty presents a new opportunity, or several such possible avenues, for responsive action. But those new paths forward are rarely obvious on the surface of the situation that confronts us. It's up to us to find them, using whatever skills of exploration and discernment we have.

Each of us needs to ask on a regular basis and in every area of our lives: Where are my best opportunities? What are the entry points around me for a novel use of my knowledge, interests, talents, and energies? How can I accomplish some good here? Where is there some new leverage for what I know and can do? Has any shift in my circumstances created an opening for innovative action? An opportunity is really just a new accessible possibility for action, personal growth, and achievement. To be used, it first has to be recognized.

Going Beyond What We Know

Whenever we face major change, many of us tend to narrow our focus precisely when we should be broadening our horizons. We stick to what we know, because it's something we're comfortable with and feel, rightly or wrongly, that we can control, even if it's the last thing the new situation needs. A challenging novel situation typically calls for a higher level of awareness in response. And

it often requires new actions. When we're in a relatively comfortable routine, operating often on automatic pilot, we can fail to
see fresh opportunities that may be appearing all around us. And
then, when our routine is interrupted, the even more unfortunate
tendency we have is to keep our heads down and avoid whatever
seems avoidable, digging a temporary storm-shelter to make us feel
safe until the winds of change blow over. But periods of big change
are precisely those times when new opportunities can most abun-
dantly present themselves as avenues for personal advancement,
improvement, and the bold launching of innovative ventures. The
churn of change creates new possibilities and paths. We need to
train ourselves to ask: "What are my new opportunities? How can
I have my best impact in this developing situation? Where should
I be looking to see what creative new directions are available?"

> Know your opportunity.
> Pittacus

Socrates believed that a life of wisdom requires asking lots of
basic questions. And so did Plato, which is presumably why he
thought it so important to depict quite extensively this aspect of
his teacher's practice and pass it along to subsequent generations.
We need to make it a habit to interrogate reality on a regular basis,
starting of course with ourselves, and then moving out into the circumstances around us. The most successful people in any changing
environment tend to be the natural investigators and detectives
who relentlessly examine reality as it transitions, morphs, and
reforms and then act on what they learn. We need to do the same,
which always means going beyond what we already know and
expanding our knowledge base.

There's a silly but instructive old story that scientists and philosophers love to tell about a man crawling around on his hands
and knees in the grass near the bottom of a lamppost late on a
moonless night. A policeman drives by and stops to ask what he's

doing. He says, "I've lost my favorite watch and I'm desperately looking for it."

The policeman parks his car, gets out, and squats down on the ground near the bright lamp and beside the man. After a minute or two of running his hands carefully through the grass and visually scrutinizing the entire area near the base of the lamppost, he says, "Are you sure you lost it here?"

The man looks very surprised and says, "Oh, no, not at all, but the light's much better here."

This little tale illustrates a number of things beyond what academics tend to think is funny. Don't do what's easy. Do what's right. What's convenient is not nearly as important as what's effective. Metaphorically, where it's now darkest may be precisely where we need to be. That's where discoveries can be made.

When there is no sun, we can see the evening stars.
Heraclitus

In times of change, it's tempting to stick with what we know and hope for the best, narrowing our focus and staying where the available light is better. But these are precisely the times when we need to broaden our search for what we should be doing and how we could be doing it. We need to be curious and open, adventurous and brave. Profound possibility often hides in the dark just beyond what we can see. If we look for opportunities outside the tight circle of the light we already have, we'll be much more likely to find what we need—a positive path forward for creative new results.

Paying Attention
To find new opportunities, we have to look in the right places, and then pay attention to what we see as a result. I'm genuinely amazed at the degree to which we ordinarily fail to be fully aware of our surroundings, and so don't notice things that are staring us in the face. This is a problem I've personally experienced many times.

A while ago, I was in a major city with a free afternoon before some meetings. At the time, I had a keen amateur interest in mechanical watches, and I knew that one of the world's most famous watch stores had an outpost that was just blocks from my hotel. So I walked down the street to admire their merchandise and see in person what the great makers are doing these days. The store's bright display cases presented the striking new creations of Patek Philippe, Jaeger Le Coultre, Breguet, Audemars Piguet, Vacheron Constantin, Girard Perregaux, Rolex, and many other top watchmakers. I stared at the beautiful faces of many incredible timepieces and even tried on a few, admiring the cases, dials, hands, numerals, and all the extraordinary craftsmanship to be seen in their construction. When I finally left the store and realized I had likely stayed much longer than I'd planned, I was shocked at the first conscious thought that ran through my head. I found myself raising my own watch into view as I pondered, "I wonder what time it is?"

I stopped in my tracks there on the sidewalk and laughed out loud. I literally didn't know what time it was. I had been looking closely and carefully at accurately set and well-running watches for nearly an hour. During all that scrutiny, I'd experienced scores and perhaps even hundreds of opportunities to see the time. I was surrounded by many of the world's finest and most coveted devices for measuring and telling me precisely what time it was. And I had not noticed this one thing at all—at least, not in such a way as to become consciously aware of it and remember what I'd seen, although it was out in plain view all around me. Incredible. Absurd. And yet, it's just so human.

We're always getting stuck in the ruts of a limited perspective. We see only a small fraction of what the world presents to us, and then we're surprised that we don't make better decisions or find the right new paths into the future.

There is only one way of seeing things rightly,
and that is, seeing the whole of them.
John Ruskin

We pay attention to our surroundings quite selectively. This is necessary to a great extent because, otherwise, we'd be constantly bombarded with an overwhelming number of sensations, perceptions, and conscious thoughts. So we have natural and unconscious principles and filters for sorting out what is and is not relevant to our current concerns. Our interests dictate to a truly surprising degree what we see and how we see it. Our beliefs, values, prejudices, attitudes, emotions, perspectives, and habits of thought can blind us from noticing exactly what we most need to see among all the things that are going on around us. That's a good part of the reason why eyewitnesses to a crime or accident can differ so dramatically on what they report, aside from the notorious vagaries of memory. And it's often why we fail to notice new opportunities right in front of us.

We shouldn't let the constraints of what we already know prevent us from noticing what we most need to see. And we can't allow a narrow mental focus to divert us from all the relevant details of the big picture we face. We need to turn on our inner radar, set it at full strength, broaden its sweep, and keep a careful eye on what it's showing us. If we'll just pay full attention to all the hints and glimmers of opportunity around us, we can position ourselves to make the most of whatever situation we're in.

Seeing Our Opportunities

We can learn something important about looking for opportunities in any time of challenge from a quick lesson in the art of fine woodcarving. The master woodcarver David Esterly once stated that in working on a new project, "A carver starts as a god and ends as a slave." What he meant is as simple as it is profound. A great woodcarver begins with an object in mind that he wants to create in the world and then starts to move from thought to existence in an almost divine manner. But he soon finds that he needs to "learn from the grain" of the wood he's using. Esterly says that the great carver ends up in a situation where, "The wood tells him what to do." The merely average woodcarver may forge ahead and attempt to force the wood to take the shape he first envisioned. The master carver, by contrast, watches the wood, listens to the grain, and partners up with it, taking direction from what he discovers. He pays attention, finds his best opportunities in the grain he confronts, and creates in collaboration with the wood.

In changing circumstances, people can easily make either of two opposite mistakes, most often depending on their personalities. On the one hand, they can freeze up with fear, unsure of how to move. That's the problem of passivity. These are the people who stay as close as they can to the light they already have, stuck in place, refusing to venture out into the dark. And then there is the opposite error, where people make snap judgments about the changes they confront, spot the first opportunity for action that seems to come around, and then rush headlong in that direction, not even glimpsing what else they might have noticed along the way if they had paid a little more attention to the details of the developing situation. This is the problem of hastiness.

Many smart, high-energy people think fast, act fast, and live in constant danger of allowing any new development to lead to disaster. They don't habitually exercise the subtle and ancient power of discernment in ascertaining the genuinely best opportunity that a new situation might present. They're in such a hurry for success-as-they-already-define-it that they rush forward without keeping their eyes open and paying enough attention to whether the path they've chosen is really the best available to them, or if they might need to adjust course along the way. Temerity without judgment is just as bad as undue timidity in the face of the new.

> The eye of prudence may never shut.
> Emerson

How often do the more aggressive go-getters among us seek to force an issue, bulling their way forward and dictating the terms of success while not really watching and listening to the grain of the situation, neglecting to monitor the detailed unfurling of events as they arise? We should all seek to be like the greatest woodcarvers and other master craftsmen who work with complete attention, and understand that while we may begin a new venture feeling like gods, there is an important sense in which we must inevitably become more like partners and even servants in order to create a true masterpiece in anything we do.

Confronted by any situation of change or difficulty, we need to ask: Where is the grain? How should we be listening? What should we be noticing? Which are the best opportunities here? This is the true art of change. An honest awareness, an openness to learn, a real humility to serve, along with our willingness to take direction and follow the grain, can lead to a greatness that's otherwise unattainable. The grain of the situation will show us what's best. When we learn to look and see and adapt, we can make the most of any change, and of any situation we face.

Take the Initiative
THE ART OF POSITIVE ACTION IS STRAIGHTFORWARD IN ITS basic components. Govern your attitudes. Look for opportunities. And then: Take the initiative. Do something new. Launch a creative response.

Demosthenes, the great ancient rhetorician, was once asked what makes for success in public speaking. He said in reply, "Action. Action. Action." It was a good answer. Action engages people. And it's ultimately the key to all real success in our world of change.

> In the arena of human life, the honors and rewards
> fall to those who show their good qualities in action.
> Aristotle

If I had to identify one quality that stands out most in the lives of highly successful people, it would be that they have a proclivity toward action. They are habitually inclined to take initiative and make things happen. They're not passive bystanders. They don't wait endlessly to see what develops. They're geared toward doing. They set a goal, create a plan, and then get going in the direction of their target. They also carefully monitor their progress along the way. They gather new information as they move forward, seeing new opportunities for action as they might develop, and they are then quick to take the initiative again to make any ongoing adjustments they might need in order to be as effective as possible. There is a pattern of their achievement:

See. Think. Act. Learn. Adjust. Repeat.

This is all as obvious as it is rare. It can sometimes seem like passivity rules the world. So, what prevents people from taking the initiative that's called for as new situations arise? Well, for one thing, the power of inertia, the metaphorical gravity of what is, along with the dulling weight of routine. Many people nearly sleepwalk through the day, not even noticing the chances they may have to do something new. Old habits of thought block their perceptions of what's possible. Familiar comforts blind them to new paths. Old disappointments can distort their judgment. But even those rare and perceptive individuals who clearly see their opportunities are often still inhibited from taking those new trails by the backward pull of inertia. There are some widespread emotional reactions we too often have in response to anything unexpected and unwanted that can block us from launching out into the positive action needed in a time of turbulence or transition. So, this is clearly a problem that deserves a closer look.

Obstacles to Proper Action
There's something going on in the world that hinders the best and appropriate action in response to change. Sometimes, it keeps people from acting at all. At other times, it generates precisely the

wrong actions. Whenever anything unwanted happens, when any unplanned or initially unwelcome change occurs, the most common reactions tend to be utterly unhelpful and counterproductive.

I recently found myself wondering what's the number one emotion or attitude to be found around the world today. Many wise people talk often about the importance of gratitude in our lives. And great thinkers of the past agreed. Some insightful advisors write provocatively about the deep value of joy. Is either of these great inner states the answer to my question? Could one of them qualify as the most pervasive emotion or attitude in the world these days? Gratitude? Joy? Unless the news we get through every journalistic medium is completely distorted in the most fundamental way and our own immediate experience of life is just as deluded, it can look as if the number one emotion or attitude around the world right now might be very different from these two quite wonderful and properly praised inclinations of the spirit. It just might be the much less uplifting psychological disposition and reaction of: Anger.

People are angry with their leaders at every level, at the leaders of other nations, and at people in different political or religious groups. Drivers are, at nearly every moment and on almost every major road, feeling anger at other drivers who seem intent on being in their way. Troubled kids are ticked off with their parents or teachers, or fellow students. People in the workplace feel hostility toward their co-workers, or their bosses. Individuals in one ethnic group are deeply disturbed with simmering rage directed at a different race. Sports coaches and fans frequently explode with fury over a player's actions or an official's decision in the context of a game. In almost every sort of context, people stomp off enraged over a perceived insult. The U.S. Congress, like most other governing bodies around the world, is full of partisan ire. The United Nations, of course, isn't united at all, due in part to international anger. Talk radio seems to broadcast on the one frequency of

"Mad." Reality TV is fueled by it, show after show. A labor union is right now incensed at management. Management is irked with them. And so it goes.

Anger clearly appears to take first place as the most common emotion or attitude of our day. And this is clearly an unfortunate feature of the human condition, resulting in very little good, while most often preventing positive outcomes. Irascibility isn't a model of wisdom, nor is it a core alchemistic trait, facilitating great lemonade. A flash of anger can goad us into action, but it should never live in us or boil inside us over time.

Anger dwells only in the bosom of fools.
Albert Einstein

The number two emotion or attitude around the globe, by my lights, is hardly better. It seems to be anxiety. People are worried. The uncertainty in our lives breeds constant concern and terrible trepidation. Almost no one feels secure. Industries are shrinking. Disruptions are everywhere. The competition is getting better, and they're out to get us. The economy appears to be more complex and fragile than we ever imagined. And in light of all this, it begins to seem somehow appropriate that our modern English word, 'business,' derives from an Old English term, 'bisignis,' which originally meant: anxiety, uneasiness, and distress. Really.

There are far too many scary diseases in the world that can strike without warning. Even minor illness and simple elective procedures in a modern medical facility can result in a terrible infection and death. Everything seems to have unanticipated side effects. Our water and food supplies are full of stuff that could harm us. The environment is threatened severely. The next bridge we drive over might collapse. Earthquakes strike without warning. Hurricanes, tornadoes, and wildfires seem to be increasing in frequency and intensity. Terrorism looms. Violent crime is capriciously unpredictable. A couple of geese can take down a commercial jet. Unhinged individuals stockpile arsenals. Mass shootings surround us. The news we hear each day feeds our alarm. Even groundless anxieties can create real problems to fret about. It sometimes seems that the entirety of civilization hangs by a thread and sharp objects are all around. Dread rules the world.

It is the nature of human affairs to be fraught with anxiety.
They never succeed perfectly, and they never remain constant.
Boethius

We worry about the project we're doing, or about the one we may not get. Young people obsess about their grades, their looks, their popularity, their futures, and about what we adults are doing to their world. We also feel great concern about them. There are so many dangers in life that we know about. And it's the ones we've never even thought of yet that really concern us. Because of all this, anxiety may be at epidemic levels. And so then is its first cousin, stress.

Too many people try to deal with all this tension by self-medicating through alcohol, drugs, and various forms of risky behavior that, ironically and inconsistently, end up giving them more to worry about than they had at the start. Many of the problems of the modern world can be traced to the high anxiety that nearly envelops us all. It's a rare personality that seems to be able to handle it well. Some turn to yoga, meditation, jogging, weight lifting, afternoon naps, massage, shopping therapy, real therapy, or, oddly, either a totally immersed, head-down fixation on the minutiae of their work, or in the opposite direction: more days off, longer vacations when possible, obsessive hobbies, and endless entertainment—anything that will help calm the nerves and assuage the stress that life seems so insistent to create. No one cure appears to work for everyone. Many of us, as a result, will try almost anything that might help.

So. Anger and anxiety could be the two most common responses to the world in our time. I've referred to both of them as either
an emotion or attitude for a reason: When they're felt, they are
unpleasant emotions; but when they simply simmer in the background beneath awareness, I see them as disruptive attitudes or
dispositions ready to manifest emotionally. In either psychological
guise, they agitate us and destroy our inner peace. And they are
definitely the most common reactions to unexpected, unwanted
change. Yet, when we stop to think about this for a second, we
quickly realize that these are not the two most positive psychological states imaginable. They don't exactly look like the twin pillars
of happiness. And they won't give us anything like a formula for
positive action in response to change. Anger often derails us. Anxiety shuts us down. Neither promotes the fresh creativity we need
to take in the face of challenge.

When we react to difficulty with ongoing anger and anxiety, we
can actually prevent ourselves from stirring up the great lemonade
we need to make. We begin brewing a poisoned potion instead,
and one we ourselves will have to drink. We seriously need to do
something about this widespread tendency, at least in our own
lives. And the good news is that it turns out we can.

There is an alternative approach to life and change that doesn't
feature these two enemies of personal peace and obstacles to positive action. And it's been around for a very long time. It comes
from some deep and simple ancient wisdom about our relationship to outer circumstances. And it's an approach that's crucial for
making life's best, most refreshing lemonade.

> Every evening, I turn my worries over to God.
> He's going to be up all night anyway.
> Mary C. Crowley

Anger, Acceptance, and Action
The first century Stoic philosopher Seneca wrote a lot about

anger because he thought of it as one of the most problematic and self-defeating inner states we can experience. He pointed out that it's never intrinsically a good thing, or a virtue. He reasoning was interesting. Any virtue, he said, is good to have, and to have more of it is always better. But the more anger a person experiences, the worse things can become, because intense anger is more powerful than any other emotion and even reason itself, and we find it very difficult, once this agitated state is given a full head of steam, to calm down and move beyond it. But, as Aristotle pointed out long before, there isn't necessarily anything inherently or morally wrong about the mere experience of anger, either. It's all a matter of our answers to some basic questions: Anger with whom, for what reason, in what measure, to what end, and lasting how long? A flash of anger in the face of injustice can move us to needed action. It can be both well motivated as an appropriate response and also motivating. But anger directed toward the wrong person, or felt for the wrong reason, in an inappropriate measure, leading to the wrong actions, or indulged for too long a time can be badly damaging. And as a pervasive, ongoing habit or settled tendency, it's horribly corrosive. It can be poisonous and debilitating. It's even strangely self-defeating. Hot temper isn't conducive to cool reason. The irascible individual tends to be an irrational person, not in full command of his or her higher and better resources. The person in a fury doesn't tend to make choices that are in his own best interest in the long run. Our ideal of a hero is a cool head responding well.

In fact, even when anger isn't wrong, it may not be optimal. And here we come to an issue that I'd like to describe as spiritual. Imagine a line representing a spectrum of measurement for the moral and spiritual nature, or value, of our actions:

-------Wrong-------/---------Acceptable---------/-------Optimal-------

One end of the spectrum represents things that are just wrong.

If you're very angry about something and your anger passes the Aristotle test, then you're not in that area with the emotion in question. Your anger isn't wrong. It's permissible. You're not what the great philosopher would have called blameworthy for it. But your emotional state still may not be morally or spiritually optimal. The most spiritually mature people rarely seem to experience this dangerous emotion. They spot wrong and wicked things better than the rest of us, and act to prevent or eliminate them, or at least mitigate them to the extent they can, but without the inner turmoil of sharp emotion that can be so corrosive to the soul.

I've come to think we should all aspire to a measure of inner calm that's rarely perturbed by the hot spike of anger. When we feel that troubling emotion, it's often a sign of some unresolved issue in our lives regarding a fear or a desire, or else it's a deeper ego problem, rather than a sign of superior righteousness confronted with an unworthy world.

It's noteworthy that the most truly spiritual or deeply mature individuals are the hardest people to insult or offend. They're like an archery target high in the air and positioned at a great distance, too elevated and far away for any arrows of intended insult or offense to hit. People still may shoot at them, and even a lot, but their shafts of snark, derision, invective, and hatred always seem to fall short. This elevation of the spirit is something we should all strive to attain. Most of us as targets are just too easy to hit. And the anger that results is often not necessary or particularly helpful in our lives.

High anxiety won't typically lead to great decision making, either. The extremely nervous individual is not in the best state for perceptive and judicious responses to the world. Excessive worry can block the clarity of mind and thoughtful perspective that's required for wise action. It can narrow and constrict our thinking precisely when we might need to broaden our sights. Any agitated apprehensiveness can detract from the calm, measured clear-headedness that's most conducive for finding and developing healthy plans of action. And again, you often find this calm in the spiritually advanced.

Disproportionate anxiety is always without power.
Aeschylus

A CEO friend recently told me that worry is an important part of his job. The day before a very big meeting where I was going to speak for an hour, as a sort of centerpiece in a major corporate celebration, I glanced over at him now and then as he oversaw a rehearsal of the program, and I could tell that he was in a state of high concern. He seemed to be experiencing anxiety about everything. I finally decided to do something to encourage and reassure him, so I walked over and said, "Hey, man. I'm really looking forward to my session tomorrow. We're going to have a great time together. It'll be awesome. You don't have to worry about my part at all."

He grimaced and said, "Whenever anybody says that, I really worry." I had to laugh. But, to some extent, he wasn't joking. I know other extremely smart, powerful, and otherwise sagacious people who seem to share this perspective. It's almost as if they see anxiety as having a vital causal role in preventing the realization of its own worries. Why? Well, perhaps the reasoning would be that intense worry results in greater vigilance and meticulous care, and those things are necessary for preventing sloppy mistakes. But if that's true, then why not skip the middle part? Grow more vigilant and careful without the unnecessary mediation of worry. The hard emotion itself is superfluous.

When we carefully analyze situations of worry, we discover that the negative agitation never, on its own, adds anything necessary or helpful to the mix that could not easily be had without it. It's utterly unnecessary. And it usually brings with it a case of frayed nerves, tension, and distraction that can make it more difficult for people to perform at their best. That's why I advise nervous people to turn their negative interpretation of the energy they're feeling into something positive. You can care about what you're doing with a passion to do it well, and without that commitment generating a negative emotion. So my advice to those who customarily embrace the emotion of worry is that this is perhaps the only thing that should worry them. And then, let it go.

> The reason why worry kills more people than work
> is that more people worry than work.
> Robert Frost

The good news of practical thinkers like Seneca, Epictetus, and Marcus Aurelius, to mention just a few like-minded sages, is that we have a pair of great alternatives to the harsh mindsets of anger or anxiety. Whenever unexpected change happens and it's even possible to doubt its positive value, we will in fact often find that anger or anxiety, or both, will naturally arise within us. But our best philosophers have advised us: If it's a situation we can't control, acceptance is better than either anger or anxiety. And if it's something we can control, action is even yet to be preferred. The key to inner resilience and outer results in the world is to accept what we can't control and take action on what we can control. Anything else is just spinning our wheels and is a serious waste of time.

The Serenity Prayer

Echoing this perspective, the influential and highly regarded twentieth century theologian, Reinhold Niebuhr, a man of deep philosophical sensibilities who was concerned with the challenge of change, is often credited for the famous words known widely as "The Serenity Prayer," a well stated and heart-felt petition that he may have first recited publicly in 1937, if not earlier. Whatever its origin, this is a prayer that has made a huge difference in the lives of people who have heard it and taken it to heart. There are several versions of it, but perhaps the best-known rendition contains the lines:

> God, grant me the serenity to
> accept the things I cannot change;
> courage to change the things I can;
> and wisdom to know the difference.

It's interesting to note that this prayer is focused on things that I can or cannot change, rather than using the concept of "control," and that the "things" under discussion are presumably difficult matters, or unpleasant situations that are less desirable than what I would like—or in other words, things that I would want to change if I could. Any new reality that comes into my life and is apparently negative should either elicit from me the courage and action to change it if it can be changed, or else it should be met by an emotion or attitude of simple acceptance. Action or acceptance are better than anxiety or anger, or any other negative response.

The famous prayer has given millions of people a sense of perspective on their problems. Its simple lines have gone on to have a tremendous cultural impact within groups like Alcoholics Anonymous and in many other contexts of addiction, challenge, and struggle. It's one of the most widely known petitions in history, and it reflects the perspectives of ancient emotional alchemists in what it seeks.

Goals and the Issue of Control

The simple philosophical contrast between things we can control or change and those we can't is crucial for a deep understanding of life and a proper response to it. Let me give an example of a common failure to acknowledge and employ this distinction. After hearing a very motivating speaker, or reading a truly inspirational book about personal or professional success, we might react by setting ourselves lofty and exciting new goals for things that are far outside our control. Such goals aren't genuinely and completely up to us, because they're either partly or mostly in the power of other people. And this common fact is important to recognize as such, because of what it implies about how we should then set out to take initiative in support of our goal.

> He that would have the fruit must climb the tree.
> Thomas Fuller

A personal goal is by definition something I intend to attain through my own initiation and efforts. In this respect, among others, a goal is different from a hope or a wish. But if a goal I choose is intrinsically outside my power to secure in any direct or immediate way, then there's a gap between where I am and where I want to be, between my starting point and my chosen end state, that will need to be bridged by some intermediate and more immediate goal setting and achievement regarding things that are within my control. And these preliminaries will have to be guided by insight, wisdom, and artful action. This additional, intermediate goal setting must also reflect the fact that I'll inevitably need the freely given cooperation of other people to attain my ultimate aim. And when I realize this, a concern can arise. Can I indeed reach out in pursuit of a goal beyond the range of my direct control and get things to happen that depend on others? Initially, the question can seem odd, because it wonders about something that appears to happen all the time. We do set sales goals, and they ultimately depend on other people. Coaches set goals for fumbles caused and passes intercepted. But again, these depend in large part on the free actions of others. How can we move forward toward such goals?

To explain the point fully, I need to make another important and related distinction. We can certainly have perfectly legitimate desires and dreams that go far beyond anything over which we have direct personal control. And dreams like these can often come true, in large part because of the realistic and more direct goals we set and attain along the way in our pursuit of them. But whenever we set immediate personal and professional goals in order to follow our bigger dreams, we need to understand the crucial difference between what's literally within our power and what isn't.

When I see a man anxious, I ask, "What does he want?"
If he did not want something that isn't in his power,
how could he be anxious?
Seneca

It can be completely fine and commendably ambitious for a film director to seek to have the number one box office hit with his next project. A salesperson can certainly aspire to be the best in her company, the recognized Number One in Sales. A writer can hope to have a top bestseller, and can work hard toward that end. But obviously these things aren't totally within the control of the individual. They require certain responses and actions by other people, and sometimes lots of other people. Because human beings have free will, as well as their own habits and interests, we can never fully determine the behavior of others or guarantee that they'll have the reactions to our efforts that we desire. When we set goals that are beyond our own power to guarantee, we give these goals the best chance of happening only if we also identify and act on things that are fully within our power and that will likely move us in the direction of our dreams.

The simple insight for goal setting here is that whenever we choose a goal that isn't wholly within our control, we should also set subordinate, supporting goals that are. But then, an interesting and powerful alchemy starts to happen. The more we work on things that are within our control, however small that circle might at first seem, our actions and their results can begin to expand our circle of influence, and ultimately extend the sweep of our actual power or control. We can start small and end big.

> Don't worry if you have built your castles in the air.
> They are where they should be.
> Now put foundations under them.
> Henry David Thoreau

The concept of influence is key. Taking care of what's within our control can help raise the probability of reaching out success-fully into the realm of things that aren't wholly within our power, where we at least might then be able to exercise a positive influ-ence. Most of life isn't about guarantees or control, anyway. It's about changing probabilities or likelihoods through wise action and personal influence. We're not omnipotent, but we're not help-less either. The range of things outside our strict control need not worry us as long as we work hard to do well with the things we can control, and that can then expand our positive influence on the inclinations of those around us. There are Dream Goals. And there are Do Goals. The latter can position us well for a more likely realization of the former.

In nearly every industry, sales people can discover at least a rough ratio between calls or contacts and sales. Whether it takes roughly seven calls to make a sale or thirty, there will be some sort of statistical guideline for the standard relationship between effort and effect, given proper training in the psychology of persuasion and the dynamics of sales in that particular industry. While a par-ticular salesperson can't guarantee that any given potential custom-er will buy, since that's something literally outside his control, he can control and guarantee his own preparation, the quality of his performance, and the frequency of his calls. If John sets it as his goal to make forty major sales this year, a goal over which he liter-ally has no direct control, then he'd better also take the initiative to set goals regarding things he can control concerning his preparation and effort, day to day. Then he can position himself to move the probabilities in his favor and more likely hit his ultimate target. To reach his big Dream Goals, he has to set plenty of small Do Goals. The pursuit of anything beyond our literal control is always a probabilistic endeavor. But it's also a form of art, so there are things we can do to raise our chance of success.

One of the reasons that change often can be so stressful is that many of the changes we experience in our lives come to us without warning and not through any dreams, desires, or decisions of our own. Change can bring us the sudden necessity of setting new goals that weren't otherwise of our choosing. When we figure out how to begin taking action to deal with these changes and set some goals that we can choose in detail, we retake a measure of felt control, however small, and this can have an enormous benefit in relieving the stress that such a situation otherwise naturally creates. It also helps us regain our inner sense of being, at least to some extent, empowered in the circumstances, in however minor a way. Even small steps taken deliberately and wisely can yield important positive results in the inner person and outer world.

> The measure of power is obstacles overcome.
> Oliver Wendell Holmes, Jr.

The ancients advise us well. We shouldn't regret what we can't control or forget what we can control. When we take initiative to do whatever is within our power in support of our goals, we can then use that action to move forward in the direction of our dreams, regardless of the obstacles that have fallen across our path. And when an old dream becomes literally impossible because of changes that have entered our lives, new things can be dreamed and new steps taken in their direction. There's always a way forward, a new path to be chosen, an enhancing adventure to be had.

Remembering this will encourage us to take initiative in the most effective ways to create good outcomes at work and in life. This is the path to great life lemonade.

Self-Control and Positive Action

We're at a juncture now where it will be good to get our bearings again. The overall art of change begins with adaptation, and this starts with the inner art and practice of self-control—where we don't rush to judgment, we value the right things, and we use our imaginations well. And then it extends into the art of positive action. If we go on to govern our attitudes, look for opportunities, and then take the initiative in the right ways to make good things happen, we become practitioners of the art of positive action, the second main component within the art of adaptation, and an important part of modern life alchemy, the making of existential lemonade. What finishes the story is then the art of achievement, to which we'll soon turn.

But first, we need to make a small and fascinating detour that will prepare us well, deepening what we've just seen and providing a more robust perspective on what's yet to come. We need a quick look at a related and vitally important concern that ties in to what we've discovered so far, and connects up with it in some surprising ways that will be of great relevance to our primary task. So, we'll now take a brief interlude to think together for a few minutes about our general human quest for happiness, which is altogether proper, since the life lemonade we desire, at its best, is a very happy drink. And this additional exploration into a state intimately intertwined with great lemonade making will give us vital new insight for attaining positive outcomes in our lives as we deal with the ongoing challenge of change and adversity in the world.

4

A Dash of Flavor

Stirring in Some Happiness

A SHORT DOCUMENTARY FILM BY THE SOCRATIC GADFLY Michael Moore explores why Finland's schools have been rated as the best in the world, despite the facts that their school days are only three to four hours long, there's practically no homework, and nobody takes standardized tests to monitor academic progress. A math teacher explained to Moore that it's all about happiness. He said that his job is to help his students find their happiness. It turns out that this immensely positive state of being has a deep double connection to the alchemy we all need to experience as we face any form of challenge.

In the last chapter, we noted how common the emotions of anger and anxiety are as reactions to the lemons of unexpected change and difficulty, and we saw that as responses they ironically make those natural lemons even more sour and hard to take. We've also seen how some very practical philosophers have recommended the very different responses of acceptance and action instead. Anger and anxiety are not usually among our most adaptive responses to the world. Properly targeted acceptance and well directed action are. There is much more to be found in these two positive concepts of acceptance and action than we ever might imagine at first glance. It's my happy task in this chapter to pause for a moment and spell out their important and powerful implications for what Plato's Chief Assistant Lemonade Maker, Aristotle, firmly believed was the fundamental, all-encompassing goal that we inevitably pursue in this life.

Understanding Happiness

MANY YEARS AGO, I WROTE A BOOK CONNECTING UP personal happiness with the quest for excellence and even greatness in our work. I've continued to ponder the topic ever since, and I've discovered something interesting. We often think of happiness as being somehow ethereal and elusive, hard to define, and nearly impossible to attain, except perhaps in quick fleeting snatches. We assume that grasping it is like trying to grab and hold a handful of smoke. Many people seem to think of it as an almost mystical state, as evanescent as it is rare. And yet, I've come to believe there's something like a simple formula for true happiness that gives us a recipe for stirring a good measure of this peak positivity into our lives in an ongoing manner. The formula is also related deeply to the art of change in some surprising and fundamentally important ways.

Happiness and positive adaptation are twins, in at least a fraternal sense. Happy people tend to adapt better to change. And those of us who deal well with change tend to be happier. Because of a primal connection between happiness and the responses of acceptance and action needed for embracing change, it will benefit us to explore the basic elements of happiness and then fold them back into our main considerations.

There's a secret ingredient in my favorite lemonade recipe. I'll reveal it later on. But first we have to look at what just might be the most hidden secret ingredients for the best life lemonade that any of us can make in response to challenge or change. They are the individual parts of a universal formula for happiness that are tied in with both the art of self-control and the art of positive action. They demonstrate how powerful some choices are that we have at all times available to us, because they're accessible within us. They don't depend on external events. And that's crucial to understand.

When we're unable to find tranquility within ourselves,
it is useless to seek it elsewhere.
La Rochefoucald

For a very long time, false and misleading beliefs about happiness have abounded throughout our culture. And they need correction. This immensely positive state of being isn't just a form of pleasure, or a feeling of being pleased. It's very different from anything like giddy delight. And it isn't merely a sensation of personal peace. In fact, it's best understood in its fundamental nature as not even a feeling or sensation at all, whether any sort of glee, or a warm sense of contentment, or a calm tranquility of emotional balance. It's much more than any of this, and when we grasp what it crucially involves, we can come to understand how to attain it more reliably in our lives.

Some Important Distinctions

THERE ARE SEVERAL DIFFERENT WORDS IN THE ENGLISH language that we often use almost interchangeably for an overall positive frame of mind, or spiritual condition, or state of being. We have such terms available as for example: happiness, contentment, fulfillment, and satisfaction. But it can be very useful and even crucially insightful to draw some careful distinctions among these words and the concepts they convey. Once they're individually clarified, we can come to see how their interrelation is almost magical. By marking a few differences here, we can provide for ourselves the basic components necessary for understanding the full contours of peak personal wellbeing.

Contentment

Let's begin with the concept of contentment. The quickest definition we can give is that contentment is an emotional acceptance of the present. It's a peaceful inner acknowledgment of your complete situation in the present, understood in such a way that this encompasses whatever is currently true about you and everything now affecting you, including your present memories of the past, along with any current implications of past events for the present and future. Contentment in this fundamental sense is emotionally allowing things to be exactly what they now are. But I should quickly add that this is completely compatible with wanting the future, even the immediate future, to be very different. We can even wish our past had been different, but in order to attain a current state of true contentment, we must also emotionally release all the weight and grip of that wish and accept the reality of what already has been. A content person indwells the present moment without experiencing the bondage of emotional negativity about what was, is, or likely will be. In order to understand accurately what such a form of acceptance involves, it's important to grasp first what it doesn't mean.

Contentment doesn't require thinking that everything is fine as it is, and that it would be equally fine for everything to stay as it is. Contentment is not complaisance, acquiescence, a defeated giving-up, or any form of "settling" for less than the best, or even less than what is good, due to a relinquishing of hope or a dull lack of ambition. Nor is it apathy or indifference. And it's not denial. It's none of these unfortunate states of belief, emotion, or attitude at all. It's quite different. It's a healthy baseline response to reality. Contentment is a form of psychological resilience and inner peace. It involves a complete absence of unproductive anger, resentment, bitterness, frustration, irritation, envy, regret, and any other hotly negative emotional reaction to your life as it is or has been, despite the occurrence of anything that might properly be judged unpleasant, undesirable, wrong, or in any other way problematic. Contentment is coming to terms with your life as it is and was, and emotionally letting go of how it could have been different up until now, and perhaps in some way better instead.

> He that would be superior to external influences must first become superior to his own passions.
> Samuel Johnson

We've all known people whose inclination to stew in anger and resentment has blocked them from seeing or pursuing what they needed to do in order to move forward positively in their organizations, their careers, or their lives. Consider a man who gets passed over for a promotion he's hoped for and even planned on, in favor of a rival candidate he views as far less deserving. First, he may emotionally collapse, and then inwardly explode. He might go on to spend much of his mental and emotional energy in the days and weeks that follow just rehashing his grievances about this grave injustice. A seething resentment can begin to poison his work and his relationships at work. As a result, he's doing nothing to cultivate the next opportunity that might come his way, but rather is digging himself into a deeper hole that puts him farther from his true goals. His inner failure to accept the realities of what has happened and move on in a positive way, working toward his next possible opportunity for advancement, signals a self-defeating pattern of emotional behavior that, if it was ever noticed before in his actions, could even be one of the reasons he was passed over in the first place. Plus, as a result of his attitudes and emotions, this person is almost sure to be unhappy in his personal life as well as at work, unless he alchemically turns it all around by coming to embrace the always available existential acceptance of his circumstances that alone can do the job.

A person who is basically content isn't balled up in negative feelings and inwardly unbalanced by unhealthy responses to reality. Contentment involves a tendency toward tranquility inside us that allows us to get into harmony with anything helpful there might be outside us, however clear or hidden. A person experiencing a powerful measure of contentment isn't distracted, blocked, or held back by bad feelings. He is in a state of positive flow. And this is of crucial significance.

> For after all, the best thing one can do when
> it is raining is let it rain.
> Henry Wadsworth Longfellow

Contentment is a form of self-empowerment. The emotional acceptance of the present and past that we're talking about is thoroughly compatible with wanting and working for change, even radical change, in our circumstances. The inwardly content person is able to do her part to usher in a better future precisely because she isn't tied down with negative feelings clouding her mind and holding her back. We all know individuals who are imprisoned in negativity to the extent that they aren't really free to venture forth and take action as they need to. Most of us have experienced this at some time ourselves. The inwardly content person is liberated from all such constraints and poised to act in whatever way is best. The more fundamentally content you are, and the more inner peace you have as a result, the better positioned you will be to practice everyday alchemy in a powerful way.

A fundamentally content individual is able to cleanse herself of all disruptive feelings like hostility, jealousy, resentment, bitterness, remorse, and regret. But she is also free of an additional affliction of the soul that blocks many accomplished and otherwise positive people from experiencing the happiness they deserve. She is blissfully liberated from what we can call a desperate craving for more—more money, power, status, respect, appreciation, recognition, pleasure, possessions, or even fun—a need that by its own nature can never be filled. The insistent call of more is endless. And it can be insidious. It's the eternal source of discontent. Enlightened, intelligent contentment, by contrast, is intimately connected with the powerful concept of enough.

The secret of life is never to have an emotion that is unbecoming.
Oscar Wilde

The content person, in his or her own heart and mind, has in a spiritual sense enough right now: enough resources, enough comfort, enough love, and enough social standing. Such a person doesn't feel a strong, insistent, demanding need for more. I've heard musicians and top athletes talk about how a craving for the approval of the crowd or the admiration of another professional can actually block their best performances, distracting them from the pure essence of what they should be focused on and deflecting them from the flow experience that alone seems to allow for their highest form of excellence. In the rare, precious times of inner contentment and flow, "in the zone," they are able to perform flawlessly. It's as if the world had actually slowed down around them to give them all the time they might need for what they were truly capable of doing. Contentment can seem to alter time. It does change our experience of its passage.

Some of the lessons in eastern philosophy about the importance of detaching ourselves from cravings may have been inspired by precisely this phenomenon. He who has no craving enjoys an enhanced and powerful state of self-control precisely because he is content. It is one of life's many wonderful paradoxes that the person who has enough right now is oddly best positioned to attain more. He is not afflicted by the distracting emotions that hold others back. Likewise, the individual with this measure of inner contentment is free of the stress produced by cravings and is able to act naturally and with a purity of power that's otherwise impossible to experience.

> All fortune belongs to him who has a contented mind.
> The Panchatantra

The content person is not so dramatically affected over and over in his inward spirit by the inevitable life changes of gain and loss. He's not stung deeply by greed or slight or failure. He is closer to the hub of the wheel in life and so doesn't spin around emotionally, up and down on the outer rim, even as it continues to turn. He's calm and steady in a turbulent, unsteady world.

Some reasonable concerns could arise about this state of contentment I'm describing. After all, aren't there many things that we just should not be content with, realities so bad that nothing other than a radical discontent is an appropriate reaction to them? Think for example of egregious injustice, or the endangerment of small children. Surely, such things should not give rise to or be met with a response of contentment.

I'm not suggesting for a second that the person experiencing an overall state of inner contentment is thereby seeing bad things in the world as good and acceptable, or even as neutral and unobjectionable. He can certainly recognize an evil or a challenge for what it is and take immediate action to solve the problem. He can know poisonous fruit for what it is and seek to protect others from it. But he also spots lemons for what they are. And he understands with the philosophers who can envision an oak in an acorn that part of what a lemon is involves the possibility of lemonade. The inwardly content person need not be a value-free, judgment-averse impassive observer of all that happens, merely noting it and moving on. Contentment doesn't require inattention, distortion, falsification, or inert apathy. To see this, we need to understand a bit more what it does involve.

Inner contentment first of all should not be thought of as an idealized, perfectly achieved psychological state. Like most things in life, it comes in degrees. It exists across a spectrum, from the very little to the truly great. Perhaps some people are in fact what we could call perfectly content. But my guess would be, not many. And yet, there's hope for all of us. Here's a crucial place where the vital concept of enough has another useful application. If you're content enough in your daily experience, if you have enough acceptance in your soul, then you are free of many negatives and are in possession of many positives. You can be said to be content.

And despite any appearances to the contrary, contentment ought not to be viewed as a purely passive state. It's more like a dynamic form of inner resilience than anything like emotional anesthesia. The content person doesn't fail to feel. She will just accept what might make others wallow in negative emotion and move on, taking whatever action she needs to take without being driven by unhealthy inner responses or needs.

> Contentment is the greatest treasure.
> Lao Tsu

A basically content person, an individual experiencing fundamental contentment in his or her life, is not by that fact someone who will be unmoved by tragedy, injustice, unfortunate events, or instances of harm. Truly bad things will most often evoke real emotional reactions, some very strong, and rightly so. The person with the inner habit and overall baseline attitude of contentment will just recover an emotional equilibrium more quickly, acknowledging clearly and without undue agitation what he confronts, and then will be able to take more effective action, rather than merely wallowing in negative reactions, nursing bad feelings, escalating his distress, and fixating on endless worries about whatever has come to light. Contentment is a powerfully positive emotional habit, or inner disposition, involving a strong tendency to let go, accept, rebound, and return to a natural state of inner calm, an equilibrium that allows for powerfully positive action.

The dynamic flow of contentment is a bit like a practice of mental and emotional judo. It's a form of yielding for the purpose of prevailing. The content person deflects the negative energy of unfortunate circumstances, harsh events, or difficult people and is then able to move forward unhindered. A truly content individual does not fight unnecessary battles but saves his energy for what's best. Contentment is a state of mind that's good in itself. It's what philosophers refer to as "intrinsically good." And it's a potent resource for making great things happen. It's also extrinsically, or instrumentally good, as it frees us up for working well toward attaining our proper achievements in life. It is an immunization against those storms of the soul that unhinge and derail too many lives from becoming what they otherwise could have been.

Fulfillment
Now let's consider another concept: fulfillment. This is something very different from contentment. I'd like to give it a particular definition. It's the progressive realization of our potential. It involves becoming who we most fully can be, through actualizing our unique potential, day-to-day. It requires learning, growth, and development. So anyone who is fulfilled by his work and in his life is a person experiencing the progressive realization of his potential in the context of that work, as well as in his other activities and relationships. Fulfillment is dynamic and ongoing. It's what progressively results from a process that matches our talents and interests to people and projects through which we can grow as individuals and make our best distinctive difference in the world.

In illustration of this important concept, I'd like to quote here my favorite poem by the insightful Samuel Menashe, in its entirety, on the topic of fulfillment:

A pot poured out
Fulfills its spout

Fulfillment is a functional and purposive concept and so, at least by analogy, it can be applied poetically to made objects like pot spouts as well as to human beings. In its best and most insightful application to our lives, the concept has an interesting inner complexity beyond anything it might connote in the case of household objects. We can appreciate this by contrasting fulfillment and contentment.

Contentment is a purely subjective psychological state. It's in the mind alone. Fulfillment is an objective process with a subjective side. Let me elaborate briefly to make this point as clear as possible. Contentment is entirely a subjective matter of inner attitude, thought, and feeling. It takes place metaphorically in our heads, and even more so in our hearts. Fulfillment is largely objective, involving as it does a real process of growing into the fullness of who we are and the best of what we can be, while carving out our niche in the world and making our proper mark in life. This takes place in an environment much larger than merely the realm of our conscious experience. It plays out progressively, as an ongoing thing, bit-by-bit in a daily drama of growth as we engage with the world. But fulfillment also has a subjective side, as an inner experience of it naturally accompanies the objective reality of its ongoing progressive attainment.

Happiness lies in the fulfillment of the spirit through the body.
Cyril Connolly

What it takes for personal fulfillment will be a bit different for each individual. There are no two completely identical people in the world. The closest of twins aren't existential duplicates. Even perfect genetic clones would be differentiated by what comes from their distinctive experiences, perspectives, and relationships. As an utterly unique individual, each of us has a chance to bring to the world and into the sweep of human history what no one else can. And we have a corresponding capacity to fill our own hearts, as a result of this process, in a uniquely individual way. This is what I think the classic American philosopher Ralph Waldo Emerson had in mind in his essay, "History," when he wrote of, "The unattained but attainable self." There is a distinctive dynamic journey for each of us, and the attainment is in the traveling itself as it goes on.

> Man is not the sum of what he has already, but rather
> of what he does not yet have, of what he could have.
> Jean Paul Sartre

There is a metaphysical and psychological distinctiveness in each of us already, but more is to come as we continue to develop and progress through our adventures in the world. As long as we're alive and conscious and learning, there is personal growth yet to be experienced, and much good remaining to be done.

It's worth pointing out that there is an interesting natural tension, but no contradiction at all, between contentment and fulfillment, or between the mindset of broadly "accepting the present" along with its current traces of the past, and the process of "progressive realization," or "progressive attainment." While emotionally accepting the past and present, we are always nonetheless essentially moving beyond them. We live in the present, necessarily, but it's a moving present, constantly sliding forward into what had been the future. We accept what is as we leave it behind. And we are content with the leaving. Accepting doesn't mean remaining. And so, acceptance is an ever-flowing stream. No moment is repeated in the ongoing passage of time, and our inner contentment throughout time is a continuing, fluid response of realization, release, and resilience.

This tension points to a deep fact about the true self that we discover as we embrace the shifting present with full awareness: the self is not inert. It's essentially becoming. Each true self is dynamic and aspirational, always moving toward its potential, or needing to become more than it already is, so that absolute presence, and an acceptance of what's already true, are not only compatible with, but actually reveal and require, an ongoing process of dynamic progress and change. Finding our true center, and accepting who we really are, means living this continual adventure into the unknown.

Satisfaction: A Quick Summary

Let's remind ourselves where we're going with these thoughts. We're making progress toward a simple formula for happiness. And at this point, we can benefit from the addition of a basic constructive definition. A useful clarification will help us along toward the next step. Consider the notion of satisfaction. I find it helpful to define personal life satisfaction, for our purposes here, as the coming together of contentment and fulfillment. Contentment plus fulfillment equals deep satisfaction.

Are you a satisfied person? Are you living a satisfying life? Are you satisfied in your work? Your answers to these questions will come from two other component questions. Do you normally enjoy some sense of overall contentment, regardless of what the day might hold, through an inner ability to accept the present for what it is? Do you experience a good measure of fulfillment in your approach to work and in your personal life? Is your adventure right now right for you? The ancient poet Ovid once said that, "Every man should remain within his own sphere." Taken one way, this statement could be limiting oppressive advice with regard to economic class or social status. But grasped differently, it simply urges us to grow within the proper bounds of our own powers and possibilities, rather than seeking to emulate others who may have talents and callings different from our own nature and journey.

Is how-you-live a nice fit for who-you-are? Then, there is a further question: Are you using your talents and powers in the right ways for the good of others as well as yourself? The self grows as it gives help. This is a requirement for objective personal fulfillment. In case you can't answer each of these questions in a positive way, you have work to do. But it's the work that's right for you. So, get to it. If on the contrary you do have positive answers to these questions, if you have a measure of both contentment and fulfillment in your life through proper work and service, then I take you to be satisfied, and as such, you're positioning yourself well for the full state of overall happiness.

> Happiness includes chiefly the idea of satisfaction
> after full honest effort.
> Arnold Bennett

In my view, beyond satisfaction, so understood, just one more thing is needed. What it is, I'll spell out in a second. First, there is a further distinction and a perhaps surprising point of connection with what we've explored earlier that needs to be clarified. The crucial distinction is this. Some people say they view satisfaction as a negative thing, asking, "Why should I be satisfied with my current success, or with the numbers my business is achieving now, or with myself as a husband or father or wife or mother, or with my current state of personal growth, or even with my golf game? Shouldn't I avoid satisfaction at all costs? Isn't it, in fact, a healthy dissatisfaction that wakes us up and pushes us on to greater things?"

This reaction simply confounds two distinct senses of the word 'satisfaction'. We need to remember what its component of contentment is and is not. In our current context, we're employing the concept of satisfaction in a precise sense that involves the coming together of contentment and fulfillment, or inner peace and outer progress. The objection just raised is using the term rather to express a form of complacency, or "settling," a version of unambitious or lazy giving-up, a dull acquiescence that refuses to be stirred to extra exertion and excellence. Deep satisfaction, in our sense, isn't about that at all, precisely because its component of contentment doesn't imply not wanting better. It only means that we're not frustrated and bitter about what is. And this is an important distinction to grasp, or else what we're building with these ideas will not be understood.

So that's the difference. Now, we can reveal a perhaps surprising point of connection with the art of adaptation. Recall from the end of the previous chapter on the art of positive action the two personal reactions of acceptance and action that were recommended to us by philosophers as always the best responses to unexpected change. These responses link up with the two profound human experiences of contentment and fulfillment. Contentment is a state of tranquil acceptance, and fulfillment is an ongoing process of action—of precisely the right sort for each of us, given the situation we're in. The exciting news then is this: the two possible responses to any difficult change that are the healthiest for us to have are also two major ingredients in the attainment of personal happiness. The best responses to change or challenge will contribute to our happiness. Now, this conclusion alone stated so simply might seem utterly obvious. But the backing insights we now have in order to fill it out are both subtle and important.

> Sometimes, the first duty of intelligent men
> is the restatement of the obvious.
> George Orwell

Acceptance and action: We might initially think of these two possible responses to challenging change in an "either/or" way, but we're now in a position to see that, at the deepest level, they actually need to serve in a "both/and" capacity. A change that can be acted on should also be emotionally accepted, in the moment, as being what it is. The practical alchemist starts with what he or she has. A lemonade maker accepts the lemons. And even a change that's completely outside our control to affect directly, and that should elicit in us the response of acceptance, should perhaps also launch, in addition to that inner equanimity, whatever actions— inner or outer—will enhance our emotional release and lead us away from any later negative behaviors of resenting and blaming that are otherwise common and that hold so many people back. It's well known, for example, that one of the best remedies for emotional pain and heartache is volunteer action in the service of others. Feeling is improved by doing, when the doing is of the right sort.

Regardless of our degree of control or influence over external circumstances, and even in situations where we seem to have no control at all, there are always actions we can take to transform ourselves, actions that can contribute to both fulfillment and contentment. Understanding the connection of acceptance with contentment, action with fulfillment, and each with the other, is a remarkable and important point of contact between our approach to change and our desired experience of happiness.

> It is neither wealth nor splendor, but tranquility
> and occupation, which give happiness.
> Thomas Jefferson

A proper response to challenge and change is tied in with what Aristotle believed is the highest state of existence we all pursue, whether we're aware of it or not, the overall condition of flourishing and wellbeing we refer to most appropriately and broadly as happiness. And this connection is crucial to see. How we deal with any difficulty is vital for our overall wellbeing. With this fact in mind, we can now go on to specify the last remaining ingredient for attaining personal happiness in our work and our lives.

Enjoyment

One more concept is needed for our happiness formula. And it requires another quick definition. Enjoyment is a kind of experience that I like to define as involving potentially both pleasure and love. To enjoy something is to take pleasure in it, or even to love it. It's to experience in some way a spark of joy. It's an important and sometimes overlooked aspect of optimal living in the world.

A fundamental part of the happy life involves taking pleasure in your work, your relationships, your surroundings, and in the best of your own inner life. Do you allow yourself to relish a new idea or a beautiful day, a good meal, or some fresh air, the sunshine on your face, a little flower illuminated by light, the song of a nearby bird, a pleasing aroma, and the many other potentially delightful sensations you might experience on a mid-day walk? Do you take a moment now and then to just soak in the greatness of the small wonders around you? I hope so. We should seek to take in and enjoy all these forms of pleasure and many others as frequently as we can, given our commitments and projects. Anyone who is missing all this is wasting a fundamental aspect of what life is to be. Our days can be a challenge. But we're built with a capacity for enjoying all those aspects of our world that can be enjoyed, and this is a capacity whose regular employment is essential to our best and highest states of being. Without it, a life is hardly more than mere existence.

> For to miss the joy is to miss all.
> Robert Louis Stevenson

There are so many ways in which we can give ourselves small moments of delight each day. You might want to keep a beautiful fountain pen on your desk with a bottle of ink in a color you like. Give yourself the small gift of writing a note to someone by hand on nice stationary. Allow yourself to feel the flow of the ink onto the paper. Be fully present and soak in the moment. Or pay special attention to how much you delight in talking with a close friend while the chat is taking place. Grow some flowers or buy some you like and arrange them in a nice vase where you can see them. Marvel at life's wonders, big and small. Laugh at its absurdities and smile at even its briefest gifts. The smallest things, noticed and loved for what they are, can bring rays of joy into our lives. This is important for anyone who wants to practice the alchemy of everyday life.

Some people will think this is silly. But it's not. There are uncountable pleasures to be had in life, if we'll just open up, seek them out, and pay attention with an open and appreciative heart. Art, music, dance, sport, meditation—even petting a dog, watching a cat, playing with a child, savoring a cool drink of water, relishing a moment's rest and stillness on a busy day—all these things and many more can be sources of authentic enjoyment, readily available in the normal course of daily events. We should never allow ourselves to miss out on the small pleasures life has to offer. The whole point of making lemonade is to taste and enjoy. And the master lemonade maker will savor not only the ultimate product, but also many of the elements and phases in the process itself.

It has long been an axiom of mine that
the little things are infinitely the most important.
Arthur Conan Doyle

I recently met a man named Abraham who had moved to America from Ethiopia when he was nineteen years old. Now about thirty years later, he is a master at enjoying the little things in life. He works for a car service in Austin, Texas as a driver, and took me around his city for two days while I was there to speak. In the course of our friendly conversations, I came to realize that he's a genius-level lemonade maker. He finds a way to enjoy almost anything that comes his way.

The greeting, "How are you this morning, Abraham?" would always be answered with something like, "Wonderful, as always! It's a great day!" He told me that one of his friends this past December hadn't seen him for a while and ventured to ask him how his Thanksgiving Day was. He had said in reply, "Which one?"

The friend looked puzzled. He asked, "What do you mean?"

Abraham then explained his own question by saying with a hearty voice and big smile, "Every day is a day of Thanksgiving for me!" I had to laugh and congratulate him.

One of my favorite college professors, an older man, once told the class that when he woke up every morning, he took a few moments to pay conscious attention to all the parts of his body that weren't in any form of pain, and that in this way he was able to begin the day with great pleasure in the glorious absence of aches. I never understood fully what he was talking about until after I turned sixty. Now, at my currently still youthful age at the lofty peak of my late sixties, I too feel grateful to start a day with this increasingly rare delight. Today in fact is such a time, and I relish it avidly. I would also urge you to take a moment now and then to enjoy any glorious absence of aches that you may have, whatever your age and stage in life might be.

Enjoyment, as I see it, can go far beyond the simple experience of sensory pleasure, however extended or intense or deepened by our conscious awareness it might be. Much deeper than the best of pleasure is the genuine experience of love. It's an active and spiritual form of enjoyment that involves an element of commitment as well as of full appreciation. It can even go deep to the heart of things in its embracing and valuing.

Never cut yourself off from the distinctive power of love. Pleasure is great. Love is greater. It's deeper, higher, richer, and fuller. It's about giving as well as getting. And it involves cherishing in addition to liking and enjoying. But then, of course, when we try to describe this sort of phenomenon, the reality of genuine love, we find that, as in the case with many of life's greatest experiences and highest attainments, words in their normal and direct use begin to fail us. We have to become poetically creative to understand or express it. And that's fine, because we also have to be creative to experience well.

There are things all around us that need to be valued and even treasured, wonders that should elicit a sense of profound gratitude as well as our deepest appreciation. Notice and honor them. Find a way to love your work, or perhaps create a new way to embrace it. Find a way to love your day, one morning, one afternoon, and one evening at a time. In the process, you'll discover new ways to embrace your life both as it is and as it aspires to be. A day without any of these forms of love is a day without genuine happiness, because it's a day devoid of the deepest form of enjoyment we can have.

> A loving heart is the truest wisdom.
> Charles Dickens

We often use a casual, abbreviated or attenuated concept of love, in the sense of a lively and even intense though superficial enjoyment, to denote a passive sentiment. I love good champagne. She loves music. He loves golf. But this derivative concept of love is in the end merely a notion of focused or enthusiastic pleasure. And pleasure is at its core a passive state, however active you might be in its pursuit and enablement. But the fullness of love is different in part because it's a distinctive blend of the active and the passive. Love always involves a commitment—a valuing, respecting, caring, honoring, cherishing, protecting preserving, and treasuring, along with a desire to benefit. And this entails attitudes that inherently involve an aim to serve and give.

Because love is the ultimate giving, it's also the ultimate gaining. The genuine mysteries of love are deeply involved in some of the equally authentic mysteries of happiness. But the undeniable secrets of each do not in the least detract from our ability to grasp the fundamental essence of both. And the true availability of love as an active and wonderful possibility for every one of us indicates that a full measure of happiness is within our potential as well. The path calls to us. And it's one we should walk.

> To love nothing is not to live; to love but feebly
> is to languish rather than live.
> François Fénelon

It's hard to find a genuinely great businessperson who doesn't in some important sense love what he or she does. There's passion. There's creative commitment. And this isn't just icing on the cake. It's a crucial ingredient of the cake. Or even better, I like to think of it as the most important element directing the alchemy of transformation, as for example, from such things as the basic ingredients of a pastry chef's confection to the very different and delightful finished product she gives us. It's nearly magical how flour, sugar, and eggs can undergo such a radical metamorphosis as to become a delicious cake. Genuine love can transform many things in analogous ways. And so, it's long been said that love makes the world go-round. It is the most magical and powerful element in every great pitcher of lemonade. And when it's there, you can almost taste its presence.

Love matters. And what's particularly crucial for us to understand is that this is just as true of things in the world of work, like sales, advertising, marketing, operations, management, manufacturing, tech support, creative coding, and customer service, as it is of anything in our personal lives. Love isn't just a committed embrace and enjoyment of what is; it's also the foundation for hope in what can be. It's contributory, as the deepest wellspring of the creative impulse and a crucial part of the happy and meaningful life.

The least of things with a meaning is worth more
than the greatest of things without it.
Carl G. Jung

Finally, the most complete form of love both sees and confers meaning. This is important, because no one can live a truly happy life in the deepest possible sense unless it's also experienced as in some way a meaningful life. We are beings who seek and give meaning. The person whose work seems like a bleak daily enactment of the Myth of Sisyphus—rolling a stone up a hill only to see it roll back down, and then starting again, with an endlessly repetitive, meaningless rhythm in service to an apparently pointless and never-ending task—clearly may not experience happiness in the job. That's why meaningful occupation is so important. We need to be able to see meaning in our work, and to give more meaning to that work. This allows for our daily exertions to be labors of love. And when love is brought to any task, the job is elevated to a new and exalted level.

Life's lemonade is best made with pleasure and love. The commitments and enjoyments of authentic love are crucial for both gaining and making meaning within the confines of our existence. Love is finally, in the broadest sense, a spiritual endeavor necessary for living a happy life. And it's a proper culmination of all the elements that are ingredient in our experience of happiness.

The Universal Formula

Now we're ready for the great unveiling of our simple overall formula for happiness. Happiness is just satisfaction and enjoyment coming together, in the precise sense in which I've defined each of them. That's the universal recipe. That's the formula. Let me lay it all out again, simply, and without further comment.

Contentment = An acceptance of the present
Fulfillment = A progressive realization of your potential
Satisfaction = Contentment + Fulfillment
Enjoyment = Pleasure + Love
Happiness = Satisfaction + Enjoyment

When we map out the elements and contours of happiness in this way, we can see how this peak human state isn't just a matter of genetics or chemistry, as some seem to fear. As important as these basic matters might be for allowing and facilitating the felt reality of a happy life, it's personal responses like acceptance and action and an enjoyment of the process along the way that create the sometimes elusive goal we all seek. The functions of the brain can admittedly enhance or inhibit our chances of attaining and experiencing this state. And many neural and genetic matters are things over which we have little or no control, at least in the period of time when I write these words. But happiness, as a condition of overall maximal wellbeing, consists, as we can see, in some important things over which we do have a good degree of power and control.

All the art of living lies in a fine mingling
of letting go and holding on.
Havelock Ellis

There is a measure of art or skilled behavior that it takes on our part to attain and experience each of the basic components of happiness. There is an art of contentment that requires a discipline of thought, emotion, and attitude facilitated by certain kinds of mental exercise as well as by various forms of physical practice, including such things as meditation, exercise, and the use of relaxation techniques. There is an art of fulfillment that's just the knack of finding ways to discover our talents, develop those talents, and deploy them into the world for the good of others as well as our selves—a process I like to call 3-D Living. And there is what we can refer to as an art of enjoyment that's simply the cultivated skill of being in the moment, paying attention to the good things around us, consciously embracing them, and savoring them all.

Taken together, these individual arts of life give us something like an art of happiness that, while not literally one of the component arts within the overall art of change that we're exploring, nonetheless connects and interacts with these arts in many ways. A few more words should make this important relationship clear. We're to be artists of happiness just as we're to be artists and alchemists of change. It should be no surprise that the best things of all come from transformative art.

A Quick Recap

OUR LOOK AT THE ART OF HAPPINESS IS IN ONE SENSE AN interlude in our quest for understanding how best to deal with difficult change, or any hardship we face, and make lemonade from all the various lemons life can give us. But it's an interlude only in the sense that this vital art of living well, as I understand it, isn't literally one of the three component arts within the art of adaptation, and so within an overarching art of change. And yet, as we've seen, it's importantly connected with the art of change in a variety of ways, and enough so as to make our small detour a very relevant one, as well as deeply entwined with what's yet to come. There is much more unity in the world than the casual glance will reveal. Things are connected in fascinating and powerful ways that our best explorations can discover and reveal. The more we understand the connections, the better we can use them well.

Masterful adaptation in life arises out of a sustained application of three core component arts. We've focused in on two of them so far. We've seen that the first art, the art of self-control, has three requirements: Don't rush to judgment; value the right things; and use your imagination well. Interestingly, an attainment of inner contentment depends on all three of these things. So, achieving contentment in our lives requires living the art of self-control. This is an important connection for us to understand, because it will provide us with motivation to engage in the sometimes-difficult discipline that a proper self-control demands. Our own personal experience of happiness is at stake.

> Our happiness depends on wisdom all the way.
> Sophocles

We've also seen that the second component in the art of adaptation, the art of positive action, has three fundamental requirements: Govern your attitudes; look for opportunities; and take the initiative to act well. What's crucial to understand here is that attaining a state of personal fulfillment in our lives also depends on these three things. So achieving both an ongoing objective state of fulfillment and the proper accompanying subjective experience of this state in everything that we do will require living the art of positive action. Again, grasping the connection can provide us with a stronger motivation to focus on the sometimes daunting demands of positive action in changing and challenging times. These same things are needed ultimately for happiness.

To show how all this is even more fully linked, I should point out in advance that enjoyment comes to us in life in the highest, most continuous ways only as we practice the third art of change, the art of achievement, which will specify that we need to do several things regularly and well in order to bring our actions to their proper forms of success. What those things are, we'll examine next.

It's worth pondering the fact that the requirements for masterful adaptation as they're captured within the overall art of change are also necessities for personal wellbeing, ongoing flourishing, and the enjoyment of a happy life. And this is something I've never seen anyone explicitly explain. It's important. And it's a discovery that each of us needs to make if we want to embody fully the power to change well. There's a deep sense in which this realization can give us access to the fresh flowing water we need for making great life lemonade. To see how this is so, please read on.

5

POURING THE WATER
The Art of Achievement

MOST OF US WHO AREN'T EXPERTS IN THE KITCHEN HAVE had the experience of following a recipe that's been recommended to us or we've found in a famous cookbook, and yet ending up with a failed experiment. And if you've ever gotten creative with mixing drinks, you can learn quickly that it's as easy to mess up a beverage as a complex main dish. Whenever we cook or mix something new, we obviously hope for success in what we're doing. We need the same thing for our lemonade making in life. Fortunately, for dealing with life's lemons, part of the recipe we have can guide us to that success.

> It is not the going out of port, but the coming in,
> that determines the success of a voyage.
> Henry Ward Beecher

In tumultuous times, if we can deal calmly with the unexpected and take the initiative to act positively, then we've already mastered two thirds of the art that's required for a life of creative adaptation. The third and final aspect of this art of change is the art of achievement. It involves a set of skills for setting and pursuing appropriate goals when things around us are in flux. Dealing well with challenging change requires all three arts: the art of self-control that gives us inner strength, the art of positive action to get us moving well, and finally the art of achievement that will incorporate the full array of techniques we have for turning positive action into satisfying accomplishment.

From before the time of Plato to the present day, the greatest practical philosophers have left us some penetrating wisdom about life success. Most of their thoughts can be summarized in the form of seven universal conditions for attaining satisfying success in the challenges and opportunities we face. I like to call these simple but powerful conditions, "The 7 Cs of Success." I'll present them briefly here, with the distinctive focus we need in order to understand their involvement in our proper relation to change. These seven conditions of success are the basic requirements for the art of achievement. They're all important for making the best lemonade out of life's lemons.

The 7 Cs of Success

In any situation of change, challenge, or new opportunity, in order to move forward productively and raise the probability that we can attain the proper personal or professional success we want, we need to have and use these seven things:

C1: A clear CONCEPTION of what we want, a vivid vision, a goal clearly imagined

C2: A strong CONFIDENCE that we can attain the goal

C3: A focused CONCENTRATION on what it will take to reach the goal

C4: A stubborn CONSISTENCY in pursuing our vision

C5: An emotional COMMITMENT to the importance of what we're doing

C6: A good CHARACTER to guide us and keep us on a proper course

C7: A CAPACITY TO ENJOY the process along the way

Let's look at each of these conditions in order. First, with any challenge, in the face of a disappointment or the midst of a struggle, or even when first presented with an invitation to blaze our way into a mostly formless future, we may need to fight to attain a basic mental clarity in our sense of direction. We have to get active right off in seeking to chart our way forward clearly and with some specificity. We should conceive a clear goal, or a set of goals. We need to begin with this first tool.

C1: A clear CONCEPTION of what we want, a vivid vision, a goal clearly imagined.

As we've noted, in times of change and challenge, many people fail to set their own goals and adopt instead a "wait and see" attitude. They either just observe what's going on, or largely try to ignore what's happening, refusing to commit themselves to any new personal aims, even for the very near future. They go into hiding until the storm of change subsides. But full attentiveness, mental clarity, a sense of direction, and the active process of personal goal setting and pursuit are most important in times of change. Otherwise, we risk being swept away by events over which we have no control and can easily end up finding ourselves somewhere we really don't want to be.

> It's disgraceful when, instead of steering your way forward,
> you find yourself carried along and suddenly,
> in a whirlpool of events, get so confused, you ask:
> "How did I get into this condition?"
> Seneca

The advice of the most practical philosophers is simple: We need to have a habit of setting goals that make sense in any changing circumstances we face. That act itself will give us some feeling of control in carving out an area for our own concerns, values, and interests, regardless of what else is happening. And, of course, we should keep in mind the larger interests of the other people around us, as well. We can't let any change shake us loose from our deepest commitments and most fundamental sense of direction. When we use those commitments and values, as well as our core sense of who we are and what we can do, to steer our own course through challenge or change, we'll more likely end up in a position of strength and deep satisfaction.

The art of achievement requires ongoing goal setting. And the most insightful high performance psychologists in our day insist that this can be done best if we have a personal dream of what we'd like our life and work to be, one that constitutes a vivid imaginative vision that's rooted in our highest ideals and deepest values. The greatest performers in any arena of life tend to be the positive dreamers who make sure their ideals percolate creatively into clear goals, and then pursue those goals with a wholehearted conviction and energy. Even if you don't have right now a big vision for your life in the future, a smaller vision for the next stretch of your path will do. What would you like to see happen as the result of your actions and energies? How can you imagine it? The path of successful achievement starts best with a clear conception of what we'd most like to see happen as a result of our efforts within the circumstances we face. This is equally important whether we're just initially launching our careers in the world or we're already far along in the journey. At every stage, we need this dynamic process in our lives.

> You are never too old to set another
> goal or to dream a new dream.
> C. S. Lewis

We need to set clear goals. There's a simple insight I've been sharing with other people for years: Vague thoughts can't motivate specific behavior. And, to anticipate any wag of a critic who might venture to suggest that there is no such thing as nonspecific behavior, I would of course agree. Vague thoughts can mess with our emotions to no end, but they tend to leave our actions alone. To improve our circumstances and reach any challenging goal requires a pattern of well-focused behavior, specific for the precise task. Positive actions won't be suggested or chosen at all without a clear aim to spark their identification. I recently saw a funny PowerPoint slide that featured the word 'Ambiguity' emblazoned across a classic lighted Las Vegas sign of the sort used by casino hotels, and under it was a play on the famous local slogan with the words, "What Happens in Vagueness, Stays in Vagueness."

Of course, there's an important cautionary note for all our goal setting. When I was fifty-six years old, the Great Recession began to envelop our economy. My professional business dropped by more than seventy-five percent. Since the day I had left university life to serve as a public philosopher, my income had been derived entirely from speaking to business groups and writing books of philosophical guidance about work and life. But in the recession, companies mostly canceled their big meetings or stopped bringing in outside speakers. And many prominent publishers seemed afraid of new projects that didn't guarantee huge audiences. Plus, they had noticed that in our time, profundity and profits tend to pull in opposite directions. So, I soon had a lot of time on my hands and decided to use the big juicy lemons that had come my way to make some life lemonade. I began to set new goals. First, I spent extra time exploring the wisdom of the ages and writing up my results for the coming time when the economy would soon right itself. And that yielded more than I ever could have imagined. But then, I thought I should also exercise more and get in better shape. I set it as a goal to go to the gym at lunchtime for two hours a day, every day for a year. Then, I'd cut back to an hour a day. I also set small goals for various exercises. Then, I met a longtime weightlifter, a man who one day came up to me and said, "You make more noise than anybody else in this gym."

I replied, "You should hear me get up out of bed and walk to the bathroom in the morning." I'd become a stiff old man prematurely, in my late fifties.

The guy announced, "I want to be your workout partner." I asked why and he explained, "You're the only one in here who's really trying, going at it hard. I want to do it with you." He introduced himself as Don. So Don and I started working out together, and we quickly made more progress than I ever could have imagined.

Let me give you an example. I had never done the exercise known as bench press, where you lie on a padded bench and lift up a bar with equal weights on each side. Our gym had a Smith machine, a setup that kept the bar in a vertical track to bypass the need for balancing it during each lift. And one day, I saw a guy about my age lifting a total of eighty-five pounds on it, so I set it as a goal to do the same weight with ten reps. I figured that any exercise you could do lying down was one for me. The next day, I repeated it, and also the day afterwards, and the following day, until someone told me you shouldn't bench every single day, but let your body recuperate for a few days between sessions. Then Don came along and suggested I aim for a slightly heavier weight. So I added a few pounds to the bar, and then days later, again on his advice, a few more. Weekly, he'd encourage me to set a new goal with more weight. And five years later, in my early sixties, I was able to bench three hundred and fifteen pounds. All my aches and pains had just disappeared along the way. And there was another unanticipated side effect. Shortly after my new personal best on the bench, I hit the floor to see how many pushups I could do in one set. I hadn't done pushups since college, when maybe I could do thirty. At age sixty-three, I managed a hundred and twenty in a row, until my shoulders started to hurt and I figured I should stop. I've been meaning to write the AARP. Your golden years can be different than you may imagine. But that will likely take some clear goals.

The journey of a thousand miles begins with a single step.
Lao Tsu

I think it's important to relate this story about goal setting in matters of fitness and strength because I didn't start by setting the clear goal of eventually lifting three hundred and fifteen pounds. That would never have occurred to me at all. If anyone had suggested such a thing, it would have struck me as laughably impossible and truly absurd. But by setting small new specific goals over time, and by attaining and augmenting them, I got to a level of fitness and strength that I never could have dreamed of reaching. At each stage, though, I had clear new goals that I could struggle to attain. And they propelled me to a level of success I could not in advance have imagined. Small steps count.

An important part of the process was that I had a workout partner, someone to hold me accountable for reaching forward and not sliding back. He gave me constant encouragement and insisted that I be consistent in my efforts. He would not let me get away with lame excuses. One day, when we had gone through an extra hard routine, we were getting ready to leave the gym, and Don said, "I'll see you in here tomorrow."

Remembering the weather forecast and looking for any reason to take a break, I said in a voice of great concern, "Well, it's supposed to rain really hard tomorrow."

He said, "Not in here." Now that's commitment. That's the no-excuses approach to life and goals. Reflecting on the role this one friend has played in my life over many years now, I remembered one day that in British universities, a Don is a tutor or teacher, derived as an honorific shortened form of the medieval 'Dominus' or Lord. And with this in mind, I realized that we all need a Don in our lives. But then, I came to the deeper insight that we all need to be a Don in the lives of others. Encourage those around you. Help them set goals, and be committed to those goals. Amazing things can happen.

After a few years of my new fitness routine, one morning at breakfast, I had the most vivid daydream of my life. I mentally saw an old man and a boy sitting in the sand under a palm tree, talking. I could hear clearly what they were saying. It was a great conversation between an uncle and his nephew in the desert in Egypt, in the summer of 1934. I somehow knew the time and place of what I was seeing and hearing. I dashed upstairs to my study and began to write what I had just seen and was continuing to witness now as an ongoing mental vision in front of the computer. I wrote about ten pages. Then the movie in my head paused. I first sat quietly and tried to figure out what I had just experienced. I had always been a daydreamer, but never with a vision this vivid and extended. I couldn't figure out what was going on at all, but I decided that the next morning, I would sit again in front of the keyboard, make my mind a blank, and see if there was any way this vision would come back to me and continue. And to make a very long story short, the inner movie did play in my head again that day, and on most other days for a period of five years. The experience has resulted, so far, in eight novels of over a million words in a genre that can only be called philosophical fiction.

I became a fiction author for the first time in my sixties. And that had never been my goal, or even a guess as to what might lie in my future. But when the movie started playing, I began to set small new goals at the prompting of a new creative urge I felt, and wonderfully unexpected things continued to happen, beyond anything I could have imagined. I would never have sat down and said, "I think I'll write eight philosophical action-and-adventure novels set in Egypt in 1934 and 1935. I'll shoot for over a million words." It could not have occurred to me. If someone had suggested such a thing, I would just have thought it crazy. And yet, in response to that initial odd vision at the breakfast table, I began to set small goals that took me on what, in many ways, has been the most surprising and engaging intellectual adventure of my life.

Keep some room in your heart for the unimaginable.
Mary Oliver

The first book that resulted, *The Oasis Within,* captures the earliest days of my inner movie as a sort of prologue to the big story, then *The Golden Palace* launches the real adventures of the series, where wisdom meets intrigue in a mode that's been described by one prominent novelist as "Harry Potter meets Indiana Jones in the company of Aristotle." In addition to the prologue, there are now seven numbered volumes in the series. Come to my website to find out more. As things creatively developed, I came up with a clear conception for each step I would take along the way in response to the new inner vision, but I never could have conceived of the entire process, or the eventual end-state as a distinct and proper goal. I tell the story because that's what most goal setting is like. We have just enough light for the part of the path we're on. As a result of things that happen, we set goals we can imagine. But as we go on, we conceive new goals that position us for more. Then, quite often, unimaginable things will result.

In fact, to get my new books out quickly, I set the goal of establishing my own publishing imprint and I found people to help with the editing, design, and creation of the books that now have their own website and already are making a difference around the world, bringing philosophy in new ways to people across a wide range of ages. And now, other topnotch writers are approaching me to publish their books through the imprint and we're launching into the world an innovative publishing venture I could never have imagined. New developments can lead to a process we can't have anticipated. And most modern advice about goal setting seems to miss this insight altogether.

In our approach to the initial conception of a new goal, we need to be in the best sense opportunistic, and properly responsive to our circumstances. We need to strive for both creativity and clarity. And we're often able to draw on our deepest creative impulses only by relaxing, releasing the normal chatter of the conscious mind, attaining a sort of inner emptiness, and then wait to see what may bubble up. This can become a distinctive practice that allows us to set the best goals that are right for us now. We initially may be confounded and confused by new developments in our lives, but if we patiently seek calm clarity amid the confusion, we can most often find it in new ideas that will as a result come to us to spark new and specific goals.

It's always the creative person who's ultimately best adapted to our world of change. And each of us has it in us to be creative, within the circle of our distinctive talents. Masterful adaptation often requires creatively conforming our lives to the world around us, and at other times, it means creatively conforming the world around us to our dreams. Either task is enhanced by knowledge. That's why constant learning should always be a part of our adventures—learning about ourselves and our work, certainly, but also learning more widely about our world and how human nature functions within it. The broader our experience and learning is, the better we're positioned for innovative goal pursuit. The most powerful goals are always rooted firmly in reality and driven by intentions that reach beyond what's already real. A clear conception of a desired attainment that arises from a broad base of knowledge and a responsibly creative vision guided by proper values can lead us powerfully in our work and our lives.

In addition to a clear conception of what we want to see happen next, a goal or group of goals vividly rooted in knowledge and imagination, we need to cultivate an inner attitude of positive expectation. We need a psychological mindset of confidence.

C2: A strong CONFIDENCE that we can attain the goal

Proper confidence breeds achievement. The most successful people in history have tended to be those who believed strongly in themselves and their prospects, at least with regard to the activities of their primary focus. This has given them the power to access more fully and use more completely the total range of their resources. It has also made them and their enterprises more attractive to other people. Confidence is compelling. And it's contagious.

As is our confidence, so is our capacity.
William Hazlitt

People are naturally attracted to anyone with a healthy measure of confidence, as long as it doesn't shade into anything remotely like arrogance or presumptuousness. And yet, oddly enough, some people seem to find even a measure of self-assurance bordering on the arrogant to be attractive, precisely because it bespeaks bold expectation and power. But that's not the norm. And arrogance isn't at all a universal condition for success. Simple confidence is. While the arrogant man may inspire some other people to believe in his prospects, his attitude will in the end alienate more than it inspires. Most people are rightly put off by arrogance, whether in words or deeds.

A top financial executive came up to me after a talk of mine and told me he worried that his employees would mistake his confidence as arrogance. I said, "Whatever you're doing, ask their opinions; sincerely seek their ideas. Arrogant people never do that." Arrogance most often blinds its primary victim to new things he needs to see and consider. The mindset is in most cases self-undermining. We can be both strongly confident and personally humble at the same time, as we believe in our projects and our prospects, while still appreciating how much we have yet to learn, and how much we need the assistance of others in order to do anything of real importance in life. A suitably strong measure of confidence is a powerful connector between people, and it has a positive influence on long-term achievement.

If Plato's teacher Socrates, who was the first truly public philosopher, made one major mistake in his life, and it ended up being fatal, it's that he often came across to bystanders as haughty and arrogant. Ironically, it may have been actually nothing more than what we might call an "aggressive humility" on his part that rubbed many people the wrong way and resulted in this perception. You may know the story. The famous oracle at Delphi had named him the wisest man in Athens. But on hearing of it, he was quick to reply that he knew hardly anything at all about the truly important matters in life. And because of this, he ultimately was convinced that his wisdom oddly must consist in merely realizing the extent of his own ignorance. Plenty of people in Athens seemed to think of themselves as extremely knowledgeable and wise. So he began to approach them with questions. And the inevitable result of his interrogations was to show that the many purported experts and sages didn't actually know a bit of what they thought they knew. Worst of all, they didn't know themselves well at all.

The doggedness with which Socrates pursued the truth through extended discussions with others, along with his lack of diplomacy in the way in which he immediately critiqued and dismissed anything that could not withstand the fiercest analytical scrutiny, are what brought him the reputation and ill regard that, unfortunately, led to his demise. Those who knew him well recognized his deep and intrinsic goodness. But because of what was misunderstood as an attitude of harsh arrogance by others who didn't really know him, he ended up with enemies who saw to it that his career and life were put to an end. The results of even an appearance of arrogance can be that bad.

Avoid Arrogance.
Wei Wu Wei

Confidence need not take the form or even the remote appearance of arrogance or presumptuousness. A confident attitude is most effective when wedded to a generously demonstrated humility of demeanor and action. A strong but humble confidence propels us properly forward and elicits the eager help of others as we pursue our goals. It will position us well to experience success rather than a Socratic demise.

Philosopher William James once examined champions across all sports to see what they might have in common, and developed as the result of his study a concept of "precursive faith," or a faith that runs ahead of the evidence. Every champion is regularly challenged to do something he's never done before—wrestle a new opponent, or break a new world record—and the evidence of his past accomplishments will always fall short of proving he's up to the new test. But, James concluded, every champion runs ahead of the evidence with faith or confidence that he can get the job done. And notice something here. James wasn't examining people with no training or skill who were just generating belief from out of the blue. He was noticing how people with great preparation go even beyond the bounds of their experience, with precursive faith or confidence in their prospects. Nothing builds proper confidence like real competence enhanced by the inwardly competitive mindset that always seeks to go above and beyond.

I should point out that it's naturally hard to generate such confidence in a goal that's not right for you, which is why every exercise in goal setting should be an exercise in self-knowledge. And while it's fine and often healthy to set big goals that push us, we can't expect our confidence to keep pace with absurdly unreasonable aims. In fact, it can be a condition for adopting a goal to ask, "Can I have a strong confidence in my ability to attain this goal?" Likewise, each of the other conditions in The 7 Cs of Success can serve the same function as a test for a possible goal. Can I be clear in this? Can I focus my concentration well on it? Can I pursue it consistently? We need goals we can believe in and pursue well, using each of the universal conditions for success.

Having set a personal goal or array of goals in any challenging situation and bringing to it a strong confidence in our prospects, we also always need, in the pursuit of each target, a particular discipline. Achievement calls for intense concentration.

C3: A focused CONCENTRATION on what it will take to reach the goal

Here's a surprising truth about the world. Many people think they have goals that they don't actually have at all. To set a goal is to embrace a new present and future, and that involves launching out into a new direction of action. An announced or assumed goal is just a fantasy unless it's both clear and specific and is also the starting point for the immediate formulation and implementation of a focused, concrete plan. The plan can change as you learn more, but what's invariant is the need for some sort of initial map to get the process going. Real goals are commitments. Goals get you going. That's their whole purpose. They set you out on a new path. And only a focused concentration of thought and action will launch you anew and keep you going as you adapt and adjust to the things you learn along the way, while moving in the direction of your quest.

If life is handing you lemons and you want to make lemonade, you have to begin to do certain things rather than others. You need to get out the right tools, line up the best ingredients, maybe find the right partners for the task, and then start to combine all these elements in the proper ways. In the kitchen, when cooking or stirring up anything, you might mentally go through a checklist. In life, it's good to do the same thing. We need to concentrate our thoughts and actions on what it will take to get the job done.

> It's amazing how much energy you can have
> once you have a plan.
> Lemony Snicket

In changing times, people often lose their concentration. They fail to plan at all, or they plan badly; or even with the best plan in mind, they get distracted by events whirling around them. If things are in a state of flux, we often have to fight hard for a focused concentration on what it will take to reach our goals. That's why I mention the idea of a checklist. From airline pilots to emergency room physicians and beyond, the simple discipline of a checklist has been found to be strikingly effective for keeping focused in pursuit of a worthy aim, amid even tumultuous distraction. Confidence without an accompanying concentration isn't enough. In fact, any tools that support our focus (C3) will enhance our confidence (C2). All these conditions for achievement are connected. And it's part of a good plan to use each of them well.

Some people despair of planning anything in rapidly changing circumstances. But this is often because they mistakenly tend to think of plans as inherently static—once they're made, they're made—and if the overall situation is dynamically fluid, they wonder how any finished and set plan could possibly help. But this worry is based on a misunderstanding of what the appropriate sort of planning amounts to, at its best.

Goals don't have to be chiseled in stone in order to rock your world. Neither do plans. They don't have to be changeless in order to be helpful. In fact, the opposite is more often the truth. Useful plans typically just get us started as well as possible along the path that initially seems best to us, after as much preliminary research and thought as the available time allows. Then, as we're out in the world enacting our plans, they position us to adjust and adapt as we go. A plan is simply a tool and a way to begin.

> The more human beings proceed by plan,
> the more effectively they may be hit by accident.
> Friedrich Dürrenmatt

If we're indeed moving forward with a focused concentration in what's even generally the right direction, we'll be getting increasingly closer to what we'd eventually like to see happen. If, however, we're initially moving in a wrong direction, but one that was reasonable to pursue given the information we had, then we'll at least be learning what doesn't work and, by contrast, what we might try instead to actually propel us in the right direction for our goals. The very best plans are never perfect, but are simply those that get us into action with the best probability we can expect for ultimate success, based on what we know. They're also sequences of actions that carry the least likelihood of disastrous results if we're wrong. They position us for good and not ill.

One of my Notre Dame students wanted to be a country music singer, and eventually a star. So she made a plan. Step one involved moving to Nashville where she would begin to perform in local clubs and perhaps meet people who could introduce her to record producers and other industry professionals. She came back to visit me in my office years later and explained what had happened. She said, "When I got to Nashville, I was so excited about my dream. And I had a great plan. But I discovered something pretty fast. The best singers in town were much better than I had imagined. And I couldn't get the work I'd been hoping to snag. Everywhere I turned, rejection was waiting for me." Life quickly handed her some big lemons. And at first, it was all bitterly disappointing. Her dream was becoming impossible. But a strange gift was on the way.

> Life is always bringing unexpected gifts.
> May Sarton

My former philosophy student then told me something I hadn't expected. Just by being around the music scene in Nashville, she learned about a job she had never even heard of before—the role of a music business attorney. These were the people who negotiated all legal contracts and in that way took care of the stars, sometimes also managing their whole personal business and overall careers. My student felt the spark of an interest in this and began to look into the possibility a bit more. Soon, she was in law school preparing to work in the industry in a completely different way than anything she ever had imagined.

She enthusiastically told me that, as of our visit, she was now good friends with many of her favorite country stars, working with them, visiting their homes, and enjoying impromptu sing-alongs and other informal music sessions along the way as she took care of their many legal needs. She was completely happy in a job that she never before could have pursued, largely because she knew nothing about it until she followed a plan directed toward another goal and, on that path, hit a detour that eventually allowed her to discover her true bliss in an unexpected place. Her initial goal and its plan got her going and brought her to a surprising new destination. Many of the best plans do.

One more point about all this: The sort of focused concentration, the insight and planning that I'm talking about, isn't easy. In a whirling world of activity, it means taking a moment at first to slow down. At its best, it calls for a measure of inner stillness. It requires mental time and space. It means standing still or sitting down and contemplating before moving forward and acting. And this is never just a one-time preparation for any goal, but must be repeated throughout the process of goal pursuit as things continue to change and we learn as we go. It can't happen at any stage without a serious expenditure of imaginative and analytical thought, and that requires a real commitment. Apart from a focused concentration on what it will take to reach our goals, our time and energy will be deflected and dispersed in a hundred different directions. Focus is power.

Focus then means awareness, discernment, order, clarity,
insight—they are like the attributes of love. The act of focusing
itself has beauty and meaning; it is the act that, continued in,
turns into meditation, into poetry. Indeed, as soon as the least of us
stands still, that is the moment something extraordinary
is seen to be going on in the world.
Eudora Welty

A well-focused concentration will get us moving with the least distraction along a process that can lead to success. And that's true even when we're dealing with a moving target in times of great flux. Governing our lives and our appropriate goal pursuits with a concentration on what it will take to reach those goals doesn't turn us into rigid robots of targeted action. We can still be quite flexible in our endeavors, and in fact, it's that baseline concentration that allows for fruitful flexibility along the way.

The art of achievement then stipulates as a fourth condition that we need a certain harmony in our actions as we pursue our goals. We need to direct our energies well, and never act at cross-purposes with our best intentions. A firm consistency is required.

C4: A stubborn CONSISTENCY in pursuing our vision

Some people may think the word 'stubborn' connotes what we wrongly call pigheadedness, in an ongoing insult to our porcine friends. That's not what I mean here at all. Most of us have heard it said of someone who just can't seem to learn from his mistakes and keeps making the same ones over and over again: "Well, at least he's consistent." This is not remotely related to the sort of personal constancy or harmony that facilitates success in times of change. I wish no one had even thought of using the word 'consistency' for a blind refusal to learn, or the firm opposition to change that never deserves this label, even in jest. The two personality traits are very different, and have wildly divergent results.

> The person who makes a success of living is the one
> who sees his goal steadily and aims for it unswervingly.
> Cecil B. De Mille

Many years ago, my son came home from high school one afternoon and told me a story I've always enjoyed recalling. He had walked with a group of boys to a friend's small car that had been parked outside the school on a very hot day. Warm weather is no anomaly at the southern coastal community where we live, and even in early summer, the days can sometimes be scorchers. The owner of the car opened the front door and the boys all stood staring at a huge mass of goopy white liquid covering the dashboard and slowly dripping down onto the floor. It was the inevitable aftermath of leaving a full stick of deodorant all day on the dash and in the blazing sun that was coming through the front windshield. The entire stick had melted into a big puddle that was spreading and dripping everywhere. The owner of the now creatively damaged vehicle stared at the sight for a moment in silence and then said, in a voice of utter exasperation, "Damn it! Not *again!*"

I had to laugh. There are some mistakes you just don't make twice. And we don't have to quote here the strangely popular but really bad "definition of insanity" that's often falsely attributed to Albert Einstein, when it's not ascribed to Benjamin Franklin or Mark Twain. Continuing to do what doesn't work, or what's created disastrous results before, and not learning at all from our mistakes is normally not behavior correlated with success. Neither is still doing what actually did work in a previous situation if things have changed in relevantly problematic ways. New and different call for new and different.

> The wise man does no wrong
> in changing his habits with the times.
> Dionysius Cato

Consistency doesn't mean continuing to do things the same way we've always done them. On the contrary, in changing times we need to be highly flexible and continuously adaptive in order to remain consistent with our highest goals and deepest values. The consistency that facilitates success is a form of faithfulness with goals and values that refuses to be derailed by either inner distractions or outer events. We should monitor ourselves in an honest and critical process of self-examination and frequently seek to assess whether our behavior is staying true to what we believe in and seek.

Several Chinese philosophers have had a wonderful and vivid image for this form of consistency. They ask us to consider the nature of water. What happens to moving water when it comes across an obstacle? It most often goes around it or over it, or under it, or else moves it aside. Running water can alter its course radically to find its way.

Now, let's consider a second instructive question. What's stronger: water, or stone? I've heard many young students of philosophy answer quickly without thinking, "Obviously, stone is much stronger. It's heavy and massive, hard, dense, and solid. It has real substance. Water is just soft, pliable, and giving, as a mere liquid." Indeed, you can throw a stone into a container of water and instantly displace the liquid, loudly splashing it out. But consider the issue more deeply. Dripping water can wear down stone. It can cut completely through a heavy, massive object. A torrent of it can roll massive boulders out of the way or smash them to bits. Waves will reshape a coastline. With these truths in mind, many Chinese philosophers have advised us, simply: Be like water.

The recommendation is profound. Be like water. Flow flexibly toward your chosen destination with the powerful harmony of this liquid force. That's a trait of our best existential alchemists. Be adaptive and patient in dealing with any obstacles that might stand in your path. And by doing this, you can be a confident force for change. As you set goals and move forward, you can be agile, prepared to adjust and change, and yet remain consistently yourself as the person you essentially are. Consistency at its best involves both flexibility and firmness. Water does what it does because it is what it is.

This powerful image can be extended even further in an illuminating way. Think about how much water can alter in changing circumstances. When the temperature drops enough, this common substance can transform from a liquid to a solid. It can also morph from solid to liquid to steam, whenever anyone sufficiently turns up the heat. And yet throughout such astonishing transitions, it never abandons its true nature. Its essence remains the same. The lesson from this is powerful and clear. We should change and adapt as circumstances demand, flex to overcome any obstacles in our way, and even radically transform what we do and how we do it in order to take full advantage of new opportunities—but, in all things, we should also stay true to who we essentially are, retaining our highest nature and best character along the way. We human beings are at our peak performance when we hold firm to the noblest of changeless ideals and principles, and within those bounds, live with open minds and hearts as essentially flexible and resilient forces that can adjust our form and course as circumstances around us change. This is the consistency that counts in our world the most.

Be like water.
Bruce Lee

To meet any new challenge well, we also need commitment. In fact, it's hard to maintain consistency in an extended, worthwhile pursuit if we're not fully committed. And in response to big problems, a genuinely passionate form of commitment is best.

C5: An emotional COMMITMENT to the importance of what we're doing

A commitment of the heart means everything. Passion pushes through obstacles. The energy that comes from inner enthusiasm facilitates positive achievement in any difficult endeavor and throughout any extended process of alchemical success.

We should never allow ourselves to merely go through the motions, caught up in a current that moves us on regardless of our values, emotions, and commitments. We need to align our activities with our best passions, pour ourselves into what we do, and do it with all our heart. This gives us the energy and inner fortitude to persist through the unexpected challenges and various forms of resistance that should always be anticipated for new and creative endeavors. As a spiritual discipline, existential alchemy is as much about the heart as it is about the head.

If I could mint my own coin, I'd be tempted to inscribe on one side, as heads: Everything's Important. And I'd likely want to put on the other side, as tails: Nothing's Easy. Of course, these succinct statements are to some extent catchy rhetorical gestures that are true only if properly interpreted and qualified. But for truth to depend on interpretation would not be unique to my coin. Its inscriptions could be worded more precisely, but then they wouldn't fit in the space allotted unless the coin was the size of a dinner plate, and flipping it would too readily confirm one of the mottos.

From a broadly spiritual perspective, everything that's in any way relevant to our lives is important—meaning: of some consequence, weight, or value—at least in principle. And everything worth doing at all is important to do as well as we can in the circumstances, given all our other commitments. In addition, on the flip side, nothing that's both important and worth doing is typically going to be a breeze. Almost anything worthwhile takes much more effort than we'd ever have thought.

When we can legitimately say of anything that, "It's not important," what we must really be taken to mean is that the thing in question is not or should not be worthy of worry, concern, or attention in the present situation, at this time, and given our other legitimate interests and commitments; and so it's all right, or even best right now, to basically ignore it and keep calm. A fully spelled out philosophical statement on either side of my coin would serve to clarify all this subtlety. But I like the short, snappy versions better. Heads: Everything's Important. Tails: Nothing's Easy.

Both of these insights about life are essential. And we deal best with either of them by remembering the other as well. Heads or Tails, we'd be confronted by a crucial bit of wisdom and never be far from its counterpart. Everything is important, and so real commitment is appropriate, whatever we're doing in support of worthy goals. Nothing is easy, and so real commitment is necessary for any valuable aim we have.

> Wherever you travel, go with all your heart.
> Confucius

We should never allow ourselves to slip into the emotional gear of neutral regarding our goals, except of course for short, occasional restorative breaks of rest and relaxation that will prepare us for the next challenge we'll face. In fact, giving ourselves the periodic opportunity to replenish our energies, especially during times of hardship or difficulty, is important precisely because we need that renewal to allow the ongoing commitment without which we can never succeed in any real challenge.

Full, sustainable emotional commitment never happens for people unless they understand the importance of not only the big things in life, but the little things as well. And commitment is often a fragile flower in the hearts of those who don't expect to have to work hard over time and in the face of obstacles to make valuable things happen. If we can go into any situation with the continual understanding that everything is important and nothing is easy, then we'll stand a better chance of attaining and sustaining the level of commitment that's such a strong facilitator of success.

Another point is important here. Whenever we face adversity, or some struggle that has entered our lives as a result of an unexpected change, negative emotions can easily arise. And most negative emotions don't help. Yet, it's hard with a negative feeling to just hit an inner delete button and make it go away. In emotions, as well as in habits, we rarely ever get rid of something unhealthy except by replacing it with a healthy alternative. When in response to change and challenge, we set our own new goals, we give our positive emotions something to rally around and support. And in this way, those positive emotions can quickly come to displace any negative ones that were sparked by the new circumstances. An emotional commitment to a new goal that we've chosen to pursue can refresh us and energize us in a distinctive way. Commitment is a deep well of flowing refreshment and energy that's beneficial in all times of transformation.

The sixth requirement for the art of achievement is that we need an inner strength of character, a personal depth to support us in adversity and power the effort required to bring any challenging task to completion. Great trees with deep roots can stand tall in fierce winds. The strength of the root system is key. Character performs this function in our life. We need good inner beginnings in order to facilitate the likelihood of good outer endings. And only a strong character is the universal guarantee for a good start.

C6: A good CHARACTER to guide us and keep us on a proper course

Our inner character is the core of who we are. A good character consists of those qualities or attributes that Aristotle called "the virtues"—a cluster of personal strengths that prepare us well for successful living: such things as courage, honesty, helpfulness, practicality, honor, and prudence. Good character facilitates success in a challenging world. Bad character by contrast undermines our greatest potential.

> There never was a good knife made of bad steel.
> Benjamin Franklin

I've often been asked the question: "Can't a bad and exceptionally corrupt character have a form of big and even flamboyant success?" My answer has always been: For a while; in a limited domain; and at the expense of what really matters in life. Bad character can't support true friendship, sustainable partnerships, or deeply perceptive interactions with the world. Corruption is self-diminishing. Unethical success is always self destructive in the long run. No lasting achievement of anything good can result from a bad character and unethical practices, except perhaps a beneficial cautionary tale.

We've seen this proved in public too many times in recent years. There are various tendencies in human nature that militate against sustaining any form of success that's built on unethical foundations. People incline to distrust anyone they've seen lying or cheating for selfish gain and will avoid, resist, and even work hard to bring down those who have treated them poorly. Apparent exceptions to this rule are always based on greed or fear (the delusion, for example, that "The enemy of my enemy is my friend") and are typically short term. The best results in life tend to arise out of strong and innovative collaborations, and such creative endeavors require a solid measure of mutual trust, an attitude that's impossible to maintain over time without a foundation of good character on all sides. Any manifestations of a bad or weak character on the part of an individual will tend to isolate him or her from the best people around, and it's precisely those people who are the most capable of contributing to the collaborative efforts that would be productive of long-term success in any legitimate and positive endeavor. Bad character can't support good outcomes in the ways needed.

The most enduring source of outer achievement is a strong inner character. The ancient pre-Socratic philosopher who famously believed, "Things are always changing" is also nearly as well known for his profound realization that, "Character is destiny." Thanks, Heraclitus. You got it right on both counts. But of course, on the level of surface appearances, karma can often seem to take its sweet time. Yet, we have the concept of karma precisely because we do see its evidence so often in life.

Character is a crucially stabilizing and foundational enterprise in an otherwise ever-changing world. I say that it's an enterprise rather than an entity because it is itself never inert, but always changing in subtle ways—growing and strengthening, or weakening and corrupting. Everything we do in one way or another contributes to the character we have. And that character will in turn either facilitate great and lasting achievement or make it impossible to reach the best that life has to offer. A good character is an important facilitating condition for positive achievement.

Aristotle surmised that character consists of qualities or virtues that prepare us well for the challenges of life. Each of these attributes is a strength we can bring to our challenging world. And his particular list has on it items you would expect, but also some things that can strike you initially as surprising. A representative summary of his ancient conceptions would have to mention such things as:

Courage: A commitment to do what's right despite the threat of danger
Temperance: A rational moderation and proper self-restraint
Liberality: a freedom in giving to others what can help to them
Magnificence: a capacity for acting on a grand scale when needed
Pride: a true sense of honor and worthiness
Good Temper: an inner calm displayed by outer behavior
Friendliness: the demeanor of treating others convivially and well
Truthfulness: a strong disposition toward honesty in all things
Wittiness: the ability to see and express humor appropriately
Justice: the fundamental disposition of treating others with fairness

Courage is obviously vital for dealing with daunting challenges. And good temper helps. So does wittiness, whenever it's used to defuse a tense situation or to bring needed relief to stressed-out people. The virtues of character do count, and matter deeply.

Aristotle once went so far as to write that the difference between an educated and an uneducated man is the difference between the living and the dead. I think the same thing can be said about the difference between a good character and a bad one. And this is something that we often, unfortunately, have to learn the hard way. But once we do learn and deeply understand it, we're empowered to move ahead more productively and make the most of any circumstances that may come our way. The path and procedure arising from good character is to deal with the many changing situations we confront by means of unchanging principles and values we can trust.

Finally, to facilitate true success and deep, lasting accomplishment in times of change, the art of achievement specifies that we need the benefit of a particular psychological capacity, the sort of ability for positive experience that we discussed briefly in our exploration of happiness. We need a capacity to take pleasure in our task.

C7: A CAPACITY TO ENJOY the process along the way

The alchemy of everyday life that's required for great lemonade making seeks to turn the apparently bad into the surprisingly good, the difficult into the useful, the ordinary into the extraordinary, and even the messy mundane into the magically magnificent— spinning golden results from nearly any experience and bringing out the best that can arise from any daunting situation. When life hands us lemons, we're to become alchemists of the spirit, and in that way we may discover to our great surprise that the activity of making lemonade can itself at many stages be a source of pleasure. Of course, the end result is great. But the reality is that the results of our work will tend to be even better as we find more ways to enjoy the process that creates them.

Here's where we come full circle back to an important element of personal happiness. Isn't it interesting how all of this is related? Despite how it might sometimes seem, life isn't just a fragmented mosaic of completely disparate activities, independent insights, and random events. It all connects up. If we have a capacity to enjoy the process along the way, our work can link up powerfully with our happiness. And so can everything else we do. A capacity to enjoy the process of our work and our life in all its most fundamental facets is in fact a foundation for sustainability and excellence in anything we do.

Obviously, not everything every day can be enjoyed. There are things that are just tough, and even awful. Some experiences are terribly difficult and painful. But if we have a robust capacity to enjoy whatever can be enjoyed throughout the process of our work and our days, we give ourselves the emotional equipment for refreshing our spirits and keeping sharp and properly focused in even the toughest times. This will make the worst of days more bearable, and the best even better than they otherwise would be.

And the further good news is that cultivating this capacity is completely up to us.

> He who enjoys doing, and enjoys what he has done, is happy.
> Goethe

In everything we seek, it's of course the process that lies behind and creates the results. If we can find a way to relish the process of our work, then we're much more likely to see the full array of positive results we want. One of the dangers for many people is a tendency to endure the process to get the results, when what we really seek are the sorts of results that only an emotionally embraced and enjoyed process can produce.

Masterful achievement always involves some love of the process in itself that then becomes a driving force in the creation of exemplary results. This seventh condition of success is not merely an elective add-on. It's not a mere decorative flourish for the making of great lemonade, but a vital part of the recipe itself. It's crucial for any sustainable endeavor that will be productive of excellence along the way. It's a prime example of how our inner approach to life can be leveraged to change the outer shape of it. Great people in any walk of life—top creators and elite performers—tend to be those individuals who most relish the process of their work, finding ways of indwelling it and enjoying it deeply. And that's where the alchemy takes place.

Countless times, I've come across a person of excellence in his or her work and I've made some version of the comment, "It seems like you really enjoy what you do." The response is almost inevitably a big smile and the words, "I love it." And that's our key. Love powers life alchemy like nothing else. As we've seen, love is an important part of the formula for life happiness, and it's precisely a happy spirit enjoying the journey that tends to deal with change the most powerfully and well.

Our Framework for Achievement

THIS FRAMEWORK OF IDEAS—THIS ORGANIZATION OF SEVEN universal conditions for success that I see as constituting the art of achievement—has been identified from the culmination of many years of research and analysis into many more centuries of thought and experiment. The framework brings together in a short and usable form some of the most helpful insights from the best diagnosticians of the human condition who have ever pondered our adventures in the world. Its ideas have stood the test of time. And as such, it can be a tool of great power in our own day for existential lemonade making. It can help anyone to adapt masterfully to the vicissitudes of this world and create a good life. But to be maximally helpful, it needs to be applied consciously, continually, and relentlessly to the challenges that life brings. Ideas without implementation are merely of interest. It's when we apply the best ideas in our experience that they can change our lives.

Other Conditions for Success

There are of course many and various other sets of principles, habits, tips, and techniques for successful achievement available in our day. Some advisors provide us with three, or five secrets. Others give us as many as a hundred discrete principles. And many of these are helpful in different ways. The real distinctiveness of The 7 Cs of Success presented here is that they offer what I think is the most completely universal advice. Whether you're struggling with a new challenge alone or working in a group, whether you're seeking new forms of success in your job or at home with your family, or even in a sport or hobby, you'll find that these seven facilitating conditions of success will apply and help you move forward in potentially useful ways.

Just as our eyes need light in order to see,
our minds need ideas in order to conceive.
Nicholas Malebranche

But is this tool kit of ideas big enough? Some clever people have asked me over the years, "Why isn't Creativity among the universal conditions for success? Or Collaboration? Or even Communication? Or Courage? And this is just to stick with words in English that start with the letter 'C'. Aren't there many other facilitating conditions for positive achievement?" In my view, the simple answer is that, as vitally important as such other things might be in the right situations, either they aren't absolutely universal (needed as a separate principle in literally every challenging goal-attainment situation), or else they can be viewed as either contained within, implied by, or an application of one of the core seven conditions in a particular set of circumstances. For example, communication as an interpersonal transaction is necessary when you're working with others, but when you're struggling with a challenge privately, it may not at all come into play. Condition C3 of The 7 Cs ("A focused Concentration on what it takes") can lead you to spot the importance of communication when it's needed, and Condition C4 ("Consistency") will urge you to apply it as required at all such times.

Courage is certainly crucial in periods of dramatic change and threat. But it's a part of good character (C6), as understood by the philosophers. So it's not listed alone. Collaboration and creativity are both often vital in times of tumultuous transition. But since our challenges don't always require these basic qualities as separate, stand-alone tools, they're not explicitly listed among the utterly universal conditions for success that I've outlined. Each is suggested or required in the appropriate circumstances by one or another of the conditions we do have.

There are many other important qualities we could highlight in any quest for positive achievement, and yet it's both simple and effective to use the framework of The 7 Cs as our fundamental organizing collection of insights to guide us in what we do. They capture the deepest practical wisdom of the great thinkers of the past, they can direct us to any other tools we might need in specific situations, and they're fairly easy to keep in mind every day. They give us an example of how simplicity and power can coincide.

I've suggested in the book *The Art of Achievement* that each of these seven conditions for successful outcomes has associated with it a distinct form of art, a skilled behavior or set of behaviors that, like any art, requires cultivation and practice. Powerful goal setting by means of the clear conception of a new target to hit isn't a simple, instantaneous action that we can perform like champions the first time we try it. It's an art. Some people are better at it than others, and we can learn from the masters. Proper confidence building is also an art. There is a distinct art of focused concentration. Those who practice it well get better at it. Likewise, there's an art of consistency, and so on for each of these primary conditions of achievement.

But the truth is, it's not the idea, it's what you do with it.
Neil Gaiman

In addition, each of the seven related arts aids in the cultivation and skilled use of the others. The art of confidence building, for example, helps with concentration. Those who are experts at expelling needless doubts from their minds eliminate important distractions and common obstacles to their practice of the art of concentration. And the better you are at concentration, in turn, the better you will be with the art of consistency. Both will help with confidence, and they also will make easier the art of cultivating a capacity to enjoy the process. Each condition can help with the others. If we understand all this at a deep level, we can see that, as in the case of any other form of art, while practice may not make perfect, a proper practice makes for progress.

Practice is nine-tenths.
Emerson

With the right sort of practice, any of us can become a true artist of achievement, an artist of adaptation, and an artist of change. That's our goal. And this is what's required for the lemonade making of everyday alchemy in the face of challenge and struggle. Self-control allows for positive action, which allows for real achievement. It will be useful to review this big picture linkage briefly now, as we've laid it out.

In any time of great change, we want to: (1) exercise proper self-control in our reactions to the twists and turns and major disruptions that come our way, (2) launch out in positive action to make the most of our newly altered situation, and then (3) achieve good results with our focused efforts. The 7 Cs of Success can help immensely in getting the best results possible from anything we do. They are the most universal facilitators of excellence and are essential for the alchemistic quest.

Change and The Keys To Success

IT'S ALL ABOUT WHAT WE DO AND HOW WE DO IT. THE MAGIC always arises from a process of implementation. The art of achievement is the skilled application of the seven conditions of success we've just outlined and, of course, the forms of art related to them, in our work and our lives. These conditions can be used to make our way forward in times of change, and they can be employed to initiate change in a masterful way. They've been understood by many of the wisest people in history, and they've proved their usefulness repeatedly throughout the human adventure, in good times and in turmoil.

For over thirty years, I've had the opportunity to introduce people to these simple but powerful concepts in many different ways through books like *True Success*, *The Art of Achievement*, and *The Stoic Art of Living*, as well as in my talks around the world. It's always a treat to hear from readers and audience members as they use these tools in whatever they're doing. The stories people tell me help me to continue to learn and more deeply understand. One day, for example, I received such a message from a man who had heard me speak on The 7 Cs to a group of 2,500 managers in his large financial services company. Tom Lakatos was one of the people in the audience who right away decided to put these ideas into action. He had a strong inclination to apply the concepts in his own life and wanted to help his associates at work by introducing them to the ideas. He went back to his office on the other side of the country and started training everyone there in The 7 Cs of Success. He then wrote me months later to tell me what he'd done.

> The greater part of progress is the desire to progress.
> Seneca

His office of six financial advisors had been struggling. Their performance had been ranked 217th out of 255 separate districts in the country for their company. Morale was down and the challenge was great. Within a few months of training his colleagues in the art of achievement, using explicitly and consciously The 7 Cs of Success and applying them relentlessly, they had managed to make some changes that tremendously grew their business. In just a short time, they had added ten more associates and were now ranked 19th in the country. Imagine that. They had gone from a national ranking of 217th to 19th in a matter of months. It was extraordinary.

My new philosophy friend told me he was particularly proud of the fact that his colleagues were enjoying their work more and that their practice of the art of achievement had enriched their lives immensely outside the boundaries of work, as well as in the office. They were not sacrificing personal life and family for the sake of the great results they were attaining in their business, but were raising the overall standard of excellence and enjoyment across all positive dimensions of their lives. Spouses and children were noticing the change and appreciating it, even mentioning it to Tom. His associates were getting such great results because they all truly desired the full range of improvements these ideas could bring.

Because of his extraordinary success in leading that office through such an amazing metamorphosis in such a short time, this enterprising man reported to me later that he had been promoted to head up another office elsewhere in the country. And I got a full update not long afterward. When Tom arrived at his new assignment, he started the process all over again, explaining The 7 Cs of Success and training people in how to use them well. In another remarkably short time, this new office grew from fourteen people to thirty-two. On his arrival, they were ranked 85th in the nation. When he next wrote me about it all, they had ended the year as number 3. He had again attained great success and still had something to shoot for. This master of life alchemy further reported that The 7 Cs of Success had become a core part of his standard orientation process for new associates, and that they use these guidelines explicitly in their business planning for each new year, even setting aside a "7 Cs Day" quarterly to check up on how they're doing in their use of these keys to achievement.

Squeezing Lemons Hard with The 7 Cs

I have seen many people change their lives with a dedicated implementation of the art of achievement, by using The 7 Cs of Success in all the right ways. One more example from many years ago can demonstrate the power and reach of these simple ideas. I had flown to Florida to give a talk to eight hundred real estate professionals on The 7 Cs. In the middle of the afternoon, I checked into my hotel room, and by dinnertime I had a full-blown case of the flu. I could barely breathe, I felt extremely dizzy, and I was quickly losing my voice. For a public speaker, this is about as unwanted a cluster of changes as you can imagine. It's lemons galore. So I started using some medication that I always carry for such remote contingencies. I ordered chicken soup and hot tea from room service, which I then drank with honey and lots of lemon juice. But nothing seemed to help. I went to bed early, hoping for a good night's sleep. And when I woke up the next morning two hours before the scheduled time of my talk, I had almost no voice at all. I could barely make a low, pathetic croaking sound. It was awful.

There is no success without hardship.
Sophocles

The entire art of adaptation became instantly relevant. Major self-control was needed. I didn't rush to judgment. I remembered to value the right things—in this case, not just my personal comfort, but the good of the people I was there to serve. I used my imagination as well as I could while sipping more hot tea, visualizing my presentation, praying hard, and hoping for the best. I was determined to try any positive action available. I was careful to govern my attitudes, not indulging in a tailspin of negativity about the apparently impossible task that I faced in less than two hours. I grabbed every opportunity for medical mitigation that my well-stocked toiletries kit and the wonders of hot liquids could provide and then, despite my condition, I began to take the initiative to dress for the talk that by all indications I shouldn't even try to give.

After I walked slowly down several impossibly long hallways and finally into the hotel's ballroom, looking every bit as bad as I felt, I met the meeting planner and revealed my full physical condition in a husky whisper to this now clearly concerned lady. But I also reassured her there was no reason for worry, and that at the appointed time, very soon, I would be able to exercise mind over matter, rise to the occasion, and do my presentation with ample voice and full energy. Mere minutes later, as I dizzily stepped on the stage, I had to take the clip-on microphone off my jacket lapel and hold it to my lips in order to be heard at all through the sound system. I used the first seconds of my time on stage to joke a bit about my obvious condition and to reassure the surprised group that our topic was so important I was nearly dying to talk about it.

> The ability to convert ideas to things
> is the secret of outward success.
> Henry Ward Beecher

Using every one of The 7 Cs just to make this thing happen at all, I whispered and croaked my way enthusiastically through my entire sixty-minute talk on the art of achievement. I was hoping only that everyone could hear me. But there was a lot of welcome laughter and loud, rousing applause throughout the session to reassure me of a real connection, and so I flew home later with a sense of contentment and acceptance concerning whatever the overall impact of the session might be. I had taken action in every way possible and had done what I could within the realm of things over which I retained some small measure of control, and I just had to live with the fact that, because of what I couldn't control, it would never qualify as my finest moment on a stage. I had no idea what would eventually result from the talk. And when I did learn of those astounding consequences, I was absolutely shocked.

A young man called me years later to report that he first heard an audio recording of me speaking on The 7 Cs when he was in his early twenties and right out of college, working in a resort real estate development. Over the years, he said, he had listened to that tape more than four hundred times. He had then based everything he did in residential sales around The 7 Cs of Success, and when he was promoted into a management position, he taught everyone else in the office these basics in the art of achievement. He had gone on to have a stellar career, moving from one success to another, opening beautiful communities, putting families in great homes, training an army of other salespeople in the wisdom of the ages, and setting new national records along the way. He didn't mean to boast about these accomplishments at all. He just wanted me to know what had resulted in his life because of using The 7 Cs.

Little by little does the trick.
Aesop

I had actually already heard of this successful man, although not about his use of my philosophical advice. Unknown to him, some of the most impressive people I knew had described him to me over the years as one of the most impressive people they knew. The wisdom of the ages had molded him into a person of stellar excellence and high reputation, as he had applied these insights little by little in all that he did.

In every challenge, this man had used the insights of the great thinkers, gently but firmly holding himself and the people around him accountable to action consistent with these principles on a weekly basis, grounding his associates in the fundamentals of sustainable achievement. He was calling me that day, he said, to report a personal milestone. He told me that when he first heard the recording of my talk all those years ago, he had quietly set himself an audacious personal goal of attaining what would have been for most highly ambitious people a long-term financial dream, allowing for early retirement and a measure of independence, a target that some big dreamers might set to attain perhaps by age 50, or even 45. But in his case, the target date for independence was the very young age of 35. And this was years before the advent of tech startups that could provide such wealth and security for people of such an age. He said that, as of our conversation in his 34th year, he wanted me to know that he had already been able to achieve his dream because of the guidance of The 7 Cs, and the art of achievement he had learned to practice so well. His plan now, he told me, was to create new opportunities to serve people in innovative ways, living and conveying even more broadly the truths that had enhanced his life. Those new forms of service would include becoming a high school basketball coach for a local Christian school where he could guide young people into lives of their own achievement and true success.

This still very young man was calling that day, he said, to thank me. But I felt like I should thank him instead. He's a shining example of ancient wisdom put to work in every aspect of life. And he has been helping throughout the years to spread the word about how that wisdom can revolutionize our approach to life. This admirably successful individual had given copies of the recording that had helped him so much to scores of people through the years, and had handed out to others in meetings, on airplanes, and at social occasions small laminated wallet cards displaying The 7 Cs, just to share the ideas that he had seen work so dramatically in his own life. The recordings, the cards, and the concepts they conveyed had then gone on to have gratifying results in the lives of many other people as well, through the actions of this one committed individual.

What we achieve inwardly will change outer reality.
Plutarch

The biggest surprise to me was to hear that the recording that had led to all this was of the talk I gave that day in Florida when I was so sick and so nearly bereft of voice that I'm shocked a taping device could pick up enough sound to record. The thought of canceling that talk from my hotel room the night before had been extremely tempting. The morning of the event, that same idea was nearly overwhelming. But I didn't give in. I didn't allow myself to be thrown by the sudden changes to my health that so obviously threatened to stop me in my tracks. Nearly buried by sour lemons,

I started making lemonade. I used all the wisdom I could muster, focused my energies to rise to the challenge, and then did the best I could on that miserably difficult day. And I have been truly amazed at what resulted, through just one person who heard that talk, and not even a audience member who was physically present in the room, but a man who, at the strong urging of someone who had been in attendance, listened to a recording of that particular session, hearing a tape I didn't even know existed. The appearances of that day, and the realities of what it would accomplish, were as different as can be possible.

It had been a day of hard lemonade making. At the grocery store not long ago, I saw on a bottle the label: *Mike's Hard Lemonade*. Well, that day's work was clearly *Tom's Hard Lemonade*. Terribly difficult things were transmuted into amazing results. And yet it wasn't clear what they were for a very long time. But I've relished those results immensely ever since I learned of them. Plus, I've also heard other great success stories that resulted from the tape of that talk in the lives of other men and women, over and over, through the years. One small pebble tossed into a pond can set up surprisingly big ripples. When we use what we have and do what we can in even the face of trouble, we provide for the possibility of great results beyond anything we could have imagined.

By telling this story, I don't mean to imply that we should never take a sick day or cancel a business commitment if our bodies are just not up to it. That's sometimes the human condition. Lemonade can be made in different ways. There are things we simply have to accept, and times we just need to rest and recover. But in order to have our best impact in the world overall, we often need to go the extra mile, put forth deeper efforts, and then trust that our best intentions will prevail and the consequences will be good.

We never know the full extent of what we can do for others in even the most trying of circumstances. It's our job to accept anything we can't control, take action on what we can control, give it our best effort, and then anticipate the results with as much contentment, equanimity, and hope as we can muster. Things are not often simply what they at first seem, and we can sometimes be quite astonished at the good we've been able to accomplish in even the most trying of conditions. This is the alchemy of life.

The Wisdom of the Ages

The great practical thinkers through the centuries have left us a wealth of insight that we can use with very positive results in our business endeavors and our lives. By giving us their best ideas, they can help each of us to become wiser and live more successfully. But they can do this for us only if we actively participate. When we ignore their advice about life and act as if we have to make it all up from scratch, we needlessly impoverish ourselves and make things more difficult than they have to be. The seven conditions of success are a focused distillation of some of this great insight we've inherited. And the art of achievement they make possible is an important culminating component within the art of change. Our guiding metaphor of lemonade making is all about the kind of change mastery that provides for positive achievement. And it's made possible by wisdom from around the world and throughout history that's never changed.

> He who knows useful things, not many things, is wise.
> Aeschylus

Unexpected change can be handled in the best possible way, and new positive change can be initiated in the most powerful way, by using these simple and effective ideas that have stood the test of time. When we employ them together as a powerful diagnostic tool and implementation guide, we position ourselves for strong outcomes, regardless of the degree of churn and challenge we may be experiencing in our lives.

The art of achievement is the third and last major component art within the overall art of adaptation, the first of the two major practices within the larger art of change, and it's an art that has helped people in almost every situation imaginable. Proper self-control (our first component within the art of adaptation) leads to appropriate positive action, and well-directed positive action (our second part of adaptation) can lead to satisfying success by the additional employment of the factors for achievement within The 7 Cs of Success (our third artistic component of adaptation). The capstone of the entire process is this third form of art that facilitates achievement.

Charles Darwin, the scientific patron saint of evolutionary change, development, and worldly flourishing despite adversity, once said:

> It's not the strongest of the species that survives,
> nor the most intelligent that survives.
> It is the one that is the most adaptable to change.

How can we be more adaptable to change, even of the most challenging varieties? By using these arts that we've examined, putting them to work in everything we do. And yet, there's more to mastering change and the overall alchemy of life than just being properly responsive and adaptable to the new things that come our way.

Half the challenge of change is, of course, in how we react to new things and difficulties that come to us. But the other half is in how we ourselves can take the initiative to create innovative new forms of positive change, whether things around us already seem to be in transition or not. This taking of initiative is captured in the latter two of our three component arts within the art of adaptation, and it's facilitated by the first art. Making the right change happen is every bit as important as reacting well to the change that occurs apart from our intent. The question then looms: How can we best become masterful originators and propagators of innovative change?

There's a bit of mystery involving this. Many people have told me they've read a book that's inspired them deeply, or they've heard a speaker who has motivated them greatly, and yet nothing ultimately happened as a result. Unlike the successful people whose stories I've told, they've found to their own puzzlement and consternation months or even years later that they'd taken no action at all on ideas that had seemed so good and powerful to them at the time, and that still seem important. Why? What kept them from acting on the new concepts they had encountered and making the changes in their lives and even in their businesses or other organizations they knew they needed to make? And how can we avoid this problem in our own experience? How can we best launch action when action is needed? How can we be transformative alchemists who go forth to set up our lemonade stands and get out our kitchen tools even before life begins handing us lemons? That's the topic of our next chapters, and the second part of this book.

Part Two

THE ART OF INNOVATION
Making And Selling Great Lemonade

6

You: The Mixologist
The Key to Personal Change

Some people appear to be natural masters at taking life's lemons and making lemonade. They seem to do just the right thing to transform any situation so that it leads to good results. What sets them apart? These are usually people who are not simply adept at responding well to change and challenge, but are also just as good at initiating positive change in their lives and work. Do they know a secret that others don't? They definitely take a distinctive approach to things. But their tendencies may be based on something that's no secret at all. The wisdom of the ages won't apply itself. The master lemonade makers understand and act in accordance with this obvious fact. They're so good at handling the ups and downs of life precisely because they've become active artists of transformation. They've developed all the right habits so that they're naturally able to adopt a good perspective and take effective action to transform themselves and their circumstances in positive ways. And they tend to do it well.

To be a man is, precisely, to be responsible.
Saint-Exupery

The basic operative insight here is simple. The best ideas in the world won't magically create their own corresponding realities, despite widely repeated claims to the contrary. Our own action is key. We can't be true masters of change or alchemists of adversity unless we understand this on a deep existential level and live in accordance with it. We're always responsible to think and take the initiative to act well in artistic innovation, to effect the transformation of our circumstances in positive ways.

In the first part of our explorations together, we've looked at the issue of how to respond best to the challenging change that comes into our lives. We've seen that there is an art of adaptation that will give us what we need. Now, we're going to look into the related question of how we can make the best changes that we need to initiate in our lives and in our activities with others. In this chapter, we'll mainly be tackling the question as it applies to individuals. We'll then go on in the next chapter to broaden our concern to group situations and organizational contexts. We'll see that there is an art of innovative transformation used by all the greatest lemonade makers. They employ it in their lives and use it to move others in a new and positive direction through the grand enterprise of making lemonade together, launching beneficial creative change into the world.

Transformative Ideas and Different Results

As a philosopher who has the rare and wonderful opportunity of working with large corporations, high impact business groups, and civic organizations of all sorts, I see people exposed to new ideas all the time. Some, with only the briefest introduction to an important new concept, will go on to deepen their understanding of it and use it to change their lives or work for the better. Others will get excited about a new perspective for a few days or even weeks, and then largely forget about what they had heard, understood, and eagerly embraced. A few people now and then simply won't see what everybody else is getting so worked up about in the first place, and will just walk away apparently unfazed. I see these three totally different reactions all the time.

What accounts for this range of responses to any new idea that could be the seed of positive change? How can we be sure that we're personally prepared to make the most of any useful new concept or perspective that comes our way? Exactly what is it that marks the difference between those who implement new ideas to transform their lives or businesses for the better and those who don't? Ideas without implementation can be educational, entertaining, and even deeply edifying, but one thing they can't be is transformative. And that's true for a simple reason. Ideas are only part of the battle. Implementation is the rest. Why then do so many people fail to implement good ideas when they could and should be doing so?

> We are responsible not only for what we do
> but for what we don't do.
> Jean-Baptiste Molière

There is a famous parable in the Bible that can give us some deep and practical answers to these questions, whatever our personal theological stance might be, or whether we have one at all. It employs an image or metaphor that has resonated with a wide variety of people for over two thousand years. Plato actually may have been the first to use it. I'll say more on that in a bit. But Jesus elaborated on it with a vivid narrative. Whether we consider ourselves in any way religious, this profound story with its central focus offers us some insights about our personal readiness for change that we can use any time we confront a need for the alchemy of innovative transformation. The theology behind it is deeply interesting, but its practical philosophy is available to us all.

The Parable of the Soils

A PARABLE IS A POWERFUL TEACHING TOOL THAT INVOLVES telling a story whose components can illuminate some aspect of our lives. Its power derives from its clear imagery, its simplicity, its narrative structure, and the fact that these three features make it easy to remember. A vivid, concise story burrows down into our imaginations and stays with us. An important additional factor to note is that the hearer or reader of a parable can't be completely passive in understanding it. Interpretation is needed. And this requires some form of creative engagement or intellectual action on the part of the person who's exposed to it and paying attention. Even a small dose of that personal investment then makes further action of some sort a little more likely. So the very process of correctly understanding a parable involves breaking, or at least gently cracking, the overall state of inertia that may be governing our lives, or a part of our lives. And this is what makes it more natural for us to engage in some appropriate form of active behavior in response to what the parable shows us. As a great teacher concerned with changing people's lives, Jesus of Nazareth was a masterful creator of parables.

The Parable of the Soils appears in the New Testament of the Christian Bible in the three Gospels of Matthew, Mark, and Luke. Some commentators have suggested that it may have a distinctive importance for the author of Mark, since it's the only parable he reports whose explicit interpretation he also records. It's not nearly as well known as the Parable of the Prodigal Son. But it's still one of the better known of such stories in the Bible and all of literature. It's every bit as illuminating as it is famous, and that's true despite the fact that the passage in which it appears contains a few statements that can seem very odd and even mysterious on a first reading. But these statements will repay careful thought with some deep insights about innovative transformation.

A Telling of the Parable
The Gospel of Mark, chapter four, begins with Jesus sitting in a boat on the edge of the water, speaking to a large crowd of people who have come down to the shore to hear him. Starting with the second verse (numbered in parentheses, and using some standard translations, with my own slight modernizing of the language), we read:

> (2) He taught them many things in parables, and in his teaching said to them: (3) "Listen: A farmer went out to sow. (4) And as he sowed, some seed fell on the path and the birds came and ate it up. (5) Other seed fell on rocky ground, where there wasn't much soil, and immediately a shoot sprang up, since the soil wasn't deep; (6) and when the sun rose, it was scorched and because it had no root, it withered away. (7) Still other seed fell among thorns, and the thorns grew and choked it, and it yielded no grain. (8) And some seed fell into good soil and brought forth grain, growing and increasing and yielding thirty-fold and six-ty-fold and a hundred-fold." (9) And he said, "He who has ears to hear, let him hear."

Ancient agricultural methods in that part of the world stan-dardly involved a farmer first scattering seed by hand, and then plowing it into the soil. Some of the seed might fall on the hard packed dirt of a well-walked pathway and have no chance to grow at all. Sitting on the surface of the ground, it would just be picked off by birds and eaten. Other seed could fall into shallow, rocky soil where it might initially grow fast, but without deep roots to support that growth long-term, the plant would wither and die. Yet other seed might fall among weeds and thorns that would steal away important nutrients and keep it from growing in a healthy way. But the seeds that Jesus is metaphorically discussing—his words, teachings, or ideas—can also fall into fertile soil and yield a huge crop, far beyond what even the most optimistic and hopeful farmer might expect.

> Nature tells every secret once.
> Emerson

We'll get to the full interpretation of this passage in a minute. For now, let's continue on and encounter our first major puzzle. The crowd has dispersed and Jesus is sitting alone, but with his close followers and twelve core disciples nearby. Someone asks him a question. A discussion arises about parables in general, and regarding this one in particular. Some of his followers even wonder about why he spoke in parables at all.

> (10) And when he was alone, those who were around him with the twelve asked him about the parables. (11) And he said to them, "To you has been given the secret of the king-dom of God, but for those outside, everything is in para-bles; (12) so that they indeed may see but not perceive, and hear but not understand; lest they should turn again and be forgiven."

Verse twelve offers the big puzzle. But before getting into it directly, let's see the rest of the passage where Jesus explains to his friends the meaning of this particular parable. He interprets it for them by using the concept of "the word" or "the word of God," by which he means the revelation of spiritual truth given by God through him and his teachings.

> (13) And he said to them, "Don't you understand this par-able? How then will you understand all the other parables?

(14) The farmer sows the word. (15) And there are people who are like the path where the word is spread; when they hear, the adversary immediately comes and takes away the word that's sown in them. (16) And in the same way others are like the rocky ground, who, when they hear the word, immediately receive it with joy: (17) but they have no root in themselves and just continue for a while; then, when trouble or difficulty arises on account of the word, they immediately fall away. (18) And others reflect the seeds sown among thorns; they are those who hear the word, (19) but the cares of the world, and a delight in riches, and a desire for other things, enter in and choke it, and it proves unfruitful. (20) But the seeds that were sown on good soil represent the people who hear the word and accept it and bear fruit, thirty-fold, and sixty-fold, and a hundred-fold."

An initial note: The phrase "the adversary" in verse fifteen can be understood to denote the devil, or Satan, or—more broadly— any quick acting primary obstacle (personal or impersonal) that can enter a life and, from first contact, uproot and carry away the seeds of transformative ideas. Comfort, or inertia, or a strongly felt need for the esteem of certain other people can act as such an adversarial force, from the outset preventing positive change and growth. This is presented as one among other possible forms of interference to an idea's taking root, growing, and bearing fruit in a life.

Now, let's turn to the first puzzle. The explanation Jesus gives in verse twelve for why he teaches publicly by using parables can strike modern readers as exceedingly strange and puzzling. He says he speaks to the multitude in parables so that they can see but not perceive and hear but not understand. Otherwise, he adds, they might turn and be forgiven. But, wait: Isn't that supposed to be the whole point of his ministry? Isn't personal change and divine forgiveness the entire purpose of his work, as reported and explained throughout the rest of the gospels? Doesn't he hope for people to turn their lives around, return to their creator, and be forgiven? Otherwise, what's going on? Why would Jesus go to the trouble of speaking in public at all if he didn't want people to perceive and understand what he was saying? This is indeed a perplexing statement. It's also a major clue to understanding the parable and seeing how it applies to our own lives.

> Perplexity is the beginning of knowledge.
> Kahlil Gibran

I love to come across a puzzling passage while reading an important text. The detective mindset comes out in me. I live with the puzzle awhile. I dig around in it. Like an original hearer of a parable, I have to get creative. I'm a lot like a dog chewing on an old shoe. I won't give up. And I always end up with more understanding. Sometimes, the problems we come across in a text are due to something in it. At other times, they're due to something in us. That parallels life in general. Problems occasionally can arise for us because of what we bring to a situation, like the enterprise of reading a text.

Much of the perplexity we experience over verse twelve is generated by assuming that the mission of Jesus was mainly about conveying new theological information and getting quick religious conversions from those who heard him. But if what he was after was quite different from that, then this passage can appear in a new and interesting light that may help us understand something important about jumping any gap between ideas and implementation, or initial challenge and subsequent change. When we open up our minds as readers and bring a dose of creativity to interpret what's going on here, we can come to see something new and surprising.

The Transformation Game

It's well known that any leader wanting to initiate a change needs to communicate all the relevant information to other people in such a way as to gain their deep personal buy-in to whatever needs to be done. People won't change unless they believe in the change. A level of personal conviction or even enthusiasm is necessary. This is an important part of any organizational or group change initiative. But simply providing information and gaining assent in such a context are always just means to greater ends. For one thing, no leader benefits from generating a merely superficial agreement or a temporary acknowledgement on the part of others that quickly will fade. That's just what I like to call "the applaud and avoid response." At the lowest level, applause can be deceptive, granted to please a leader or fit in, but also actually used to mask an intention to avoid the consequences of what's being proclaimed. And there's a less disingenuous version of such a dynamic as well. People can applaud something from their minds, and yet avoid it in their hearts. Intellectual assent is never by itself enough. Leaders have to be able to create in other people, or at least elicit from them, deeper levels of sustained commitment to new goals as mutual aims, as well as to any associated process. Great leadership is never just informative and transactional, but also fundamentally transformational in profoundly positive ways. The best leaders are able to spark basic and sometimes radical changes, and that requires gaining something deeper than mere intellectual agreement or assent.

> If your actions inspire others to dream more, learn more,
> do more, and become more, you are a leader.
> John Quincy Adams

We can learn something important and highly relevant to our perplexity over the words of Jesus we just encountered by pondering a famous nighttime meeting that took place between him and a socially prominent man named Nicodemus, as recorded in the Gospel of John, chapter three. But don't worry: In consulting a second New Testament document, we're not at all yet in danger of becoming biblical scholars. It just happens that the Bible, like many great texts, and especially large compilations of various related component documents, such as it is, contains in different places interconnecting insights on certain central topics like our current concern about transformation. When we put the various scattered puzzle pieces together, we can see new things and perhaps shed new light on some old things as well.

Throughout his ministry, it's clear that Jesus was focused on changing people's lives at the most fundamental level. He wanted to bring what we can call a measure of spiritual alchemy to everyone, helping us turn life's most fundamental lemons into great lemonade—as odd as that might sound in reference to an individual much better known for transforming water into wine. But remembering this alchemical endeavor is crucial for understanding what happens in the remarkable short conversation between Jesus and Nicodemus that we're now going to examine.

Nicodemus and the Need for Change

The writer of the Gospel of John tells us that Nicodemus was a leader of the Jews who came to visit the highly controversial itinerant preacher at night, presumably to avoid being seen with him by many other people. The religious powers of the day were not at all keen on this new and popular public speaker, but disparaged him and his followers as lower class troublemakers. So, the respectable Nicodemus ventured out to see Jesus on this occasion under the mask of darkness, and then revealed to him quietly what he personally had observed and concluded about him and his work.

In the account we have of their meeting, Nicodemus displays some simple reasoning he's gone through when, in his opening words to Jesus, he says, "Rabbi, we know you're a teacher sent from God, for unless a man came from God, he couldn't do the things you do." For any careful reader of the New Testament, this looks like a major breakthrough. As far as we know, none of the other top religious leaders of the time had previously thought of Jesus as a man sent from God. Many had viewed him as a blatant sinner, a dangerous blasphemer, a rabble-rouser, and even as a demon-possessed maniac. But here's one of those leaders going to the trouble of visiting this figure of controversy in person to express his distinctive, contrary, and remarkably true beliefs, from the viewpoint of the gospel writer. Perhaps he's come to Jesus with the hope of having his beliefs confirmed, and then gaining even more information.

The surprise then, for most informed readers, is that Jesus doesn't say something to him in response like: "Nicodemus! Congratulations! You're right! I'm impressed. I am indeed a man sent from God. And there's even more to the story that I'd like to tell you now. But first I want to commend you for the perceptive observations and impeccable reasoning that have gotten you this much of the truth. You certainly seem to stand above your peers in observational acuity, logical reasoning, and theological insight."

We don't see Jesus saying anything remotely like this. He speaks to his remarkable and presumably sincere visitor in a way that simply seems to ignore the content of what the man has just said to him. Jesus replies, point blank and without any preliminary explanation: "Truly, truly, I say to you, unless a man is born again, he cannot see the kingdom of God." A moment of puzzled silence most likely followed.

This response is a bit unexpected, to put it mildly. How can such a statement-out-of-the-blue even count as a reply to Nicodemus? This astute visitor has overcome any personal prejudice he might have had, looked at Jesus carefully, ventured to draw a conclusion based on what he's seen, and has offered the man in question a brief example of his reasoning, and then Jesus seems to just ignore it all, and he starts talking instead about something that's not just completely different, but utterly strange on its own terms as well. Has Jesus listened to the man at all? And more: Has he genuinely heard him?

> The art of conversation is the art of hearing
> as well as of being heard.
> William Hazlitt

Do we have here an egregiously inexplicable failure to communicate? As arguably one of the leading ethical lights in history, and especially as an extraordinary person presenting himself as the Son of God, surely Jesus can't be displaying a rude disregard to answer straightforwardly a well-intentioned and curious visitor. Likewise, it's not likely that he's simply distracted or unable to understand what counts as an appropriate reply, on hearing such a stunning and insightful revelation from this top religious leader. So, what on earth, or in heaven's name, is Jesus doing?

The answer is a key that will unlock our puzzles. Jesus has actually listened carefully, heard well, and understood fully. He's also responding directly and quite deeply to what his visitor has said. The freelance rabbi is conveying to Nicodemus in reply to his remarks that the intrinsically valuable actions of observing, reasoning, and drawing true conclusions are not the most important activities for understanding him and relating to him properly. Changing your life is. Rather than commending the intellectual game Nicodemus has played well, Jesus instantly challenges him to redirect his energies and become more concerned with his heart than his head. His focus should be on the opportunity for personal metamorphosis that Jesus provides. Nicodemus needs to engage in a change so fundamental that it can be described insightfully as being born a second time. Jesus is more interested in transformational actions than in intellectual conclusions.

> The living self has one purpose only:
> to come into its own fullness of being.
> D.H. Lawrence

I can get my dog's attention and point to a beautifully yellow full moon just visible over the trees, but rather than directing her gaze heavenward and joining me in my cosmic musings, she'll just lick my finger. And such reactions aren't confined to our canine friends. As a university professor, I once returned home from a retreat with several corporation presidents after we had philosophized together in a famous cloud forest and then at a small fishing village on the coast of Costa Rica where I had come to some incredible and life-changing insights. I shared a few of these exciting discoveries with great exuberance the next day in my advanced senior seminar at Notre Dame. I expected faces of astonishment and wonder around the table, and perhaps even exclamations of heart-felt delight from some of the more deeply contemplative students, but all I experienced as a result of my dramatic revelations was the sight of them hunched over their notebooks, quickly writing down what I was saying, in presumed preparation for the next exam. I couldn't get them to see the moon that day, either. The exciting ideas I was pointing to and expounding didn't seem to have any bite. I had forgotten the basic truth that some insights won't resonate deeply in us until we've had a sufficiently rich and relevant range of experience in the world. The ideas that for one person constitute no more than new information can spark for another a mind-blowing and life-altering realization.

If I were to bring a group of people some powerful ideas that could change their lives for the better and all they were concerned about in response was the scholarly history of how I had come to discover these things and in what way the concepts I'd articulated might reflect on the lives and thoughts of the great philosophers in the past who first hinted at crucial aspects of these notions, then I would have failed. Or, perhaps, we all would have failed.

For their part, my conversation partners would not be taking full advantage of the opportunity they had. The whole point of my presentation would have been derailed and we would have gone off the tracks into the surrounding underbrush. I would be extremely disappointed. And in at least this regard, I could understand how Jesus must have felt when he was dealing with smart people like Nicodemus who just didn't get what was supposed to be happening. The man wanted information. Jesus offered radical change. The real issue at stake was alchemy.

> Thoughts, like fleas, jump from man to man.
> But they don't bite everybody.
> Stanislaw Lec

This brings us back to the surprising and problematic passage in Mark's Gospel, chapter four, where Jesus says that he teaches the crowds in parables, "so that they indeed may see but not perceive, and hear but not understand; lest they should turn again, and be forgiven." This perplexing verse can be understood in the light of what we've learned from the exchange between Jesus and Nicodemus.

The mission of Jesus was not one of communicating simple information and then motivating people to quick assent and superficial affiliation. He preferred to teach them in a way that would require their active participation while listening, so that genuine, deep, and transformative understanding more likely could result. To this end then, his discourse became parabolic. Parables engage the imagination and not just the intellect. They touch the heart. And this is important because the imagination is always more apt than mere intellect to elicit emotion and move the will. In addition, parables sometimes puzzle and always entice. They invite an investment of thought and inner energy. In fact, they demand it. And they somehow indicate modes of appropriate action that we can take in our lives as a result of what we come to understand by their narration. They remind us how inner seeing can at times suggest or even require personal becoming.

The true seeing is within.
George Eliot

We'll circle back to a related issue in the next chapter when we explore together what a leader needs to do to motivate real change in an organization or with any group of people, including his or her own family. Without a compelling story that draws people in, a simple tale that conveys a vision of what can be and how we can make it happen, we're rarely able to help people initiate major change in their behavior. On a subjectively personal level, unless we construct for ourselves such a simple and vivid tale about the need for a new pattern of action in our own lives, we rarely convince ourselves in a visceral and emotional way that any big change we're considering is really important. And yet, that's often a necessary condition for accomplishing genuine transformation. A parable conveys a vivid vision of what is and can be. It does so in such a way as to reach us emotionally and move us with its warnings or its portrayal of positive possibilities. A good parable is precisely a story aimed at commitment and action.

Jesus explains to his close disciples that he talks to them in one way and to the crowds in another way. Why? For one thing, the disciples have already undergone an inner transformation and have made a major commitment to follow him. The crowds are full of people who are merely curious, looking for novel ideas to tickle their ears. They're hoping for some simple answers with magical results. In this respect, they're like many people in our own culture, and even within the world of business today. Everyone's eager to hear The Next Big Idea. We're all consumers of bold concepts. The brightest of us go around collecting ideas that we find interesting. But then what do we do with them?

To dispose a soul to action, we must upset its equilibrium.
Eric Hoffer

Jesus seeks to stimulate people's thoughts, excite their imaginations, capture their hearts, and help them start down a path of genuine change. He wants them to become active in what they do with his words. His aims with his already committed disciples are subtly different. He's speaking to them in a distinctive way—that is, more plainly and straightforwardly at this stage—because the right fundamental changes have already happened in their lives, and he's preparing them now for their own teaching missions. They're hearing everything the crowds are hearing, because they're present on such public occasions, but they're also being told more. They get the story behind the stories in order to prepare them to be teachers and transformative leaders in their own right.

Jesus isn't trying to mystify and confuse the bigger crowds with his parables. He's not seeking to hide the truth from them. If he were, then indeed what would be the point of speaking at all? Obviously, he's going to some trouble to talk to them and teach them well. He's dedicated himself to this. He's even risking his life to do it. He cares deeply about the people he addresses. He knows he has limited time with them and he's trying to make the most of it in order to have a major impact within them. He's presenting the truth and cloaking it only enough that his listeners will have to work a bit to uncover and understand it. He's encouraging a personal investment regarding that truth.

Investing in the Truth
The Gospel of Mark, chapter four, continues like this:

> (21) And he said to them, "Is a lamp brought in to be put under a bushel basket, or under a bed and not on a stand? (22) For there is nothing hid, except to be made manifest;

nor is anything secret, except to come to light. (23) If any man has ears to hear, let him hear."

Jesus wants the truth he's teaching to be known at the right time and in the proper way for each of his listeners. Then it can provide the light for their lives that they need, as well as important illumination for the people they're around. The next two verses from the passage are crucial:

> (24) And he said to them, "Take heed what you hear— the measure you give will be the measure you get, and still more will be given to you. (25) For to him who has will more be given; and from him who has not, even what he has will be taken away."

This is another statement that can seem problematic on a casual reading of the text. People who already have much will be given even more, and those who have little will lose even that? This sounds more like a badly unfair tax policy and overall economic agenda than anything like the announcement of a divinely fair conception of giving and taking. But we should read this passage in the light of its overall context.

If you bring much to the hearing of Jesus' words—attention, concentration, commitment, and active implementation—then you'll be given even more in your life as a result. You will be changed. If you bring little to the hearing of those words, then what little you have brought will be lost. The time you spent in passive listening, for one thing, will be wasted and gone. Nothing new will spring forth as a result. The situation will be one of net loss. And the same will be true of a casual, half-hearted attempt to understand and implement. It's only those who put in the ample time, energy, and creative effort to fully grasp and use what they've heard who will reap a good return from their investment.

Strongly spent is synonymous with kept.
Robert Frost

Think of this again in terms of soil. Jesus is sowing some meta-phorical seed. If you bring him fertile soil, you'll end up with that good soil and lots of crops, which means a great increase. If you bring him poor soil, and even worse, very little of it, you'll not only fail to get the crops you need, but you'll eventually lose even the meager amount of bad soil you had. When poor or shallow soil can't support plant life with root systems to hold that soil in place, any water or even wind that comes along can erode it all away. This is the way of physical nature. It's human nature as well.

In the dialogue *Phaedrus*, composed at some time after Plato's more famous works, the *Republic* and the *Symposium*, and nearly four hundred years before Jesus tells his parable of the soils, the great philosopher represents Socrates as using this same image. This is during a conversation with an individual of his acquaintance for whom the dialogue is named, a man called Phaedrus. Interestingly, it's the only Platonic dialogue whose setting is outside the city of Athens. It takes place when Socrates and Phaedrus take a long walk to catch up with each other and talk in the countryside. Socrates later on in the conversation seems to reflect their surroundings by using this agricultural image of seeds and soil. While examining together the most effective forms of communication by which any productive knowledge can be conveyed, Socrates suggests that a good teacher, like a good farmer, "will follow the true principles of agriculture and sow his seed in soil that suits it," and that he will then be well satisfied when a harvest comes at some properly later time. But what exactly is suitable soil for any particular seed? What is it to be good soil? And how is this to be determined and applied in the crucial matter of ideas, implementation, and per-sonal change? What exactly can it mean for our lives? That's our next question. And it's crucial to understand.

The Essence of Good Soil

Here then is my overall suggestion in a nutshell, or perhaps a seed-ling, to use our guiding image from Plato and Jesus: The secret to using any seed of good advice or sound philosophy in such a way as to generate real results in your life is simply bringing it to good soil. The key to getting the most from any new idea or helpful recommendation you come across is the same. Provide good soil. Or, to be more precise: Be good soil. So then, the vital question would be: Is there good soil in your life? And to put the question more directly: Are you good soil? Or are you, right now, a fairly poor locus or receptacle for any intellectual, spiritual, or concep-tual planting?

Masters of innovative change and deep transformation are always good, rich soil. Because of that, they are the ideal partners for great ideas and new possibilities. So it's important to explore this powerful metaphor just a bit more. Its lesson is vital.

Good Soil in Your Life

Healthy change, or positive transformation in the form of personal growth, is not possible without good soil. But think about soil for a minute. Initially, it can seem like the most inert thing imaginable. It's dirt. It just lies there. It appears completely and absolutely pas-sive. The farmer sows the seed, and the soil is present to receive it.

On this understanding, in order to be good soil, you'd just need to be an open-minded, passive receptacle, allowing new ideas to enter your awareness and germinate. You'd have to be a little like the philosopher John Locke's famous image of the mind as a blank tablet on which experience can write. And even such a minimal requirement as this isn't easy for many people. Unfortunately, some of us seem to be more like impermeable, slick, and almost self-erasing surfaces. It's indeed important to be able to take in and retain what we encounter. But being good soil requires much more than that.

There is life in the ground; it goes into the seeds; and
it also, when it is stirred up, goes into the man who stirs it.
Charles Dudley Warner

To the casual glance, soil can indeed look passive and inert. But appearances can be misleading, and they're very deceptive here. I once asked a biologist what makes for good soil. He said that the best way to express it is to contrast fertile soil with its sterile counterpart. Sterile soil has no microbes, no bacteria, no decaying matter, and no grubs and earthworms or any other active life forms in it. Good soil, fertile soil, has in it all these things. According to Paul Bogard, the author of *The Ground Beneath Us*: "A teaspoon of healthy soil holds millions of species, and far more microorganisms than there are people on earth." There's tremendous energy in good soil. There's always immense activity and the dynamic becoming of real life in it.

To be good soil you have to bring your own personal energy and activity to reading or hearing new ideas, and then to processing and using them. You can't be passive or inert. There's an activist imperative at work. Good soil actually partners up with the seed to create a plant. It's a cosmic collaboration, or something metaphorically akin to a team effort. A good listener or reader is a partner with the teacher or text. A great existential alchemist is always ready to invest mental and emotional energy into a real collaboration with ideas and opportunities, and by doing this he or she can bring new things to life. Real life metamorphosis is always a dynamic process that's engaged in and even performed by an energized agent of change.

The energy of the mind is the essence of life.
Aristotle

Many years ago in the large auditoriums where I lectured at the University of Notre Dame, I sometimes could tell that my students wanted to view me as a philosophical performer, an enlightened entertainer of sorts, and they correspondingly liked to think of themselves as the astute and demanding, yet always appreciative, audience. It was "The Tom Morris Show," and they were season ticket holders. I was at work, and they were there to relax and enjoy the show. Because of this, one of the things I tried to impress on them at the start of each semester is that every great learning experience is a partnership. I was more like an Outward Bound guide than a Broadway performer. I had been up the mountain many times before and knew the terrain well, so I'd be able to help them with their ascent. But ultimately, they had to work hard to pull themselves up the side of the peak alongside me, and of course with my encouragement and direction. We were supposed to be genuine partners. If my students and I didn't all think of ourselves in this way as partners within a joint enterprise and act accordingly, something important would be lost and we could never create the fundamental changes that a great education can produce. Their energy and action was every bit as important as mine. They had to be good soil or else we couldn't produce something great.

The Results of Good Soil

Good ideas need to have fertile soil in which to grow. Are you rich and fertile soil? It's not enough to contain decaying matter. That would be far too easy. You need to embody positive energy. You have to bring a lot to the mix. Then, the parable of the soils tells us, you'll get much more as a result of your investment than what you had at the start. You can experience a tremendous increase. And in that manner, working with the right ideas in small or large ways, your business, career, relationships, and life can in various respects be born anew. This, and nothing less, is the point.

It's really no surprise that such a powerful metaphor for personal alchemy should come from agriculture. In the sweep of our early history, one of the first experiences of alchemistic transformation must have been the observed metamorphosis of seed to

plant to harvest, and of harvest grain to flour, and then of flour
to bread. The alchemy of the field, farm, mill, and kitchen, and
then ultimately, of digestion and human growth and power can
appear to be a surprisingly magical result that comes from the
bread, flour, grain, and of course, the seed and soil. The laws of
transformation lie deep in the cosmic dust and all the universal
processes around us. We are not called to do something in our
dealings with change or challenge that's unnatural and out of step
with the universal matrix within which we live. In fact, alchemy is
all around us. It's within us. And nothing could be more natural
than its apparent magic. We're just called to take it up and use it
well in our work and lives. Then we become the agents of alchemy
we're meant to be.

And now, believe it or not, we still need to finish the passage
in The Gospel of Mark, chapter four where we've been digging
around for wisdom. There's important insight yet to be harvested.
Verse twenty-six continues the presentation of a crucial idea, as
Jesus once more uses his now familiar farming images:

> (26) And he said, "The kingdom of God is as if a man
> should scatter seed on the ground, (27) and should sleep
> and rise night and day, and the seed should sprout and
> grow, he knows not how. (28) The earth produces of itself,
> first the blade, then the ear, and then finally the full grain
> in the ear. (29) But when the grain is ripe, he then puts it
> to the blade, because the harvest has come."

Once real wisdom gets into properly fertile personal soil, it will
grow. This will happen when we're awake and while we're asleep.
We don't have to know exactly or even approximately how it grows.
It still will do so. That's the way this works. And what's really great
is that the growth will lead to a harvest. This represents the point
where what has been growing becomes useful, for example to make
bread and to feed the people around us, as well as ourselves. That's

the intended purpose of the words of Jesus, and of any sound wisdom teaching: to yield a harvest of usefulness that will enhance
our lives in a broad way. We can even be assured that great things
can result:

> (30) And he said, "With what can we compare the king-
> dom of God, or what parable shall we use for it? (31) It's like
> a grain of mustard seed, which, when sown on the ground,
> is the smallest of all the seeds on earth; (32) yet, when it's
> sown, it grows up and becomes the greatest of all shrubs,
> and puts forth large branches, so that the birds of the air
> can make nests in its shade."

Of course, if these are the same birds that are so keen on plucking up any stray seed that falls along the path, we'd better continue
to be on our guard. But it's indeed reassuring to be told that even
the smallest of seeds can yield great results. That's the hope of any
dedicated teacher and of every change agent. It's the desire of any
leader with a new and innovative vision that he or she wants to
share with other people. And it's always my aspiration as a philosopher, public speaker, and advisor, whenever I bring the seeds of
useful ideas on any topic to a group of people. Within the claims
of the text in front of us, it's only the kingdom of God that's guar-
anteed to grow with such impressive magnitude. But I believe we
can have a parallel well-grounded expectation for any great ideas if
we introduce them to authentically good soil.

Do what you can, with what you have, where you are.
Theodore Roosevelt

We can facilitate change in all the ways we need to if we are
good soil. The equally reassuring news is that even if we haven't
been good soil in the past, we can become so at any time by being

more open, humble, and eager, and by bringing a new energy and activity to the ideas we see or hear that can make a positive difference in our lives. Part of our own inner good soil will be the several individual elements from the art of adaptation that we've been discussing: our self-control, our positive action, and our use of the universal facilitating conditions for achievement recognized by the great practical philosophers. Another part will be the depth and extent of our personal engagement and investment in the process.

This is the secret to transformative work of any kind. And, to shift back to our large scale governing metaphor, this is what it takes to be an exceptional lemonade maker. We need to open, active, and personally committed to producing something great. The art of innovative transformation always begins within us. And it's ultimately in our nature to practice it well.

7

TEAM LEMONADE

Juicing It Up Together

IT'S HARD ENOUGH TO HANDLE THE CHALLENGE OF CHANGE
well in our own lives as individuals, or to initiate something very
new for you when no one else's involvement is required. But it's
another level of difficulty when we try to help other people change
in basic ways. It can be surprisingly hard to convince others to alter
their behavior in even trivial respects. They may experience any of
our efforts in this regard, at least initially, as if we were handing
them a bunch of sour lemons. And those, in turn, they'll quickly
toss back to us. So, launching change well with others can mean
making lemonade together.

In this chapter, we're going to examine what it takes to lead
change, encourage innovation, and make transformative lemonade
with any group of people, whether it's a global business, a national
company, a regional enterprise, a local store, a community organization, a small office, or even your own family. We're going to identify
the most common obstacles to any social change effort and look at
the best strategies for overcoming them. People sometimes disap-
point us. And we can let them down. But if we can come to understand more deeply what we all need, we can do great things together.
The path isn't always smooth, but it can lead to spectacular results.

To be social is to be forgiving.
Robert Frost

A business consultant I met years ago told me that he was writing a book on "The Three Stages of Change." But he didn't go on to explain what he meant. The first thing that ran through my mind was that in many organizations, those stages far too often seem to be resistance, reluctance, and relapse. But it need not be that way at all. We can team up to create something new and astonishing together, if we just understand how.

Initiating Change
IN HIS BOOK *CHANGING MINDS,* THE INSIGHTFUL HARVARD psychologist Howard Gardner considers in some depth how we can help others to change. At one juncture, he points out that there are several basic and very different ways to create change in the lives of other people, or throughout a group. He sums it up by saying, "Classically, change takes place through compulsion, manipulation, persuasion, or through some combination thereof." His statement will repay a bit of reflection.

Compulsion, Manipulation, and Persuasion
Compulsion involves force or fear, or both. Manipulation, as distinct from compulsion and persuasion, typically depends on praise, pressure, or promises, and even sometimes, subtle warnings, and it requires a measure of deception. In most cases, a person being manipulated would resist it and rebel in anger if he knew it was going on. So, the manipulator has to hide the realities of the process, to at least some extent. As a result, both compulsion and manipulation involve treating other people not as rational centers of free choice, but rather as objects to be pushed or pulled into whatever new behaviors we desire. Persuasion, by contrast, at least in principle treats others with a measure of respect as autonomous

individuals who have minds that need to understand and value a new course of action as a condition of being properly motivated to engage in it. Throughout history, the best leaders have been great teachers, and the best teachers have always used the techniques of persuasion in a spirit of respect, in order to change the thought and behavior of others for the better. Persuasion creates allies in a way that compulsion and manipulation cannot. And this arises in part as a result of the element of respect, as well as from a meeting of minds through shared values.

If you have some respect for people as they are, you can be more effective in helping them to become better than they are.
John Gardner

People respond most favorably to leaders who treat them well, show them respect, and act toward them with honor. We're all more open to moving in new directions when we're being asked to do so by individuals who demonstrate they care about us and appreciate us for who we are, as well as for what we can do and be.

If we seek to force others into changed behavior or attempt to manipulate them into doing something new, we face some basic problems. People don't like to be pushed into anything. And we all naturally resent most forms of manipulation. Plus, in most circumstances, either of these approaches is just wrong because of how it devalues people. Honest persuasion is the high road or fully ethical path to eliciting altered behavior in others. And, as such, it's the only sustainable method by which to launch and maintain important forms of change. But even it bumps up against problems.

We all have obstacles in our lives that can hinder us from changing when we need to change. Unfortunately, not everyone is equally prepared for, or open at all times to, positive transformation. Not many people stand poised and ready to approach a chance to change with enthusiasm. A leader needs to keep in mind the enormous variety of life influences that can either help or hinder any effort at transformation. If we ignore the important emotional and psychological side of change, we can be shocked at how some particular and much needed innovation that obviously seems so right can get diffused and watered down, and end up not being made by the people we've trusted with its implementation. We can often be surprised to the point of incomprehension at how difficult it is to lead change.

> Difficulty gives all things their value.
> Montaigne

But that's Ok. We don't often celebrate easy things. Deep satisfaction doesn't typically arise from our accomplishment of things that are simple or nearly effortless. When a good and needed change has been difficult to make, we can all grow from the experience and even come to an eventual pride in the result that would not have been the same without what we had to overcome along the way. Some of the difficulties we face can strengthen and enrich us as we pursue worthy goals. Doing what's hard cultivates the virtue of hardihood, which then prepares us for better handling things that lie ahead.

The Challenge of Leading Change
Challenging change almost always meets some form of resistance. If we neglect to deal with that resistance or underestimate its strength, we won't likely gain the degree of transformation we may want to see in the lives and behaviors of the people around us. I wasn't just joking to wonder about whether the three stages of change in many organizations might not be simply resistance, reluctance, and relapse. This is too often the exact sequence we see taking place.

Of course, there are times when it can seem like it's almost too easy to effect a change and make a big difference in other people's lives, and that can mislead us into thinking that helping others initiate important changes is going to be much simpler than it most often is. A casual conversation can transform a life. A book recommendation can alter a business. Hearing just the right talk by the right speaker can revolutionize a career. A new colleague can arrive and energize a department. But as we all know, these are relatively rare situations. It's not usually that easy to bring lasting change to others.

Let's briefly use some of the images from the parable of the soils that we explored in the previous chapter. Clearly, a best-case scenario for leading change in the lives of others comes about when (1) a seasoned spreader of change (2) expertly introduces (3) high-quality seed into (4) very good soil, and then (5) tends the garden well, under (6) highly favorable conditions. Sometimes, four of these factors will get the job done. And occasionally, just three may do. And yet, in all cases, good soil has to be in the mix.

> We cannot make it rain, but we can see to it
> that the rain falls on prepared soil.
> Henry J. Nouwen

The parable of the soils warns us about assuming that the issue of success or failure with the propagation of change always turns on questions regarding the sower, the sowing, or the seed. Very often, the most basic issue is the soil. When we seek to do our jobs as change agents, we have to keep in mind that there are many kinds of soil in the world and in our group or organization, and all sorts of conditions that may promote or prevent our ideas and efforts from taking hold and growing in other people's lives. Obviously, we need to do whatever we can to sow well the best seed for change, while knowing at the same time that the results lie ultimately in the soil. The work we do when we act as leaders of change should be as high in quality as possible from the very first moment we begin to seek transformation, since things that start badly more often than not tend to end in exactly the same way. But not even our best efforts as change initiators can guarantee the results we want if we've started out with poor soil.

A bad beginning makes for a bad ending.
Euripides

Ultimately, it's the soil that will most crucially determine whether a new planting has any chance of success at all. And this truth carries important implications. First, if you occupy an executive, managerial, or supervisory role, or any other form of official leadership position in an organization, this is one more reason to make sure you hire the best people you can find and place them in positions that are right for them. Only that will begin to give your enterprise the best soil you can provide. In a family situation or in a fully volunteer organization, of course, the approach has to mostly skip this stage. You can't advertise for, interview, and hire your kids, in-laws, cousins, or your parents. You work with what you have and try to encourage the people involved to provide the best soil they can for whatever changes are needed.

Then ideally, with a healthy measure of the right soil in place, you need to cultivate and fertilize it on a regular basis, but not with the meager compost of scraps and leavings that many companies toss at employees. That's not the fertilizer I have in mind. You need to use the very best soil enhancers understood by all our greatest philosophers and wisest leaders—such fundamental factors as I've described and explained in the book *If Aristotle Ran General Motors: The New Soul of Business*. These elements of enrichment are, quite simply, the transcendent universal values of: Truth, Beauty, Goodness, and Unity. When you attend to the intellectual, aesthetic, moral, and spiritual needs of people—showing a little care, kindness, and respect to others by doing whatever you can to provide these four foundations of greatness in their environment, it can be amazing how fertile the soil in their lives and throughout the group may become.

We should always, in the most general and empathetic sense, treat people the way we would want to be treated if we were in their place, with all their morally legitimate interests and preferences, following the ancient Golden Rule along each of the four most fundamental dimensions of our experience: the intellectual dimension (targeting Truth), the aesthetic dimension (aiming at Beauty), the moral dimension (requiring Goodness), and the spiritual dimension (moving toward Unity).

> The seeds must be carefully chosen;
> they must fall on good ground;
> they must be sedulously tended, if the vivifying fruits
> are to be at hand when needed.
> Winston Churchill

When we treat others in all the ways we would want to be treated with respect to Truth, Beauty, Goodness, and Unity, we cultivate and enhance the spiritual soil in their lives. By acting in these ways, we'll tend our garden well. Then, when we want something new and different and powerfully good to grow, the conditions will be the best we can create for it to happen. We'll have positioned everyone well for metamorphosis.

The Transformative Leader

Any of us in leadership positions should be asking ourselves on a regular basis what kind of soil we are as individuals and initiators of innovation. We often need to be engaged in the age-old Socratic challenge of self-examination, making sure that at all times we are preparing the best soil in our own lives that we can have, so that we can make the most of any new seed of insight or opportunity that we come across along the way. The simple truth is that we can't do our best to help others create the change they need unless we're first living as artists of transformative change ourselves.

It's nearly a psychological truism. Leaders should model the excellence of adaptation and change initiation they want to see in others. In fact, many students of positive transformation have pointed out that the two most important things any leader can do to encourage beneficial change in an organization are, first, to tell a simple but powerful story about the change that's needed—why it's important, and what good it will produce for everyone involved—and, second, to show that this story resonates in his or her own life. Tell and show. Show and tell. People tend to follow those who practice what they preach and live what they teach. The most powerfully persuasive factor of all in moving others, and the most potent testimony that a particular path is indeed the right way is the sight of a life lived in harmony with its own advice.

> Example is the best instruction.
> Aesop

Most of us know that to understand what another person really believes, we should pay attention to his actions far more than his words. A leader attempting to persuade others to change needs to remember this and take care to live the elements of that change in every relevant way within the bounds of his life and work. Then he can inspire others to change as well. This is so important that there has actually been a website selling T-shirts, caps, tote-bags, sweat shirts, kitchen aprons, coffee mugs, and, believe it or not, classic white cotton thongs emblazoned with the slogan, in various font sizes: "Practice What You Preach." Modeling a new behavior is the best first step toward persuading others to adopt it. We have to show it to share it.

Why do new programs work in some companies but not in others? Why are some change initiatives successful in one context but not in another? The parable of the soils has given us some helpful insights we can use to understand this. In any organizational context, we're dealing with real people who have habits, hopes, fears, and such attitudes as anxiety and pride. We ourselves have all of that in us. We need to remember the importance of cultivating good soil in all our lives, in season and out, so that when the time is right for a new direction, an innovation, a fundamental transformation, or a change of any sort, we'll be people who are prepared to respond well and fully do our part. Any great change leader first leads the way in preparation, then in transition.

Whenever you want to plant a new idea or policy and reap great results, ask yourself, "Have I properly prepared the soil?" If the honest answer is yes, then you're in the best position for launching a new change. If the answer is no, then you have some important preliminary work to do before you can take on the challenge of promoting change. Any grower's greatest resource is the soil.

Change And The Power of Habit

THERE'S A CENTRAL REASON IT'S NORMALLY NOT AS EASY AS we'd like to bring new ideas into the lives of the people around us and see those ideas make the difference we have in mind. Implementing a new way of thinking, shifting a major focus, or introducing a novel procedure for doing things in any organizational context involves changing people's habits of thought and action. And, as we all know well from personal experience, habits have a certain inner weight that produces a real resistance to change. Until the novel ideas or new proposals can overcome that resistance and replace habitual ways of thinking, feeling, and acting, they are, in effect, inert. When new ideas do manage to get a real grip on people and inspire actual change, they can provide a powerful leverage for needed growth and new forms of effective action. They provide the seeds of new habits.

Habit is oddly both a difficulty and a necessity. It makes change hard. But then it makes change stick. Old habits are tough to break.

New habits are challenging to create. But once fresh habits are up and running over a period of time and with a new stability of their own, real change successfully has been made. We've engaged the help of a new and powerful force to push the new behavior forward.

The Natural Purpose of Habit
A primary difficulty we face in launching any change is that we have to overcome and alter current habit, and habit can be one of the strongest forces in life. It's easy to understand why. After exposure to a novel situation has elicited a new behavioral response, for instance, a solution to a problem or a new form of action with a successful outcome, our minds store up the connection. A further situation that can be seen as similar to the one already handled well will then evoke a similar response without all the time, energy, thought, or risk that dealing with the initial circumstances might have required. This automatic natural process of recognition and repetition frees up our mental energy and conscious decision-making skills precisely for the purpose of handling any genuinely new situations that we can identify as something we haven't seen before.

Habit takes care of the familiar so that we can use our energy on the new. And this makes a lot of sense. But the deep irony of human psychology here is that the habits of thought and action meant to deal with familiar ground can at times prevent us from recognizing true novelty when it does cross our paths. The mind is so keen to view a new situation as really not that different at all, but as version of what it's already handled well that it will tend to highlight common patterns in what's new and discount the less familiar aspects of the situation, which can be a big problem.

> Man like every other animal is by nature indolent.
> If nothing spurs him on, then he will hardly think,
> and will behave from habit like an automaton.
> Albert Einstein

The mind is a most paradoxical device. On the one hand, it's ever changing, dealing with new stimuli and varying perceptual data moment-to-moment, continually regulating the body under subtly new conditions, and constantly seeking to acquire any fresh information or insight that will protect and help us. On the other hand, all this continuous activity requires so much energy and focus that the mind naturally tends to maintain an inherent reticence concerning any apparent novelty of considerable magnitude that's proposed to it. It won't be prepared to change in any major way unless it's convinced that the change is either strictly necessary or at least overwhelmingly useful. Because of this, it has a stubbornly strong unconscious tendency to perceive and interpret new situations in terms of old ones, and react accordingly.

This tendency to favor already established and proven behaviors would not have developed and survived through the multitude of generations past unless it was generally an effective way of relating to the world. But here's the twist. The mind is so set on using what it already knows to illuminate any new situation that this can actually distort what it sees and present us with a misleading gloss of similarity when we should be noting the differences. In this way, our preexisting categories and tendencies of thought can prevent our recognizing the need for change when it genuinely confronts us. And these categories, along with their associated habits of response, can offer serious resistance to making a change of any kind, however genuinely beneficial and even urgent it might be.

The prominent twentieth century British philosopher Bertrand Russell once told a simple story about a chicken who had so often seen his owner approaching him each day carrying a bucket of delectable food, that he had developed a firm habit of dinner expectation connected with the man's appearance in the coop, an expectation that inclined him to run to the farmer in eager anticipation of the presumed treat. Then one day, the farmer approached him carrying something notably different, but the chicken, more taken with the similarities of the situation than the differences of this particular development, ended up to his great surprise not having but being dinner.

Habit can keep us from seeing what's new and different and calls for a stark alteration of behavior. What we need to understand is that our natural resistance to change can be operative even when we do see a need for change, or it can work much more subversively to keep us from noticing any need for change at all. At either juncture, it inhibits us from the transformative alchemy that we otherwise could be performing to our own advantage and to the great benefit of others around us. The past range of experience that ought to help us move forward can instead be a force that holds us back.

> Everyone is a prisoner of his own experiences.
> Edward R. Murrow

Our innate mental inertia also creates a natural slippage for new behavior to revert back to old patterns. That's why the natural arc of change is so often indeed the three stages of resistance, reluctance, and relapse. The emotional lure of the comfortable, known, and proven is strong, and easily gives rise to deep anxiety whenever we seriously contemplate or actually enter the foreign territory of the new and unknown. A natural aversion to the cause of that anxiety pulls us back to familiar routines.

Like many other natural processes, the mind's fundamental and reasonable tendency to use habit as much as possible is not infallible in its functioning. It can misfire and produce precisely the opposite results from what we need, and from what it evolved to provide. Because of this, we should always be watching for those times when the normally effective conservative impulse of the mind that's meant to free up our time and energy for spotting and dealing with the new actually inhibits our perception of new things, and prevents a prompt and proper response to them.

If the world was mostly stable and change was relatively rare, the conservative tendency of the mind would not present much of a problem. In primal societies living with the regular cycles of nature, it functioned well. But at the current stage of human history, rapid and continual change is our new undeniable reality, so we have to train our minds to get with the program and go with the flow of adaptation and innovation. And yet, reversing such long embedded tendencies isn't fast or easy. So the question arises: How can we most effectively act to change our habits of thought and conduct?

The Two Kinds of Habit Change

We first should bear this in mind. In addition to the inner mechanisms that make innovation in our behavior difficult, the world around us sometimes seems to rise up and resist any effort on our part to do things very differently. Our environment may contain endless reminders of the old ways, and these marks of the past can have what seems like a strong gravitational force pulling us back. For every circle of people around us that we do manage to convince to try something new, there are others they deal with outside that circle who may question their new direction and plant in their minds many convincing seeds of doubt. Sometimes, the world around us seems to demand new things. And at other times, it appears to resist them just as mightily.

> There is always an inertia to overcome in striking out
> a new line of conduct—not more in ourselves, it seems,
> than in circumscribing events, which appear as if leagued
> together to allow no novelties in the way of amelioration.
> Thomas Hardy

So for many reasons, the common human resistance to change isn't hard to understand. It stems from diverse sources, including deeply entrenched mechanisms of the mind. And because of this, we don't need to conclude from any initially recalcitrant behavior that the people around us are just acting like idiots in the face of either opportunity or challenge. If we approach helping others to change, as well as helping ourselves, through being part psychologist, part therapist, part coach, and even part cheerleader, with a baseline of sound philosophy as our guide, we can actually enjoy a strong chance of making the difference we want to make with real change.

But just explaining things clearly and using reason with others, as well as within our own minds, is never alone enough to create a transformation in habitual behaviors. We also need to use the one power we have that's greater than reason: the imagination.

As we've already seen, imagination is vitally important for dealing well with the change that comes to us. It could even be even more important for launching the change that will happen only because of us. We'll have to do something to get our own imaginations in gear and then spark the imaginations of others, and work hard to put in place and reinforce the new patterns of behavior that are needed. Imagination is key.

> The world of reality has its bounds;
> the world of imagination is boundless.
> Jean-Jacques Rousseau

Only a proper use of this vivid mental and moral faculty can powerfully move us from new information and ideas to a real and positive change of habits and genuinely new behavior. An involvement of the imagination is always crucial. We'll explore this more in the next section. But unless we first grasp the full nature of the challenge we're up against when we try to facilitate change among others, we'll typically fall short when we attempt to create something new. With a greater understanding of the obstacles we face, we can make a more targeted and effective use of the tools we have.

There are two kinds of habit change: augmentation and replacement. Current habits can be augmented by new behaviors into an expanded set of routines, or old habits can be eliminated and replaced by new ones. It's often hard enough to create positive new habits in augmentation of what we're already doing. Such habits get established and thrive only with effort, reinforcement, repetition, experience, and time. But what's even harder is habit replacement, which involves both uprooting the old and creating the new.

One of the most difficult challenges in life generally is to get rid of bad habits, or established tendencies to act in particular ways that are pleasant or comfortable but are not currently effective, and substitute for them better patterns instead. The hardest bad habits to abandon are those that were once good to have in a very different environment. First of all, it can be tough to convince anyone that a long-term positive habit has become outdated and ineffective. Habits of thought and feeling track and support habits of behavior, and the thoughts and feelings attached to a particular habit can distort or prevent any perception that it needs to be changed. This is perhaps why so perceptive an intellect as Samuel Beckett once wrote that, "Habit is the great deadener." A firmly entrenched pattern of thought and action can indeed deaden us to new realizations we need. And then, the resistance goes even deeper. When we do finally become convinced that our old habits need to change, we can still find ourselves oddly acting in accordance with the exact patterns we want to drop. The Apostle Paul, who was one of the major evangelists of the new Christian movement when it was just beginning to take root in the world and who also authored many of the earliest New Testament writings, famously admitted in his letter to the Romans that he often found himself doing what he didn't want to do and not doing what he did want. Habit can be that powerful in our lives.

Habit couldn't be as helpful as it needs to be unless it was as strong as it is. The people around us aren't stubbornly set in their ways just to be difficult and drive us crazy, at least, not most of the time. Their widespread aversion to change has deep and tangled roots. As we've seen, the strongest natural resistance to anything new is based in ancient tendencies of the mind that have worked fairly well in most situations through history. But those very same tendencies can make it unexpectedly hard for us to do what needs to be done in novel circumstances that call out for innovative change.

We are as much automaton as reason.
Blaise Pascal

Once we fundamentally understand this inclination of the mind in its normal operations, however, and see clearly how it can act as an unhelpful obstacle to needed innovation, we can gain better control over the exact nature of the challenge we face when working to launch something new.

Helping Others Change

HABIT CHANGE OF EITHER BASIC KIND, AUGMENTATION OR replacement, can be accomplished in either of two ways: First, by a powerful single event that galvanizes people's imaginations and sets their emotions on fire, or else by a series of smaller events over time. In principle, a highly motivating single event could be either positive or negative in its nature, or in its perception by those needing to change. A positive example might be the one-time offer of a large financial bonus to any who would change their behavior in a desired way. But the resources for this sort of incentive are not readily available at most times in most organizations. And even when they are, such extrinsic motivators as one-time incentives have a surprisingly short shelf life. The behavior they launch tends not to last. Once the money's changed hands, the motivation eventually dwindles.

Unfortunately, the only commonly available kind of single event that typically has any chance of resulting in a full, effective, and lasting habit change is something very different and disruptive—the occurrence of a disaster, or else the sudden realization that such an event looms menacingly near on the horizon. It will be useful for us at this point to examine this sort of one-time negative event and how it can function effectively, or else also fail to motivate and sustain needed change.

Catastrophe and Behavior Modification
The connection between catastrophe and change is simple. A disaster tends to wake people up from their often-customary level of nearly sleepwalking through life. It can jump-start the drowsy or even dead imaginations of everyone involved. After the wonder years of childhood and early adolescence, throughout adulthood most people's imaginations are in many respects at least moribund, if not actually resting in peace. And that's a tragedy, since the imagination can be a unique source of power. A crisis that's bad enough can spark people's imaginations back to life. And once their imaginations are back up and running, even radical change can happen.

For a long time, philosophers have understood basically how this works. The imagination engages the emotions, and in this world it's mainly the emotions that move the will. This connection of cause and effect is simple and often decisive. Disasters can do the needed work of opening us up to change by way of rousing our imaginations and enlisting our emotions in the enterprise. To revert to our overarching metaphor, the mere arrival of lemons in sufficient quantity and size can goad our imaginations toward visions of how we might need to begin to use them to make lemonade.

> Disaster is virtue's opportunity.
> Seneca

Of course, I would never recommend intentionally creating the conditions for this avenue of change initiation, for reasons that can be obvious. Life throws enough disasters at us without our help. A leader who deliberately creates disaster so that good may result isn't a wise and careful guide. Like gives rise to like, and anyone who would do this is typically a disaster himself. The end does not always justify the means. A person in a position of power who thinks he can orchestrate a carefully controlled catastrophe to create positive change often finds that he badly misjudged the potential consequences of the manufactured calamity and ends up in a much worse situation than he had when he started. Devising disasters as a motivational tool is itself a disastrous approach.

There are, of course, many leaders who won't go so far as to create an actual catastrophe in order to inaugurate change, but they will contrive at least the appearance of one to motivate others. It's well known among students of organizational transformation that people aren't usually willing to buy into major change without feeling a sense of urgency about it. So the advice is often given to business executives and managers seeking major change to "create a sense of urgency." This can be very good counsel, as long as it's not misapplied or overdone. It's hard to persuade people to change unless we connect with their emotions. And creating a sense of urgency in the right way can do that well. But it's also easy to do this in a completely wrong way.

I've often heard CEOs use an interesting metaphor here and say that they've seen change best implemented from "a burning platform." If where you're standing is a platform on fire, then naturally you're moved to make a change and go somewhere else as fast as you can. It's a matter of safety and self-preservation that draws on some of the most fundamental human drives. So, in order to facilitate a new program involving change, many executives will work to create a sense of urgency by portraying current conditions in terms that the local Fire Department would recognize.

If it's true that things around you are burning down, then broadcasting that truth as clearly and quickly as possible is a fine way of motivating people to change. But shouting, "Fire!" when

there are no flames is a fast way to lose trust and diminish or eliminate your ability to communicate such information well if it ever
were to be true in the future. Truth is the foundation of trust. And
so we should never be irresponsible about it, but rather always
design our motivational efforts in accordance with it.

Great is the power of truth.
Cicero

The top team doctor at a famous football program once told
me that one of the best known head coaches he had worked for
was comfortable only as a crisis manager. So, he said, whenever
there wasn't a crisis, the coach would create one. But stirring up a
crisis as a management technique is inherently dangerous, ethically
dubious, and even self-defeating over the long run. Orchestrating
merely the appearance of a crisis isn't a good idea either, and is not
a sustainable practice, in addition to its own ethical problems.

Most people are pretty smart—and I include in my general-
ization here even the beefiest members of the offensive line on the
coach's team—and they'll eventually figure out what's going on.
When they do, the credibility of the coach or leader plummets. And
this procedure in any case inevitably becomes increasingly less effective with time. As we've noted, people don't like feeling manipulated. They resent it, and rightly so. Manipulation isn't a path of
respect. Any strategy for creating change that depends on concoct-
ing a catastrophe, a crisis, a false appearance of such a problem, or
even just deceptive rumors of impending doom, is simply a bad idea.

Disasters, Dire Threats, and Real Change
When things are actually bad, and perhaps worse than most of
the people around us might suspect, when even true disaster likely
looms, then it's a necessary and often courageous act to become the
bearer of that news to anyone who will listen. Physicians do this all
the time for their patients. If an individual's weight or unhealthy

habits will soon generate serious problems with blood pressure or perhaps prompt a debilitating disease that can have dire consequences, a doctor should convey this message to the patient in a form that's as engaging and dramatic as possible, while at the same time being professionally responsible and also encouraging as to the potential power of change to turn it all around. And yet, one of the ongoing frustrations faced by primary-care physicians and cardiologists is that even those patients who have been given the most serious warnings will, more often than not, fail to change their behavior as a result. Such is the power of habit. And if a strong threat of likely death issued by a recognized authority won't reliably motivate people to change their ways, then even the most dire warnings of serious trouble in other settings clearly may have their shortcomings.

> Habit puts to sleep the eye of our judgment.
> Montaigne

This leads to an important point. Despite the generally widespread assumption that a real disaster, or even credible warnings of imminent peril, will move people to new patterns of action like nothing else, there is actually a surprisingly high threshold for any catastrophe, or threat of a catastrophe, to act effectively as lasting change agent. It's instructive to recall how, right after the terrorist attacks of September 11, 2001, nearly all journalists and pundits said, "Now, everything's changed." And just months later, it began to be clear around the nation that very little had really changed at all. Then, many years after the fact, recognizing that our ports are still not secure, illegal border crossings are rampant, and little beyond the cosmetic had been done to enhance air travel safety or create a higher level of protection for our cities and crucial infrastructure, from bridges and the electric grid to water supplies and the internet, we can conclude without a doubt that disaster motivation is much less reliable than we ever would have guessed.

Let's consider for a moment the general relationship between threats and behavior change. Many parents seek to motivate children to alter their behavior through issuing threats of various kinds. So do some teachers. Nations threaten nations, and neighbors, each other. Managers and executives have been known to issue threats to employees. Customers sometimes do the same with vendors. The assumption behind all this is that threats can effectively cause change. But we need to examine that belief.

First, there are two kinds of threats. Unfortunately, bad bosses often issue direct threats in a loud voice or with scathing emails as a motivational technique: "Do it or you're done!" What they fail to realize is that the people they've threatened will usually be more offended and alienated than positively motivated, and will then figure out the very least they can do in response to the threat that will still likely allow them to avoid any negative consequences. So, this is not in general an effective maximization strategy for human behavior. It breeds resentment and erodes morale. It also results in people looking for ways to leave and get themselves into a better work environment. And worse yet, those most likely to achieve success in departing will typically be the best people, and so the precise individuals who are normally most likely to succeed in anything.

> There are two great levers for moving men: interest and fear.
> Napoleon

Such a threat tactic is typically inadvisable on simple moral grounds as well. It fails to honor people as people. It doesn't treat them with respect. Pointing out behavioral consequences is one thing. That's just a matter of passing along information. Making a threat goes beyond that, and is ordinarily perceived as both aggressively hostile and also demeaning. And yet, a second kind of threat announcement is quite different. Not all threats are morally or psychologically the same. And the behavioral consequences can be quite different.

An objective, developing situation that involves potential danger can itself properly be considered as a threat. And when people are apprised of the danger, a threat is not made or issued, contrary to the previous example of the bad boss, but we can say that it's conveyed, announced, or described. Warning others of an objective threat is very different from the intentional action of personally and offensively threatening them. And this radically changes the psychological dynamics of the situation. Whenever a manager or executive sees danger looming unless changes are made and explains this clearly to his or her associates, we can think of this as the announcement of a threat or warning, rather than as the making of a threat. And this can have a fully positive impact, under three conditions, which were pointed out to me long ago by my old friend and fellow philosopher, Michael Murray, a man who has since helped to run some of the best philanthropic organizations in the world. So, now, let's turn to Mike's distinctions.

The Three Features of An Effective Threat Warning
To create behavioral change, a threat must be seen as:
1. Credible
2. Imminent
3. Strong

A threat of any sort is more or less effective for inspiring change to the extent that it has the three qualities of credibility, imminence, and strength. First, there must be a credible threat. The report of it or warning about it should be believable. It has to be conveyed by someone who is trusted and is in a position to know and, if at all possible, it should be relayed with clear, supporting evidence that everyone can see. An effective threat announcement or warning needs to be backed by significant probability and to be perceived as such. Few people change their behavior because of mere possibilities, but the high likelihood of a coming disaster can put a crimp in your day and transform your actions immediately. In a famous children's story, the little boy who cried, "Wolf!" too many times lost his credibility and so couldn't issue an effective warning when a dangerous wolf was in fact nearby. Credibility is crucial.

Second, a threat is motivating to the extent that it's perceived as being in some sense imminent, and an effective warning has to convey this. People aren't often moved by remote, far-off dangers. Something that threatens harm this year, or this month, this week, or the next moment will be a more powerful motivator than anything that promises harm ten or twenty years from now. This is one main reason why it's so hard to motivate people to change their behavior in ways relevant to the protection of our natural world. The dangers we face can seem so distant, no matter how extreme they are.

> People live for tomorrow because
> the day after tomorrow is doubtful.
> Nietzsche

We've evolved in such a way that proximity matters for motivation, a perceived closeness in space or time. We react differently to the proximate, nearby, or imminent than we do to the distant or remote. It's a natural, unconscious prioritization program that's always running in our brains. And that's a fact we need to respect if we hope to launch major change. Remote eventualities rarely move people to action now. What's distant won't often excite the imagination to spur instant action.

Immediate danger is different. If a thief puts a gun to your head and demands your wallet, the threat imminence is about as great as it can be. This is a clear example of maximum proximity in space and time. The same is true of a robber who accosts you and merely conveys what his nearby, clearly visible, and well-armed colleagues will do if you don't present him with your cash and credit cards right away. As a result, you'll likely respond with compliance, altering on the spot your presumably otherwise firm habit of not handing your wallet to strangers with the idea that they'll keep the contents. The remote future seems abstract. The immediate future looks real.

So, in order to change behavior, a threat has to be both credible and imminent. And then, third, it has to be strong, in the sense that the danger at issue is associated with consequences that would be substantially damaging in ways that matter greatly to the person or group threatened. A simple example can make this clear.

Imagine that a physically unimpressive criminal approaches you in a parking lot late at night, not with a gun or knife or any other implement of physical violence, but with a sudden demand for your wallet that's accompanied by the unusual threat warning that if you don't comply, he'll spit on your shoes. This threat would lack what I'm calling strength. Even if the threat is credible—from sizing up the man in the available light, you realize that if you decline to comply, there is a high expectation of expectoration— and the threat is imminent in its immediacy, because there he is, inches from your loafers, you still mostly likely won't find this to be a highly motivating threat, unless you're wearing extremely expensive and quite delicate shoes. A threat that involves severe bodily harm or death has, by contrast, what I'm calling high strength. So does a threat of sudden unemployment due to a business or product failure.

Self-preservation is the first law of nature.
Samuel Butler

If there is a serious danger to a business in the context of the current market or due to developing competition and someone in a leadership position needs to convey that threat effectively in order to motivate behavior change and avert disaster, then the threat needs to be perceived by everyone as credible, imminent, and strong. But even when all three of these qualifications are met to the extent that the context will allow, it's still sometimes hard for the single extended event of a likely catastrophe brewing, or a single warning of such a danger, to bring about sustained behavioral change for everyone involved. Especially in difficult business circumstances, but where there is typically no likely chance of bodily harm or death, there is a tendency on the part of people to preserve their comfort and protect their current habits of thought and action by a selective use of skepticism and rationalization, which can operate as a form of self-deception.

People in a leadership position can be warning of huge sour lemons on the way in massive quantities out just beyond the horizon, and end up astonished that no one as a result starts gathering the tools and ingredients needed to make large amounts of lemonade. For most business dangers, it's possible for those hearing the bad news to doubt the true credibility of the threat or its real imminence, or its likely continued strength through time. Denial and avoidance thought can take many forms. Unanticipated circumstances might intervene to block the danger or mitigate its impact. The market may change again. The competition could stumble. A number of things could possibly happen to improve the seemingly dire situation, even without any dramatic change on our part. Enough doubt can creep into the minds of those who are being called to change so that they are able to rationalize dragging their feet and adopting a "wait and see" attitude.

Because of the deep comfort and tremendous power of habit, aided by these strong supporting tendencies in the mind, the motivational threshold for real change can be very high for any single event disaster warning or dire threat to make the difference it may need to make. Of course, wise individuals respond well to even subtle feedback from the world around them. Because of this, they're generally more likely than most people to avoid calamity.

And when a calamitous threat motivator does loom or actually occur, the wise person will most likely see and respond with quick and heroic change.

> The misfortune of the wise is better than
> the prosperity of the fool.
> Epicurus

The implication of this is simple. As far as possible, surround yourself with wise people. The problem we face in most contexts, however, is that genuine wisdom isn't nearly as widespread throughout our environment as we would like it to be. As a result, generally, inertia is harder to defeat than we might anticipate. Big changes aren't made easily, even with a real or likely crisis as a catalyst. A disaster on almost any scale, or the threat of such an event, isn't as reliably effective in motivating change over the long run as we might have supposed. This is the unfortunate ultimate limit of the one-event motivator. So, even when there is a crisis or one big impending danger, we'll often still find that significant change can be initiated successfully to avoid or solve the problem only by launching a multi-event process of transformation. And so this is what we should explore next. But first, a quick note is needed.

One thing that can be said about a crisis is that it gets people's attention. And that attention can be important if we use it to launch a process of transformation. I don't want to discount the role that a crisis can play in sparking attention and opening people up to a need for change. So I should summarize my baseline advice to leaders about the proper use of crisis in change motivation: Don't make it, don't fake it, but when a real crisis happens, don't fail to take it and use it well. We even have a relatively new old saying: Never let a good crisis go to waste. But you'll typically have to go far beyond the single looming event of the crisis and its announcement and seek to devise an ongoing process in order to create lasting change. And even apart from crisis management, a proper process is always best in launching innovation. The most effective forms of alchemy require an extended process in order to work. There's power in a good process.

> Life is a process of becoming, a combination
> of states we have to go through.
> Anais Nin

Before we move on to examine the sort of process that helps to facilitate change, I need to consider a potential objection that's related to an idea we briefly touched on earlier. Isn't it always possible for there to be a single positive event or wonderful opportunity, instead of a crisis, that jump-starts tremendous transformation and change? Suppose that, in the place of a one-time offer of a huge bonus or financial windfall for changing behavior, the people in a business are told of a major, tremendously great opportunity that is a unique possibility. In order to take this opportunity and reap the many substantive benefits it promises, behaviors are going to have to change radically and soon. Couldn't people be expected to respond positively to such a chance with real change and not require any sort of follow-up process? Couldn't the dream itself deliver the results we want?

First, it should be said that a sudden, unique, and limited availability opportunity, however positive, in itself creates what's actually a crisis of sorts, a focal decision point where suddenly options have to be weighed and distinctive actions taken. Gain and loss are in the balance. It's not that it needs to be seen as primarily threat driven, with the implicit threat being the loss of the new opportunity if certain things aren't done differently right away. But such a situation still can be thought of as a one-time crisis, in the sense of a turning point where something may be lost forever if the needed actions aren't taken. And something very similar to what we've said about any negative crisis will also have to be said about this.

In order for a one-time, single event, positive opportunity to elicit major change, it would have to satisfy the same three criteria of credibility, imminence, and strength that we've just examined in connection with threats. The portrayal of such an opportunity is itself much like a promise, and a promise is in some ways like a threat, however much more positive it might be. Anyone proposing the opportunity would have to realize that everyone who is expected to change in order to take advantage of it will be asking, at some conscious or unconscious level, the same questions: Is the portrayal of this opportunity by leadership credible? Is there good evidence that it is what it seems to be? Is the opportunity also imminent? Or would any promised benefits be a long time in coming, with those theoretical boons being vulnerable to circumstantial alterations, diminishment, or even blockage in the meantime? And third, does this opportunity involve things that truly matter, and matter strongly to us, and to me?

A long history of change initiatives in modern organizations teaches us something important. Even if all these questions can be answered in a positive way and everyone comes to accept those answers at least initially, human nature is sufficiently recalcitrant and fickle that a supporting process will still have to be established to lead and undergird the change effort, supporting it along the way, in order for it to be truly effective for the long haul. Some things, and especially major change, can be accomplished and secured only by an extended campaign over time. And so, the process or campaign required needs to be understood. It would then be helpful to have a model for the sort of powerful multiple-event process that's normally necessary for group transformation.

The Power of A Process

The only alternative for relying on the occurrence, warning, or positive announcement of a single event as a way of motivating group change, and the only proper augmentation to this when you do have a big wakeup call or an overwhelmingly convincing one-time opportunity, is to launch a multiple event transformation process. The agricultural metaphor we've consulted that's focused on good soil even suggests this. Standing in the long line of philosophers who find wisdom in our interactions with nature, the Roman Stoic Seneca once wrote:

> The farmer will lose all that he has sown if he ends his labors with putting in the seed. It's only after much care that crops are brought to their yield. Nothing that's not encouraged by constant cultivation from the first day to the last ever reaches the state of fruit. (*On Benefits*, II. xi. 4)

We've seen why the single event approach to creating change in most group circumstances will typically have to be augmented by a process of reinforcement in order to be effective. We almost always need to work over time to fight and overcome the ongoing possibilities of skeptical doubt and rationalization that are the natural accompaniments and psychological defenses of inertia. And perhaps the most important benefit to approaching change through a process is that the process approach to transformation can also be used effectively in normal circumstances where there is no captivating big single event, positive or negative, to galvanize the change. Typically, anything worth doing in life requires an extended process of supporting action.

Any process for turning new ideas into firm new habits of thought and action must involve an extended endeavor of education, imagination, inspiration, appreciation, reinforcement, accountability, and personal growth. New ideas meant to effect change should be presented clearly and vividly, with strength and passion, and communicated repeatedly, in more than one way, and with great patience through time. And we can't always wait for some huge initiating event to force the issue. We need to learn how to launch such a process ourselves. The passion we may have for what we'd like to see needs to be matched by a patience for the process that will play out only over time.

> Patience and time do more than strength or passion.
> Jean de La Fortaine

Change implementation in any social context requires relentless communication and reinforcement on every level possible. One of the most common mistakes in organizational change efforts is the failure to communicate often and well, and with consistent actions firmly augmenting all the words of guidance and inspiration. Soundly executed repetition and ongoing reinforcement are crucial for getting the message across clearly and making sure it's understood, as well as for keeping the desired new behaviors top-of-mind and convincing everyone that you're really serious about the new program or procedure that's being launched. Creative repetition is crucial.

Several times in my long career, so far, of serving major corporations and smaller businesses with the wisdom for new levels of performance, I've heard someone in a top leadership position say of a major change initiative something like, "We stopped talking about it too soon. We assumed wrongly that everyone had gotten the message. And then things drifted backward." It's almost impossible to overestimate the amount of good communication needed to effect lasting change, and especially of any major sort. Effective teachers repeat. Great leaders reinforce. We all need reminders along the way of what's important. Our attention needs to be reclaimed periodically, and our energy needs to be refocused and renewed on what we're seeking to attain. There's a fickleness in human nature that only a repeatedly reinforced focus can tame.

What if one does say the same things—of course, in a different form
each time—over and over? If he has anything to say
worth saying, that is just what he ought to do.
Oliver Wendell Holmes, Sr.

An extended process of repetition and reinforcement that's done
right can have at least two effects. It can establish and firmly root
the new ideas in the minds and memories of everyone involved,
and it can provide for a deeper understanding of what exactly the
ideas mean and how they should be applied in concrete situations.
This process takes time and typically a lot more effort than we
might expect. But patience with the process and a committed,
determined use of it is the most productive way to approach the
challenge of initiating change throughout a group of people.

The best leaders of change are compelling storytellers. They're
able to communicate a simple and powerful narrative about where
things are, where they need to be, and what can be done to bridge
the gap. A great leader tells the truth about the present reality in a
compelling and empowering way. An account of how things now
stand has to be simple, penetrating, and engaging. A description
then of how things instead need to be should evoke a sense of
excitement about that clearly portrayed and possible future. And
a prescription for how we can get from here to there must be perceived as presenting a path that's both possible, desirable, and even,
in best case scenarios, necessary.

A. → B.
Where we are now.   Where we need to be.
C.
How we can get from A to B.

This three-fold story of where we are, where we need to be, and
how to get from here to there is the structural form of the basic

message in every great religion and philosophy of life. It's also the blueprint for leading change well. The leader in any context, as the resident alchemist-in-chief, has to tell a story that makes sense, rings true, and inspires people with a conviction of noble endeavor, touching their imaginations and emotions as well as their intellects. Motivation is always about the heart and the mind. And it grows best in the rich soil of desire and longing for what seems great.

> If you want to build a ship, don't drum up people together
> to collect wood and don't assign them tasks and work, but
> rather teach them to long for the endless immensity of the sea.
> Saint-Exupery

The life of the leader should resonate with the story he or she tells, and the more resonance there is, the better things will go. To the extent that a leader of change can set an example and imaginatively lure, inspire, and encourage others to adopt a certain vision of the future, they will more likely become partners in the innovative effort to get there and actively look for ways forward in even more depth and richness than the leader could have had in mind. When anyone known to be a master lemonade maker invites you to join in stirring up a new libation, you'll be more likely to partner up with enthusiasm and your own creative spark than if the opportunity were coming from someone not recognized for such a talent. Who a leader is always speaks louder than anything she says. But being and telling ideally work best together when transformation is in the air.

A powerful story can launch an effective process. I've learned a lot about the importance of an ongoing and multifaceted process to generate real transformation as I've watched people implement new ideas in their businesses and lives over the past decades. I've seen that the best procedure for taking any newly understood ideas and using them to create new and powerful habits of thought and action is a multi-media, multi-level ongoing educational experience spread throughout an organization, a process that consists in repeatedly supporting and deepening everyone's understanding of both the ideas involved and the behaviors needed, as well as of what's ultimately at stake.

When companies (1) use a wide variety of communication tools to spread a new initiative, (2) work to integrate the new ideas into the normal rhythms of the organization, and (3) review the use of these new ideas on a regular basis, (4) positively holding people accountable for the change that's desired and (5) showing appreciation through praise and other forms of reinforcement for those who make progress in the new direction, then there is a much higher probability that important workplace habits will be changed for the better and over the long run.

> Change is not a decision; it is a campaign.
> Rosabeth Moss Kanter

To sum up: Any program to launch change should be both a multi-media and multi-faceted process extending though time and reinforcing core ideas and desired behaviors until they become second nature. The process should be carefully monitored along the way and altered or enhanced at any stage if the need is detected. Change leaders should be as focused and committed at all later times during the process as they were at the outset and initial launch. And this all adds up. A successful change campaign creates successful new habits that will endure.

The leaders who succeed at innovative transformations tend to be those who are personally excited about what they're bringing to everyone else. Nothing can replace genuine enthusiasm at the top for a newly announced change. This positive energy can then spread through the culture of a company. To reinforce and propagate it properly, champions of change should be recruited early on in the process at every level, even well in advance of the launch date itself, and their efforts throughout the endeavor should be recognized and celebrated at every stage. They should feel responsible for the change within their own domains—sparking, cheering, and monitoring it. No one person or small group can alone energize a large community without developing pockets of strong support throughout it. That support should be garnered early, used well, and reenergized regularly throughout every stage of the enterprise. In the very strongest change efforts, the leader personally recruits change champions throughout the organization for his or her attention and guidance, and they in turn recruit their own small groups of champions. The more positive touch points throughout the organization that are actively engaged in championing the change, the stronger and more effective the effort can be. This is an application of what I think of as The Proximity Principle: Close, face-to-face contact can encourage transformative innovation like nothing else.

All the champions and leaders of change should then also be counseled early on about their need for patience and resilience to match their enthusiasm, so that they won't easily become discouraged with difficulties or setbacks they will encounter along the way. The more people there are who understand the extended nature of the process of effecting change, the better the process can proceed. If we know up-front that something will be difficult, then we're much better prepared to handle any challenges well. And in any major change, there will be obstacles encountered and mistakes made as time goes by. The more people we have around us who are prepared to anticipate and understand this, and who can then periodically help to relight the fire of the process, the more likely it will result in all the changes we want.

The Three Ways of Propagating Change
We've long known that the practices and traditions of corporate cultures are generally propagated in three basic ways. Not surprisingly, change initiatives also get spread through any organization

in the same three ways. They are as easy to define as they are difficult to use well.

Corporate Change is sparked and spread by:
1. Formal communications
2. Informal conversations
3. Constant observation

We too often think of these three paths for spreading culture or change as if they're being listed here in an order of decreasing importance, with formal communication always being the most important way of launching or disseminating both culture and change, while informal conversation is a useful mechanism of secondary importance, and a consideration of what people actually see going on around them is indeed relevant, and even perhaps important, but at a lesser level than the other two matters. I've come to believe quite firmly that it's the other way around.

As important as formal communications are—and they are extremely important in their content, tone, frequency, variety, and consistency—the informal conversations that people are having throughout the organization every day about the change initiative, its seriousness, need, and probability of success, as well as concerning the likely benefits it will lead to for everyone involved, are even more important and by a very large margin. But most vital of all is what people actually see others doing all around them. Are the organization's leaders acting in accordance with their public statements, showing that they really care about the new initiative and clearly giving their valuable time and energy to the process? Are recruiting, evaluation, and reward structures being adjusted to acknowledge and highlight the importance of the new ideas and newly desired actions and habits? Are people throughout the organization signing on to the initiative and actually acting in new ways? Or are lots of people just treading water to see whether the whole issue will eventually blow over?

Well done is better than well said.
Benjamin Franklin

The process of inaugurating transformative change will not be effective unless those undertaking the effort make sure that as much as possible comes together in support of the goal. However crucial the right words are for announcing any innovation and stressing its importance, actions always do speak with more authority. A great leader of change remembers this and is vigilant to watch how people behave, quickly recognizing, praising and rewarding the right actions, while also actively discouraging contrary or unhelpful behavior. All through the process, an ongoing display of rewards for consistent behavior, along with an understood warning or credible reminder of the potentially negative consequences for recalcitrant conduct, expressed in accordance with the three needed threat attributes of credibility, imminence, and strength, will encourage and support the efforts of all toward the transformed conduct needed for lasting change.

Group change is not just a simple aggregate of individual change, but is a genuine social phenomenon. It's always best effected by a well thought out and properly executed social process involving as many people as possible, as soon as possible in the unfolding sequence of events. Then, the psychological mechanism of social tuning can kick in and assist the transformative effort. Small gains will begin to establish momentum, and as the conduct of the people in the organization begins to change, that momentum will grow. When people see the changes begin to happen around them, and a new normal comes to be established, any residual resistance they may have felt will begin to diminish, more often than not. When people do what they say, it gets our attention.

The conduct of our lives is the true mirror of our doctrine.
Montaigne

Getting all this to happen effectively takes thorough planning, careful monitoring, constant reinforcement, and the very important element of time. And that's something we need to reflect on for a moment. We can't approach an extended process with the patience that's typically needed to see it through if we lack a sufficient understanding of the temporal element that can be so important. A good grasp of this is distinctively empowering. Time is, after all, one of the most important elements in our lives. When you know roughly how long a difficult or painful experience will last, you'll typically find it easier to endure. When you also know, before it ends, basically how long a brief pleasant experience will continue, you're often equally motivated to enjoy it more deeply while you actually have it. We can benefit from grasping the time a thing will take.

Time and Change

Time is usually just as important a factor in organizational change as it is in all forms of personal transformation. And we easily underestimate the amount of time that a substantial change in long-term habits may take. A man wrote to me years ago, saying that he had heard one of my talks on "True Success" and had gotten so excited as a result that he went right out and bought my book of the same title and read it immediately. As soon as he finished it, he read it again cover-to-cover, underlining and highlighting it throughout. He made it a point to tell anyone who would listen about what he was learning. He then confessed to me that the one thing he didn't do was to make any of the changes he needed to make in his life in order to implement the ideas he was getting from the book. He didn't consciously realize it at the time, but he just wasn't yet ready for that. Then, months later, he said, he carefully read the book for a third time. And finally, he said, he was prepared to take action.

Time ripens all things.
Cervantes

It wasn't just one dramatic exposure to new ideas that brought about the needed change in this man's life and, fortunately, it wasn't any sort of traumatic personal crisis that made the difference. It was a process over time that allowed it to happen. And when the time was right for his reading and thinking to bear fruit, things fell into place and old habits were altered for the better. My enthusiastic reader used some vivid imagery in his letter to me. He said that the road of his life had gotten into pretty bad shape and that, as a result, he was always busy patching potholes. Any patch he made would last for a while, and then it would eventually require his attention again. When he finally became ready to confront the deeper and more fundamental changes he needed to make, he realized that piecemeal pothole patching was not good enough. He had to rip up all the old asphalt and repave the entire road with a new surface. My book, he said, had helped him do this, but only when the time was right. Even without all the details, I got what he was saying.

I love the image of roadwork that he used. It's a vivid metaphor for what many businesses experience all the time. They're patching holes when they need to be replacing the old surface altogether. The man writing me about all this wanted to tell me his story, he explained, because he thought I should know that whenever I was speaking to an audience or writing a book that would be published for lots of people to read, I was just planting seeds, and that I should expect them, like any seeds, to take time to grow. Here we are with our farming image again. He went on with the metaphor. Some of the seeds I was bringing to the world might sprout up right away, and others might take months, or even years, to germinate. But there is one simple guarantee. When the time is right, the right ideas will make their proper difference.

> Time is the greatest innovator.
> Francis Bacon

This was a lesson important for me to learn, and it's one I've taken to heart and tried to remember in everything I do. If needed change takes time in an individual life, then we should also expect time to be an important factor for seeing any form of real change happen in organizations, which are obviously just structured communities of individuals. And across networks of individuals, there will be a wide spectrum of readiness regarding change. Some people and groups will take more time than others to implement change well. In even the lives of the most eager early adopters, we should remember that lasting change is always the result of a process extended through time.

And yet, there's a big problem connected with this important fact. In many business contexts, changes have to be made quickly, and sometimes even quite radical transformations need to take place rapidly. The market demands speed. Or our particular circumstances require it. We can't wait until everyone is good and ready, in their own time, to initiate and consummate the personal changes required for the organizational innovation. And so, to continue to use my correspondent's fruitful image, any leader has to be prepared to help the process along and encourage all relevant associates to rip up the old asphalt and rebuild their road together.

It's crucial here to realize that if we've been cultivating the right attitudes in people all along, helping to prepare them to be receptive to our leadership in times of change, and we've subsequently been launching the right sort of process with all the proper forms of reinforcement available to us, then the challenge of implementing something new will typically be easier and faster when that's needed. But it will always take time. Remembering this helps us to calibrate our efforts with the preparation, patience, and persistence it takes to see great change made well.

Greatness takes time. To revert back to our original big-scale governing metaphor, the creation of great lemonade requires an extended process through time, whereas a poor or mediocre swill can be quick and easy to stir up. But if you're in a well-equipped kitchen with talented friends who've been trained in great lemonade making techniques, getting a superior libation made in sufficient quantities for a big crowd can happen more easily and expeditiously than otherwise would have been the case. Any patience you still have to exercise will be amply justified and rewarded. And then you can set up your lemonade stand and serve your delightful creation with pride.

8

A Small Dash of Magic

The Wizardly Innovation

At this point, it will be useful to review briefly what we've just learned about launching change together, and then add a quick dash of magic to the process. There are a few secrets to innovation that are every bit as simple as they are potent when used well. The trick is to understand these ideas and employ them consistently in support of any needed innovation or group transformation.

> Ideas are, in truth, forces.
> Henry James

We've recently been instructed on some ideas we need, and they've been presented both memorably and well in a surprising set of popular books that aren't typically thought of as presenting philosophy or psychology, or tips for life or business success. But they offer exactly that. And, indeed, an entire generation or two in the workplace now has been exposed to these books and their ideas, often at a formative age, but perhaps didn't realize what they were learning and how it all can be put into practice. When grasped and used in all the right ways, these ideas can indeed be magical. So to them, we'll soon turn. But first, we need to get our bearings and sum up what we've seen.

The Basics of Transformative Efforts

WHEN WE SEEK TO INSTILL NEW HABITS OF THOUGHT AND practice in our workplace or within any group of people, we need to remember and use all the basics for a philosophy of transformative change. We've seen that there are two ways in principle that significant change can get made: through a crisis and through a process. But even when a crisis threatens or erupts, the most lasting changes nonetheless will come as a result of using the occasion to launch a process. And this can be done in the utter absence of any sort of disaster or catastrophe, and without any radical new opportunity suddenly appearing over the horizon. What's typically most effective for transforming our behavior together is a well-directed process, whether in our lives, our families, or our businesses, launched with imagination and followed up with patient persistence.

We need to tell a vivid story about the value of new ideas, the need for new directions and actions, and the goals they will help us attain. We should clearly and imaginatively define the changes we want to make and the future we desire to reach, highlighting the benefits of the innovations for all involved. We need to gather strong support from others, make sure everyone knows what's at stake, and provide a context in which people are encouraged to succeed, which includes being willing to listen empathetically to any complaints, to validate people's feelings of struggle or frustration in the early stages of the change, and to encourage them as much as we can along the way. And, of course, as initiators of any innovation, we need to live consistently every day the exciting story that we're telling in order to create a reality that will match it.

If we're leaders, it's our job to prepare people for any big change we need to make together. We have to point out clearly where we are, where we need to be, and what it will take to get there. We should reinforce the message in as many ways as we can to train everyone's thoughts, habituate them to the new ideas, and ground them in the choices day-to-day that will accomplish the task. We need to remember that, for them, any innovation that we're launching may be perceived as an unexpected change and challenge being dropped in their path, and can be seen as an obstacle or difficulty they need to surmount. It can look like a high mound of sour lemons. And so it can be useful to introduce them to, or remind them of, all the steps in the art of adaptation. They will benefit greatly, as we shall too, if they can practice the art of self-control, the art of positive action, and the art of achievement regarding the innovations and transformations that we need to make. And all along the way, we should be quick to praise and reward the steps of adaptation and transition that we see, while dealing effectively with any recalcitrant conduct that impedes the process. When we do the right things, we can initiate real change in the least time possible and have a great chance of making it stick.

> Philosophy's work is finding the shortest path
> between two points.
> Kahlil Gibran

Finally, we should still expect the process, even guided by the best philosophy of change and under the most favorable conditions, to take more effort than we ever would have guessed. And we should be prepared to keep at it, with unflagging positive energy and a determination to see it through. This is the way to position new ideas and launch new behaviors in order to make a real and lasting difference. This is the path of the true alchemist who successfully creates the elixir of great change.

The Five Steps to Courageous Change

AND NOW WE NEED TO GET TO THE SIMPLE, UNIVERSAL magic. We have one more tool, or framework of ideas, to examine and use well. And when put into everyone's hands, it can have amazing results.

A few years ago and to my great surprise, I found myself writing a book about all the life and leadership wisdom to be found in the popular Harry Potter stories, a project called *If Harry Potter Ran General Electric: Leadership Wisdom From the World of the Wizards*. It wasn't anything I'd planned. I hadn't even read any of the Potter books until fairly late in the game, at about the midpoint for the original publication of the seven books in the extraordinarily famous series. But a younger friend who is also a philosopher convinced me to take a look at the first installment and I was hooked. I quickly had to read them all, and did so with great excitement six-times through, at least for most of the books. I was astonished at the genuine life wisdom they contain. Not long after I wrote my own book about it all, I ended up giving talk in Las Vegas at a big international conference held in honor of the young wizard by his most enthusiastic fans from around the world, who surprised me again with a long, loud standing ovation for my presentation on the philosophical side of the magic in and around Hogwarts. It was all I could do not to put on a long billowing robe, spontaneously grow an impressive beard, and go shop for a wand.

It didn't take me long to discover that the talented author of the Potter stories, the former classics major J. K. Rowling, is in a sense one of the most highly skilled practical thinkers and public philosophers of our time. She's managed to capture deep wisdom in her engaging tales, and has introduced a new generation to the importance of the ancient virtues delineated long ago by such great thinkers as Plato, Aristotle, and Seneca, among many others. In particular, her main character, Harry, shows us that without the distinct virtue of courage, so loved and promoted by Aristotle, it's impossible to prevail in a world of ongoing and difficult challenge.

Courage in danger is half the battle.
Plautus

Harry Potter displays the quality of courage in a uniquely dramatic way. When we first meet him, he's a young boy as sensitive to danger and susceptible to fear and anxiety as any of us could be. And yet, when confronted with the very worst dangers of his day, he's always able to step up and do the right thing, over and over again. In addition, he leads his friends to follow him into repeated confrontations with the many stunningly awful threats of their time. I was intrigued. How does he manage it?

As I read the stories and carefully pondered their details, I began to see a pattern in Harry's conduct over time. He doesn't seem to realize that he's giving himself the basic conditions for the attribute of courage. He just intuitively does everything necessary to muster the bravery he needs when he needs it. And by doing this, he also becomes a natural leader when a lot is at stake. His confidence and courage inspire those around him to try more and accomplish more beyond anything they would have thought themselves capable of achieving. To take the understanding we can gain from his effective actions, fictional as they are, and then apply it to our own challenge with change and transformation in the real world is immensely illuminating and helpful.

The Wizard's Way

Big changes can be scary. The unknowns and uncertainties that lie beyond our experience can spark great anxiety. One of the primary difficulties people have with initiating change in their lives is the problem of how to have courage in the face of fear and move forward to do new things and effect the changes that should be made. The young wizard's way of approaching this, distilled into a simple formula, is exactly what we need. So allow me to present his recipe for courageous resolve in daunting times:

Harry Potter's 5 Steps to Courage

(1) Prepare for the challenge.
(2) Surround yourself with support.
(3) Engage in positive self-talk.
(4) Focus on what's at stake.
(5) Take appropriate action.

By doing these five things well, we can all position ourselves to summon the courage we need when we need it, and do the right thing when it has to be done. But there is an implication of this relevant to our present concern that reaches far beyond the original context. What I didn't realize when I was first identifying these five simple steps and writing about them is that they have a more universal application outside the range of what might be needed for courage in the face of danger. They are deeply relevant to the issue of everyday alchemy and transformative change in more than one way. These five steps provide us with tools that we need for leading and managing change.

Give us the tools, and we will finish the job.
Winston Churchill

One night on the Internet right after my book was published, I was googling the title, "If Harry Potter Ran General Electric." And yes, whether they admit it or not, authors do such things to see what people are saying about a book in the early days of its public life. Somewhere on the Google Results page thirty-seven or so, I happened to come across a Power-Point presentation that had just been created by a British physician and professor of medicine to accompany his talks to hospital Emergency Room staffs in the United Kingdom on how to launch and manage change in their procedures, and in the process, perhaps save more lives. I wondered what this had to do with my new book. And the answer first stunned me and then made me smile. It turned out that the doctor saw my Potter book while on vacation in Canada, read it carefully, and found in it some ideas he knew he could use. I clicked through his presentation to see what he had to say. He was obviously doing important work. And then on one of his slides, I saw something that I had not expected. It laid out the exact framework of ideas I had extracted from young Mr. Potter's behavior in difficult situations, but with a new heading:

Harry Potter's 5 Steps to Managing Change
(1) Prepare for the challenge.
(2) Surround yourself with support.
(3) Engage in positive self-talk.
(4) Focus on what's at stake.
(5) Take appropriate action.

These were the steps to courage I had identified from all the Potter stories, but now repurposed with a different and broader concept and application. It struck me immediately that the professor of medicine was right. Our famous young wizard's actions capture some of the most important insights for anyone getting ready for a major change, undergoing a difficult transition, or on the verge of launching any new effort toward an innovative transformation. It was a connection I honestly hadn't seen. And it was a small but important revelation to me.

The things Harry Potter does and that we all need to do in order to position ourselves for courageous action in any challenge are precisely what we should do to initiate any major change in an organization or even in our own personal lives. And since courage is so important for dealing well with any big change, we shouldn't be surprised at this connection. Because the young Hogwarts student of magic is a master of courage, he's also a master of change, and a wizard of transformation. That's a key to his success.

The original five steps are centered on what an individual needs for courage, or to handle tough change well. We can tweak some of them just a touch to broaden them out so that they encompass as well the challenge of leading innovative transformation in a group. This is a minor restatement that goes beyond the initial context, and will sum up the main outlines of what we've previously seen to be necessary for the art of innovation. This great art has five requirements:

The Art of Innovation
Prepare for the Challenge.
Gather Strong Support.
Communicate Positively and Well.
Focus on What's at Stake.
Take Action to Launch New Habits.

When change efforts fail, it's usually because one or more of these five steps has been ignored. When such efforts work, it's typically because all five steps have been taken and are being monitored on an ongoing basis. They focus and extend what we've already seen in our look at making change happen with others. They summarize the most basic elements involved in what we're calling the art of innovation.

Let's consider for just a moment how each step works. Even a brief examination will underline the importance of these simple activities for both personal and team alchemy in the launching of new change. They'll sum up much of what we've learned, and give us a useful checklist for the things we need to concern ourselves with in any new enterprise of transformation.

The Five Steps of Innovation

   1. *Prepare for the Challenge.* As the author and change consultant Jeanie Daniel Duck makes clear in her book *The Change Monster*, too many executives who are keen on initiating some sort of innovation neglect the genuinely human side of the challenge, the emotional and psychological preparation that's needed to make any difficult change happen and last. It's only when people have been adequately prepared for a new project that they're likely to be able to do what's necessary to work through it well and succeed. And in every effective process of preparation, people should be helped to realize that they're acquiring the skills they will need for the adventure ahead. Understood in this way, Harry Potter's first step of preparing for the challenge is vital.

> Success depends on previous preparation, and
> without such preparation, there is sure to be failure.
> Confucius

   Preparation creates competence and confidence, and both these qualities are crucial for success in any new endeavor. Before any change initiative in an organization is announced, lots of preparatory work should be done to see to it that the process can be successful. When we suddenly spring things on people without a proper time of cultivated preparation, we all too often merely set them up for failure and ourselves for disappointment. The importance of proper preparation can't be overstated. This is something that's been understood by the wisest people for a very long time. In the best of modern agricultural methods, the soil is prepped thoroughly before any seed is sown.

   In an individual life as well as in a social group or business, we best initiate lasting change when we've prepared for the challenge well in advance. The man I described in the last chapter who wrote me an email about repeatedly reading one of my books was really telling me a tale of preparation for change. It's likely that in the months between his initial introduction to the ideas I had discovered and the actual making of the changes he had long needed, many things had happened in his life to help prepare him for the moment when his own alchemical transformation could begin. Preparation is vital. But we need a second factor as well, both for personal and professional transformation.

2. *Gather Strong Support.* As we've seen, the support of others is crucial for launching change. No change agent can, like Atlas, hold the world up on his or her shoulders. No one can go it alone in bringing bold and innovative change to a group of people. In order to see any innovation effected properly and woven fully into the fabric of an organization, or any group, we need a broad basis of support for the change. Properly focused and sustainable transformation within a group context is always a collaborative effort. It arises out of partnership. Without the right support, it just won't happen, even if it initially appears to be occurring. When we carefully secure the active support of others, we greatly raise our chance of success. This is Harry's second step and the second requirement in the art of transformation. Surround yourself with support.

And, of course, support is just as important for success in efforts of personal change as it is in an organizational context. It's hard for anyone to quit smoking, curtail unhealthy drinking or drug use, adopt a better diet, or engage in a new fitness routine without the encouragement and help of others. The more difficult a change is that we're seeking to make, the more we need the assistance of trusted others. Even though all worthwhile change starts from within, most effective change, even in an individual life, is in some way a group endeavor.

3. *Communicate Positively and Well.* The most commonly misunderstood link in any organizational change effort is the importance of the ongoing need for clear and helpful positive communication, repeated and reinforced in every way possible. And this is important

for a number of reasons. As we've seen, the full story of where we are, where we need to be, and how we can get there should be described imaginatively, well, and often. But even this is not enough. There's a second vital form of communication that we see going on in Harry Potter's cultivation of his own courage, as well as the courage of his friends. And it's just as crucial for launching transformative change. He thinks and speaks in such a way as to communicate an attitude of strong confidence in his prospects for success in the challenge he faces.

> Whatever words we speak should be chosen
> with care, for people will hear them
> and be influenced for good or ill.
> Buddha

In response to any major change effort, it's nearly inevitable that at some point a bit of discouragement can set in due to setbacks, reversals, complications, the time it ends up taking to see clear results, or the sheer difficulty we find ourselves facing along the way. But these things are to be expected. And that's fine. As we've seen earlier, effort and satisfaction do tend to be directly correlated in life. The harder something is, the better we'll feel about our accomplishments once they're finally attained. And yet, without a positive psychology of confidence to power us forward, we're likely to give up before our change efforts have had a full enough chance to succeed. Each of us needs to engage in a process of inner cheerleading for our own efforts and bring that optimism to bear in what we say to those around us who may be struggling in their efforts at transformation. Leadership is always a process of inside out. First, as a leader of change, go out of your way to communicate to yourself positive messages of confident expectation, and then you can bring such messages more convincingly to others. The benefits of positive self-talk in any tough challenge are well known. And then an external communication of confident assurance is needed to encourage everyone involved in the change.

> Much unhappiness has come into the world
> because of bewilderment and things unsaid.
> Dostoevsky

The prominent British writer, philosopher, and theologian G.K Chesterton once said, "If a thing is worth doing, it is worth doing badly." And that's true—at first, and for a while, until we get the hang of the new activity. This often characterizes the early stages of any change effort. We rarely start off doing something different and innovative at a level of peak mastery and excellence. We're outside our comfort zones. We're departing from old skills and habits. We're trying something new. We'll likely struggle a bit at first, make some mistakes, and trip up several times. We'll surely feel frustrated now and then. And so, we'll need a psychological preparation and ongoing support along the way that won't let this take all the wind out of our sails and stop us, dead in the water.

Any change implementation process requires an attitude of resilience and positive expectation on the part of the people engaged in that endeavor, along with a properly noble sense for the importance of what's being done. Because improvement in almost anything involves both bursts of progress and times of diminished returns, with periods of frustration and even backsliding now and then, it can help to remind ourselves and each other of these facts and use the inevitable universality of this general pattern in order to bolster our confidence in the process. The young Harry Potter's use of positive self-talk throughout many of his adventures can spark and guide our overall thought and talk in our own challenges. Frequent positive communications geared to the psychology of the challenge can pay off important dividends in every phase of the effort. The third requirement for the art of transformation is to communicate positively and well.

4. *Focus on what's at stake.* It's easy to get distracted and lose focus during any extended change process. Inertial forces will block us and pull us back to old ways of working, if we don't keep our focus on the values at stake in the process and on the things we should do to honor those values. We need to remember "The Why" behind it all. We will have to remind ourselves of the reason the change we're working to implement is important, and then reinforce that regularly to all who involved in the process with us. Everyone wants a worthy cause to believe in and support. So we have to focus and refocus on what's at stake in the changes being made. That keeps people's hearts as well as their minds engaged in the effort. Everyone needs a noble task to pursue. Whenever a change effort can be parsed as a classic hero's quest and each of us can play at least a small heroic role, we're ennobled and strengthened for the effort, day to day. Our deep need to be heroic and to be engaged in a noble cause is one of the most overlooked sources of motivation in the world today. And it's one of the most important.

> A good cause makes a stout heart and a strong arm.
> Thomas Fuller

The Odyssey is a book that's been read and loved for three thousand years, across at least one hundred and fifty generations of human beings. Why? Now that I've read it many times throughout my own life, I think the answer is easy. It's all about how to be a hero. It's about never giving up on the noble cause you have, on the mission and purpose that drives you forward. Our tragic hero Odysseus is described many times as "the storm tossed man," and as "a man of many sorrows." He's even said to be the unluckiest man alive. He certainly goes through one awful and fantastical struggle after another in his effort to return home to Ithaca after the Trojan War, where he has served with distinction as one of the top Greek leaders and strategists. He never gives up his quest for home despite ten years of incredible obstacles that would have stopped most people many times over. He keeps up his valiant struggle with apparently endless adversity because of his noble goal, to reunite with those he loves—his wife, son, father, and friends. Something we value deeply and with our whole hearts can shore up our courage and motivate us on toward our goal, no matter how extremely hard it may turn out to be.

Here's a simple image of struggle and adventure of a different sort that's meant a lot to me over the years. Imagine that you're out in the woods on a hike and around you there are some steep hills. Suppose you're leading a group of hikers, and together you set the goal of getting to the highest point in the area, from which you'll be able to survey all the surrounding terrain. Imagine now that the highest hill you can see from where you stand is one right in front of you. Let's call it Hill A. You want to get to the highest spot, and it looks like that point is atop Hill A. So you lead the group up the side of the hill. On the ascent, you trip and slip and struggle and occasionally fall, but you help each other along and with all your hard work, you get to the top together. All of you feel great about what you've managed to accomplish. You may have a celebration and enjoy together the new view, at least until some fog lifts and suddenly, from your new vantage point, you can now see a hill nearby that's much higher. Let's call it Hill B.

If your goal is truly to get to the highest point in the area, then, after resting and taking in the view you already have, you'll need to lead the group onward. But what does that initially mean? If you now stand perched atop Hill A and want to get to what's actually the highest point in the area, the first thing that you'll have to do is go downhill. And when you as the leader point this out to everyone else, you can imagine how they'll react. The response is almost universal. People tend to say or at least think things like, "What do you mean, we have to go downhill? It took us a long time to get up to where we are, it was quite a climb, and it's actually very good here. We can see plenty from where we're already perched. Let's just stay right here and enjoy our success!"

At any given time, there are vastly many people and organizations and even families stuck on some version of Hill A, because nobody wants to go downhill. What does going downhill metaphorically represent? Changing what you've most recently been doing. Going forth to something new. Getting out of your current comfort zone. It can even mean leaving your main knowledge zone or your skill zone, and launching into something uncertain. And, in virtue of all that, it means descending from the success you've already had, striking into the unknown, encountering new struggles, and likely stumbling in new ways. Furthermore, it's important to notice one aspect of our picture that's both surprising and revelatory: In the initial downhill phase, you'll superficially appear to be getting farther from your true goal. You'll be going lower, not higher.

In almost any change effort, there's an initial downhill phase where people will seem to have left behind their former mastery and success and even basic competence in exchange for a new, potentially difficult struggle where things can at first appear to be getting worse and not better. Because of the near inevitability of this transitional time of trouble and discomfort, anxiety and regret and even dismay can become widespread, people may get genuinely discouraged, and it will be easy at some point for all of us to lose track of the importance of what we're doing, along with the loftiness and nobility of our ultimate goal that depends on this change, with all that it now involves.

As a leader, you'll need to help people focus on what's at stake throughout the entire process of making any major new change. And at the time when people are most discouraged, just being able to point out the rough universality of this initial downhill struggle in any new adventure can help calm nerves, settle dispositions, dispel negativity, and allow people to focus on the noble value of their quest.

> When I have reached a summit, I leave it with great reluctance, unless it is to reach for another, higher one.
> Gustav Mahler

In his book *Managing the Dynamics of Change,* the social psychologist Jerald Jellison lays out what he calls "The J Curve of Change." He suggests that there is a common psychological shape to any major change effort. From any high ground of familiar accomplishment and habit, any big transformation to something new will go through five stages, from Stage One, The Plateau (what I'm calling the top of Hill A), to Stage Two, The Cliff (and its descent downhill), to Stage Three, The Valley (whatever lowest area there is between Hill A and Hill B), to Stage Four, The Ascent (the stage of progress up the new hill in which things are getting better amid ongoing struggle and there are at last more clear improvements to celebrate than mistakes from which to learn), and finally to Stage Five, The Mountaintop (or the higher peak of Hill B, where at last everything is much better, and perhaps even great, thereby justifying for everyone all the difficulties of the entire arduous trek). What Jellison calls the J Curve pattern can be mapped onto our image of the transition from the smaller Hill A, where things may be good, to the bigger Hill B, where things are better, and sometimes even best.

> After climbing a great hill, one only finds that there are many more hills to climb.
> Nelson Mandela

Before his death in 2002, the distinguished Harvard philosopher Robert Nozick had spoken of this general distinction as, in principle, one between "a local maximum" and what he called "a global maximum." The great thinkers and alchemists of life would caution us not to allow what's very good to keep us from what's best, not to let our first success, or resulting habits and comforts, prevent us from the next adventure we need to launch. What Nozick called a local maximum may just be a stage along the way to the greater global maximum we might need to pursue.

Inevitably, a higher Hill B, a loftier summit of some sort, awaits us. Those who are not willing to go downhill initially from where they now are and struggle to get to that higher point will miss all the great value that's to be attained only along the path and finally up at the loftier summit. And this is a vital point not to miss. In any such journey, the value is to be found not just at the peak, but also on the trail. It's ultimately the quest itself, the journey or adventure, that forms us into the people we're capable of being. And in any business context, a lot may be at stake if you can't persevere through the ups and downs of the sometimes-arduous expedition to get to where you need to go. Some competitors almost inevitably will. And as a result, the market will come to reflect the attainments of the most courageous and adventurous, and then require such innovative journeys from any others who would prosper in that domain. Life moves forward, whether we're willing to do so or not. Those who hang back too long almost always miss out on the great good they could have attained.

One of the chief sources of wisdom in life is to know what to embrace and what to release. The best approach to our professional and personal lives is to keep on the lookout for the next great adventure we may need to embrace, and to be open to whatever initial descent it might take to release our current peak or plateau of success, and let go enough to make the new journey happen, to move from the known into the unknown. To get to what's best, we most often have to give and do our best.

It's a funny thing about life; if you refuse to accept anything
but the best, you very often get it.
W. Somerset Maugham

To revert to our larger scale governing metaphor, we're not just
dealing with the lemons of life, cutting them, squeezing their juice,
measuring out some sugar, heating up the needed water, and stirring things well, we're doing something great together and making
world-class lemonade. We should never allow ourselves to forget
the importance of the task we're undertaking, in any challenge we
face. This is the fourth step in the art of innovation, a crucial element in the leader's overall toolkit for launching change well.

5. *Take Action to Create New Habits.* Finally, the only way we
can produce major positive change is by taking the right actions
to cultivate whatever new habits are needed. It's all about personal initiative and consistency with our goals, two qualities we've
discussed in part one of this book. We have to roll the cart down
the road a little farther each day until it gains a good momentum
of its own. We'll likely trip up and get off track at times along
the way, but that's normal. We learn by doing. Innovation obviously can't happen without launching new action. And when it's
done right, today's innovation can become tomorrow's routine, the
new normal preparing us for the yet next adventure. But to get to
that point always takes the energy of determined and appropriate action, completed and then repeated. This fifth requirement or
step of taking specific action to create new habits is in some ways
the most obvious and most important one of all.

The key to transformative and innovative change in whatever
we do is action, perception, adjustment, and more action, repeated
and refined. The more we do, the more we learn, and the better we
get as a result. The process done well can produce the changes we
want, as well as those we need. Creativity emerges from a dynamic
enterprise of initiative and engagement. Great new ideas seem to

strike most often in the minds and hearts of those who are on the move along a path, going up or down a hill.

One of the great realizations of modern psychology is that we don't have to wait to act in a new way until we feel like doing so. Taking action regardless of our feelings can nudge and lure and pull our feelings toward where they need to be. The young fictional wizard Harry Potter often showed me the truth of this connection, and we can display it in our own lives, as well. We may feel uncertainty, anxiety, and fear, but courage can lead us to step out toward what's right and what we need to do. Even the smallest of steps can begin to take us to where we need to go.

> Great things are not done by impulse, but by a series
> of small things brought together.
> George Eliot

These five requirements in the art of innovation are all adumbrated by the intuitive actions of the most popular imaginary character in recent times. Who would have guessed that a fanciful wizard could teach us all a thing or two, or five, about courage, change, and the challenge of launching any innovative transformation we might face? Harry Potter's five steps to courage have given us the basics for encapsulating the entire art of innovation, as it needs to be practiced by anyone wanting to launch new change. Following his lead, like his literary creator herself and certain emergency room physicians and staff who now act on the wisdom of the wizards, we can make great things happen in our world. We can stir up together the new, refreshing lemonade we need. And as a result, we can enjoy, at a very deep level, a job well done.

9

THE ULTIMATE LEMONADE STAND

A Philosophy to Live By

HAVE YOU EVER READ SOMETHING OR HEARD SOMEONE MAKE a statement that affected you so deeply, it transformed how you think in a fundamental way? There are some ideas so powerful that they instantly bring us a completely new perspective on life and work. As soon as we come across such a concept or thought, it immediately affects the way we understand everything else. The light bulb goes on over our heads, the sun breaks through the clouds, the music swells, and everything suddenly looks different. One such idea can change us profoundly and forever.

> A moment's insight is sometimes worth a life's experience.
> Oliver Wendell Holmes, Sr.

We're going to draw near to the end of our look at how to make lemonade out of life's lemons with just that kind of idea—a broad, powerful, transformative insight that will provide us with an overarching context for everything that's come before in this book, and for whatever's to come next in our lives. It may be the single most important piece of wisdom I ever heard articulated in a classroom. And, so that you can appreciate the significance of that claim, I should point out that I'm a person who had six years of classroom experience in elementary school, another six years of junior high and high school (not six years of each, I should hasten to add; I was never held back), but the normal six years total, plus four years of college, six more years of graduate school, and then a decade and a half of living, lecturing, and learning more in the classrooms of Notre Dame where I was a professor, as well as in other great universities where I was often a guest at conferences or an invited speaker. For the next quarter century, I've also continued to have amazing classroom experiences as I've visited schools, colleges, and universities to talk about my books or my joyful work as a public philosopher. And I've learned from every visit. But I didn't have to wait very long in the course of my extended journey through formal education settings to encounter the greatest piece of wisdom I would ever find in such a context. It came my way on the very first day of school that I ever experienced, during the first few minutes of the first hour of the first class session held in the first grade, when I was six years old. Maybe I just peaked early.

Wisdom for the Journey

I WANT TO TAKE YOU BACK TO THAT INAUGURAL DAY OF MY long educational career in the first grade in Ms. Anders' class at the Calvert Method School, which was a year later to be renamed Durham Academy, in Durham, North Carolina. The year was 1958. This was a period of time, at least in my neck of the woods, when kids didn't go to preschool or kindergarten. We kept busy running around barefoot, chasing dogs up and down the road, which is where we get such TV classics as *The Andy Griffith Show*. It was a different era for early childhood development for both Opie and me. The first day of the first grade was my initial experience in a formal academic setting of any kind. This was the first time I ever walked through a classroom door and sat in a schoolroom chair, not knowing that it would be followed by many thousands of such times yet to come. And I had no idea that I was about to hear something that would change the course of my life.

My First Glimpse of The Lemonade Making Art
Let me set the stage further and give you a bit more of a sense of the period in history I'm talking about. 1958 was quite a year. Nikita Khrushchev became premier of The Soviet Union. Fallout Shelter signs were all around. Duck and Cover drills were common in schools. Elvis the pelvis Presley went into the army. The Bank of America issued the world's first fully functional credit card. Jerry Lee Lewis created a huge scandal by marrying his very young cousin. I encountered for the first time the unexpected and daunting concept of homework, and Connie Francis had a big hit song called, appropriately, "Who's Sorry Now?" For various reasons, this was a sentiment many people could understand, and especially those of us with schoolwork to do when we could be out playing in the sunshine.

The roots of education are bitter, but the fruit is sweet.
Aristotle

It was a very interesting time in the world, in America, and in my little life. For one thing, Ms. Anders was a very beautiful teacher. Even at my tender age, I could see that. As she stood before us in the classroom, she had a sort of Jackie Kennedy thing going on. Sitting in my little desk looking up at her on that first morning, I suddenly had a sort of Jack Kennedy thing going on, with my first twinges of attraction to the female gender, but of course, I didn't know at the time what it all meant. Some important transformative changes in my life were still yet to occur.

My teacher smiled at us all from the front of the classroom, greeted us graciously, and then wrote a sentence on the board. We had no idea why. None of us could read. But then she read it out loud and I remember to this day what it said. This one sentence from the first few minutes of that first day of school has stuck with me for all these years.

Ms. Anders wrote across the board the words:

Life is not what you want it to be; it is what you make it.

She read it aloud to us with feeling. Then she read it again, slowly. It took a moment for the big ideas in that profound statement to begin to sink in. And even at such an early developmental stage, I think I intuitively understood at least a part of what my teacher was saying. Our desires alone don't determine our experience of the world, but rather it's our decisions and deeds that do. Life is up to each of us to carve out and create. This world may hand us lots of lemons along the way, but only we can decide whether we'll turn them into the treat of astonishing and refreshing lemonade.

This was quite a striking insight about the nature of our existence in the cosmos to get on the first day of first grade, and at such a tender age. It could be construed as a little bit like hitting a bunch of six year olds with an existential brick. How could our teacher ever follow that? "And class, tomorrow, Johnny's dad will come in to talk about his new book on death, despair, and the possibility of hope." No. It never actually got quite that deep. But still, it should be no surprise that I eventually became a philosopher. How could I help it? It's all been an effort to cope with first grade. The most fundamental transformations can happen at almost any age.

We didn't get too existentially engaged on that first day of school, but we did gain a pretty heavy insight that morning. It caused me to start wondering, at even that early stage of my journey: Why isn't life what we want it to be? What's going on? Why do we have difficulties? What's the reason for any of our challenges? Is there anything I can do to solve all the problems I'll face along the way and make my life into something, as a result of all my efforts, that I'll actually want it to be? One short sentence led to a flock of big questions and big ideas. It planted seeds. And I was good soil.

All great ideas are dangerous.
Oscar Wilde

Of course, I didn't get all the answers that day, even in part, and I still don't have them all, but Ms. Anders, by presenting us with the simple essence or core from the mindset of everyday alchemy, started me along the path of deep and practical philosophy. It's a road that can take any of us to an understanding of change and challenge, difficulty and adversity and hardship and struggle we all need, whatever our position in life and work might be, whether we labor on the front lines of the world in what we do or serve in management positions, or even hold the ultimate levers of power in an organization, state, or nation. The practical side of philosophy is absolutely universal in its reach.

A Philosophy for Life and Lemonade
The word 'philosophy' comes from two root words: 'Philo'—meaning "the love of;" and 'Sophia'—meaning "wisdom." And wisdom is just embodied insight about life that helps with living it well. Philosophy is then, etymologically, the love of wisdom. Think about that for a second. An object of love is special, it's distinctive, and perhaps it falls into a category that's unique. When you lack it, you pursue it. When you have it, you embrace it. Philosophy is fundamentally the pursuit and embracing of wisdom, or insight for living. It's not just a bunch of questions or theories. It's an active engagement along an elevated path. It's all about commitment, power, growth, and good deeds. It deepens and broadens and raises your life to what it's capable of being.

Wisdom gives life to those who have it.
Ecclesiastes

You might not glean that understanding of philosophy from most introductory classes in a college or university context at present. There are two distinct streams feeding the river of wisdom that runs through the ages: a strong theoretical stream, and a bubbling brook of practical thought. Most academic contexts focus on the theoretical side of philosophy. In university classes or introductory books, you'll typically hear about epistemology, metaphysics, or logic, and perhaps you'll encounter theories of ethics and social or political thought. Philosophy of religion and the philosophy of science may come up. Many domains of life suggest questions and elements of theoretical philosophy. But my first dip into this cool water of the mind was completely practical at the young age of six.

My first grade teacher gave me on that first day of school, and offered to the rest of the class, a tremendous piece of practical wisdom about life. It's become a reliable touchstone for how I think about such things as success, desire, struggle, choice, action, attitude, hope, disappointment, achievement, and change. It has helped me to survive large-scale tectonic shifts in my own life, involving both great goods and real tragedies, as well as to experience many successful adaptations and wonderful, unexpected transformations along the way. The wise people who have lived before us, the insights they've had, and the techniques of thought and action they've bequeathed to us can guide us mightily along our own challenges in the world today. Transformed by wisdom, even the worst of times can surprise us and lead us into the best of times.

In short, everything that the human spirit undertakes or suffers
will lead to happiness when it's guided by wisdom,
but to the opposite, when guided by folly.
Socrates

And here's one of the main bits of wisdom we have: "When life hands you lemons, make lemonade." Life is not what you want it to be; it is what you make it. This is the core philosophy of the world's great existential lemonade makers. My first grade teacher gave us all this bit of profoundly useful wisdom that can change the way we approach almost anything in life. It can revolutionize our attitudes and actions along with our assumptions. It can guide us and provide us with an impulse toward wise initiative and patient persistence that's vital in the adventures of life. It's a key to living well. And, in that sense, it's a secret to the essence of life itself.

Ok, Just One More Story
A college freshman from Tennessee felt totally alone in her fancy New York school environment. She knew only her advisor, and so decided in the great southern manner to bake him some cookies. She walked all the way into town and returned to the dorm with a heavy bag full of ingredients that she carefully prepared and mixed, only to discover that her dorm oven was broken. Life can hand you lemons even when you're trying to make cookies. She remembered seeing a fancy house across the street and knew it must have a working kitchen, so she carried her full pans of well-formed cookie dough over to it and somehow rang the bell. The new president of the college was just moving in and unpacking boxes, but she took a moment and listened to the explanation for the urgent need of the moment and invited the determined young girl to come inside and use anything she needed. Ann baked her cookies and her new president was so impressed that she invited her to be the regular baby sitter for her young daughter, as well as to cook and serve at her many official and personal parties. The surprised freshman had no idea how all that would prepare her for the first job she would get after her expensive and elite college education, working in another kitchen at a restaurant. Lemons again?

She was soon in the much bigger commercial kitchen, scrubbing everything in sight. But one day while cleaning a steam table on the job she got burned and was fired, "for her own good." More lemons. Life is not what you want it to be. She decided to go to graduate school to study writing for a Master's Degree at one of the most prestigious creative writing programs in the world, and knew this would surely launch her into the dream life she wanted. It surprisingly took her into a job ... at a restaurant, as a waitress. This time, she interacted with customers and learned more than she could have imagined about people and life. To some, that would have been one more load of sour lemons for a girl with big dreams, but to her, it was just one more ingredient for the big pitcher of lemonade she was about to make as the novelist we all know and love, Ann Patchett.

So. Life is indeed not what you want it to be; it is what you make it one step at a time. Ann tells the wonderful story of her adventures, filled with additional wisdom for all our journeys, in her inspiring little book called *What Now?* It's all about the choices we make and how we react to what happens to us along the way. Every apparent obstacle can be an opportunity for learning, for growth, and perhaps for a new path toward great things in ways we never expected, as long as we make the most of every twist and turn.

Looking Forward

THE PROMINENT STAGE AND SCREEN ACTOR ALAN ALDA wrote some years ago a surprisingly philosophical memoir entitled *Never Have Your Dog Stuffed*, a book actually meant for a broader audience than just those of us who might be contemplating domestic taxidermy. In one section, he describes a point in his life at mid-career when he realized how radically different the mundane reality of his work was from his youthful visions of acting. He'd just left a performance at a theatre in Boston where he'd been working in a play, not by the likes of Shakespeare or Ibsen or Pinter, or even representing a piece of modern, experimental drama, or anything remotely as noble as any of that. It was rather just something he considered small and demeaning, and that required him to play a role involving, in his words, a silly wig and tights. In the midst of the play, he'd suddenly become profoundly self-conscious about the embarrassing and even humiliating absurdity of it all. He said that he felt depressed to the point of tears. Then, as he walked away from the scene of what had become his own inner shame and defeat, he suddenly experienced an unexpected epiphany of insight, and he reflected on it well. He tells us this:

> I realized that I was never going to have things the way I wanted them, no matter how vivid they seemed in my imagination. In a way, life itself was an improvisation in which I was going to have to deal with what came to me and not think about what should have come. I went back to the show the next night with more energy than I'd ever had. (129)

This man who would one day go on to become a major icon of television and film as well as the stage, had realized in his own profound experience at this moment, that life is not what we want it to be, but what we make it. And empowered by the realization, as the rest of his book intimates and his subsequent history has proved, he's ended up making it great. He turned his major lemons into amazing lemonade. He's lived his life and career as an artist of change and transformation. This is the power and purchase on our lives that a single great philosophical insight can have. Real wisdom can turn us around and give us new eyes for seeing the world both as it is at present and as it can become next. Then that wisdom can guide us into a better future.

The concept that I came to understand on the first day of first grade, as conveyed to me by my wise and gracious teacher, was a pivotal one for me, and can be the same for all of us. It was to be the philosophical basis for the construction and operation of all the best things in my life. I hope it will serve in exactly the same way for you. Adversities come. Challenges loom. Hardship and humiliation and heartache can show up at any time as uninvited guests. We get jolted out of comfortable routines. We're launched into the unknown and uncertain. We face more than we think we can handle. And that's a universal element of the human condition. So we all need a concept, an idea, a tool that we can use to be transformative.

> The secret of life is to find a pivot, the pivot of a concept
> on which you can make your stand.
> Luigi Pirandello

Life is not what you want it to be; it is what you make it. With that simple and powerful understanding, we can be motivated to go and do and make our lives great. We can be inspired to work as alchemists of the possible. And, as I philosopher, I always have one basic question to ask: Why should we ever settle for anything less?

A Conclusion

Throughout this book, we've been exploring the wisdom we have about change, challenge, and adversity, and for dealing well with any such difficulties on a very personal level, as well as with other people. We've been able to sort through and organize what some of the wisest thinkers in history have discovered and told us about the ups and downs of change in this world. And we've reflected on how these insights can alter us in deeply positive ways. The result has been something like a manual or a guidebook on how to handle change and challenge well, how to deal with any struggle and go beyond even the best of resilience and grit, into a mode of innovative transformation.

> Human beings are works in progress
> that mistakenly think they're finished.
> The person you are right now is as transient,
> as fleeting and as temporary
> as all the people you've ever been.
> The one constant in our lives is change.
> Daniel Gilbert

Alan Alda's clever book title echoes in its recommendation some of the best wisdom there is: *Never Have Your Dog Stuffed*. Having your dog stuffed is to be taken metaphorically as looking backward, trying desperately but with inevitable futility to keep things being at least an approximation of how they once were. Nostalgia can be a proper and sometimes wonderful thing. But it's not to be our driving force. It should never just hold us back. The past prepares us, but shouldn't simply define us.

Alda realizes that we all need to move forward, enjoying what we have when we have it, or enduring what we need to when we must, and then transformatively launching out into the new reality that always yet awaits our wise action and engagement. Life does hand us lemons. And sometimes, it gives us a lot of them. But it also provides us with many other things, including deep insight about how to best deal with its most bitter fruit. So with the right tools of art, we can indeed follow Plato and the other practical philosophers in the quest to make great and enjoyable lemonade, and set up a stand, and share the amazing results with others. A lemonade stand is an inherently social thing. And that itself is worth pondering. We're all in this together. There are lemons everywhere, and we all need a refreshing drink now and then. Your own lemonade making is then something that you can do not only for yourself, but also for those around you, and even in your own small way for the world and its cumulative good. We need you as a fellow alchemist engaged in creative transformation.

It doesn't have to be perfect, and you don't have to be Plato.
Elizabeth Gilbert

And then finally, we can perhaps come to realize the most surprising ultimate truth, and at least an important part of the greatest wisdom of all:

We are the lemons.

We're to be cut and squeezed and stirred by life and made into something great. This is the lesson of all the deepest spiritual traditions and is at the core of my own Christian faith. I'm writing these closing words on the day after Easter Sunday. And I have just come to realize anew the full import of this great day in the Christian calendar. The most fundamental philosophical message from Easter may be about the transformative power of real love, the ultimate spiritual alchemy that knows no bounds and that calls each of us to allow it to work in our hearts and, through them, to embody it to do great work in the world. This is the pinnacle of loving wisdom, and truly wise love.

And here's a thought. What if all of wisdom, virtue, work, play, and culture are supposed to be about love? What if growing in a capacity for deeper and broader love for your source, your self, and the spiritual siblings all around you and across the globe is the aim and intent of it all? What if that's meant to be the great litmus test for anything we ever think, feel, do, or aspire to be? Imagine how different the world and its own history through time would look if we were all convinced of this and sought to embody it every day. It's something to ponder. And it's certainly something to seek to live.

I believe we're here to change the world, in however small or extensive a way. But we're also here to be changed and made into the best of what we're capable of being. The alchemy of life is most powerful within us and for us. We're to be transformed. As the traveling rabbi Jesus revealed to his visitor Nicodemus, all of our physical and emotional life is meant to contribute to a metamorphosis that can lead to a second and spiritual birth as what we're meant to be. So, this life is really all about what can be made of us, which is, hopefully, the best spiritual lemonade of all. Cheers.

Appendix

A Philosopher's Favorite Lemonade Recipe

This is our very favorite lemonade recipe in the Morris family. You may like to experiment with others. There are lots of variations on the classics, not to mention the many "Tear open this bag and mix with water" versions available to us where you can outsource the whole process of dealing directly with the lemons. The kids in my neighborhood with lemonade stands probably use this division of labor so they can focus more on the selling than the making of the product. But there are plenty of juicy lemons all around. So here's our best recipe for using them to make really good lemonade.

First, go pick out the finest fruit you can find, which is something that life doesn't always allow. We like Meyer Lemons picked from our own tree the best, but with them you have to increase the number of lemons used to 11, with no other changes to the ingredients, except that you can reduce the added sugar to about one cup, depending on your taste.

Ingredients

• 1 1/2 cups of sugar (But if you have Meyer Lemons, cut back a bit.)
• 1/2 cup of boiling water (Ah. We start with something hot to get to something cool.)
• 1 tablespoon of grated lemon rind (You didn't see this coming, did you?)
• 1 1/2 cups of fresh lemon juice (8 large lemons, cut in half and squeezed well)
• 1 teaspoon of high quality vanilla extract (Another surprise? Good!)
• 5 cups of clear, cool, high quality water (Tap will do fine. Filtered is also great.)

Preparation

Stir together the sugar and 1/2 cup of boiling water until the sugar dissolves. Stir in the grated lemon rind, lemon juice, vanilla extract, and 5 cups of water. Cool it all down. Put it in a nice pitcher, perhaps garnished with three thin floating lemon slices. Then serve it over ice. Its lemonaciousness will be aesthetically supreme, metaphysically sublime, and perhaps even epistemologically amazing, and of course, spiritually great. So then, go enjoy what you've made.

Acknowledgments

I love it when people call or email me to ask whether the great philosophers of the past have had any insights about something they're going through in their lives, or in their companies now. The answer is always yes. Right before a large national bank merger several years ago, an executive from the smaller of the institutions involved called and wondered if I could put together a talk for several hundred of their top people on how to handle the change well. I enthusiastically agreed to the challenge and found that it launched me on a fascinating journey. This book is the result. I want to thank all those seasoned professionals for inviting me to explore the topic of change with them, and then for sharing their excitement about the treatment of it that's ultimately to be found here.

One young executive in the bank that had invited me to explore this topic told me minutes after my talk on the art of change that I had managed to say in one hour what all her coaches had long tried to communicate to her over the years they prepared her for competition as an Olympic athlete on the United States Team. She said the philosophers got it right. And Plato took the gold.

I also want to thank all the other companies and groups who

have subsequently invited me to bring them these thoughts on challenge and change. I've learned from every opportunity to speak on these ideas, and from every reaction to those talks. Without the enthusiastic support of my speaking agents throughout many years and the ongoing assistance of all my great friends at the top speaking bureaus throughout America and around the world, this adventure of bringing people ideas they can use would not have been nearly as much fun as it has been and continues to be. I heartily thank them all for their important work of helping to bring wisdom into people's lives all the time, and including my own life.

I had never thought I would write a book on the difficulties of change and the importance of transforming challenge into something great. And the difficulties I've gone through while writing it have been epic. For years, I thought the book would never get finished. If memory serves correctly here, it's been turned down at least forty-four times by some of the best editors at the top publishing firms in America who are revered for knowing what they're doing. It's had four literary agents, each of whom had to finally give up on it. It's a crazy, wonderful irony that I've never had such a hard time completing a project on the hard times that adversity and change can cause for us. I've rewritten the book with major changes through at least twenty-five versions over a period of about fifteen years. It's had at least five or six totally different titles. Two of my three dogs and a great cat passed on while I worked and struggled with it. And don't get me started on the economy during The Great Recession when some of the research and writing was done. Plus, there were more other kinds of turmoil roiling around me while I wrote and rewrote these pages than I have otherwise ever experienced in my entire life. During the years of writing and rewriting this book, I've had to use every concept in it to stay afloat and get safely to shore. It's a good thing the ideas here work so well.

Philosopher Dave Baggett read the first draft of these ideas long ago in the middle of a busy semester of teaching and made many perceptive comments that helped a lot in my first major effort of rewriting. I deeply appreciate all his supererogatory work on it, which, among its many other benefits, allowed me to find a way to use here that rare and scintillating word.

Notre Dame philosopher and Morris Institute Senior Fellow David O'Connor gave me masterful comments on an earlier draft of this book, helping me to put a number of things into perspective. I'm always grateful for David's prodigious insight. The immensely popular speaker, and author of *The Freak Factor*, among other books, Dave Rendall also helpfully commented on an earlier version and gave me some freakishly good suggestions. I appreciate his quick and thorough attention during a very busy time in his own global touring. Dan Golombek, Chief of Staff at the Space Telescope Science Institute at the Johns Hopkins University, where I was once honored to do The Meridian Lecture to their physicists, astrophysicists, cosmologists, and planetary scientists, along with the Hubble Telescope staff, also read an early draft and offered me some sagacious advice that was really out of this world, and of astronomical value. I'm in his cosmic debt.

Michael Brannick, the energetic former CEO of Prometric, worked through a later draft and made many incisive comments that goaded me on to several additions and changes. He deserves a hearty word of thanks for providing me with the most extensive set of comments on a manuscript I've ever received from a busy and highly accomplished corporate leader and innovator. He also happens to be quite a philosopher who has generously shared with me over several years some of his favorite wines.

True Crime author Scott Whisnant and a close circle of his friends served as a weekly focus group for fine-tuning the ideas in the book in one of its many early drafts. I appreciate their personal reactions to the topics in it. Scott's suggestions meant a lot to the book. I also gratefully thank Dr. Bruce May who provided many great challenges and thoughts.

My son Matt was the first to suggest that I connect up with the old adage about lemons and lemonade in writing such a book as this. It was an idea of great merit for which I'm grateful. I also deeply appreciate all the helpful things that my wife and daughter have done during the long writing of this little book to make life a bit easier for me. My wife Mary is a master lemonade maker in the kitchen and in life. A great poet could have been speaking of her when he wrote centuries before our time these words:

You are that Alchimist which alwaies had Wit,
whose one spark could make good things of bad.
John Donne, 1633

I've appreciated that wit and ability throughout our now forty-six years together. I have also, across this period of years working on the book, had many great times with my granddaughter Grayson Teague Morris. Being around her is always a joy. May she grow to become a master life alchemist and lemonade maker throughout all of her days.

Sara Morris for cover design, and Abby Chiaramonte for interior book design did their magic as always. I'm very grateful to them for the quality and speed of their work.

Finally, I'd like to thank The Library of American for their kind permission to quote from *Samuel Menashe: New and Selected Poems*, edited by Christopher Ricks. Copyright © 1971, 1973, 1986, 2004, 2005, 2008 by Samuel Menashe. Used by permission of Library of America, www.loa.org. All rights reserved.

Please visit me for more practical philosophy and even a little wisdom now and then, at www.TomVMorris.com. Or come look at the new novels through which I'm now exploring wisdom, at www.TheOasisWithin.com.

"But it's no use talking. Ring the bell for lemons, and don't look dull anymore ..."
Walter Vincy, *Middlemarch*

"Eh, gentlemen, let us recon upon accidents!
Life is a chapelet of little miseries
which the philosopher counts with a smile.
Be philosophers, as I am, gentlemen;
sit down at the table and let us drink."
Athos to D'Artagnan, in *The Three Musketeers*

I'll be with you in the squeezing of a lemon.
Oliver Goldsmith
1773

The Books of Wisdom/Works

Wisdom/Works is a new cooperative, cutting edge imprint and resource for publishing books by practical philosophers and innovative thinkers who can have a positive cultural impact in our time. We turn the procedures of traditional publishing upside down and put more power, a vastly higher speed of delivery, and greater rewards into the hands of our authors.

The imprint was launched with the Morris Institute for Human Values, founded by Tom Morris (Ph.D. Yale), a former professor of philosophy at Notre Dame and a public philosopher who has given over a thousand talks on the wisdom of the ages. Wisdom/Works was established to serve both his audiences and the broader culture. From the imprint's first projects, it began to attract the attention of other like-minded authors.

Wisdom/Works occupies a distinctive territory outside most traditional publishing domains. Its main concern is high quality expedited production and release, with affordability for buyers. We seek to serve a broad audience of intelligent readers with the best of ancient and modern wisdom. Subjects will touch on such issues as success, ethics, happiness, meaning, work, and how best to live a good life.

As an imprint, we have created a process for working with a few high quality projects a year compatible with our position in the market, and making available to our authors a well-guided and streamlined process for launching their books into the world. For more information, email Tom Morris, Editor-in-Chief, through his reliable address of: TomVMorris@aol.com. You can also learn more at the editor's website, www.TomVMorris.com.

Made in the USA
Monee, IL
07 July 2020